Diplomatic Ladies

To Sarah with much love,

Diplomatic Ladies

NEW ZEALAND'S UNSUNG ENVOYS

Joanna Woods

Joanna

OTAGO

Published by Otago University Press
PO Box 56 / Level 1, 398 Cumberland Street
Dunedin, New Zealand
E: university.press@otago.ac.nz
F: 64 3 479 8385
W: www.otago.ac.nz/press

First published 2012
P: ISBN 978 1 877578 30 4
E: ISBN 978 1 877578 75 5

Front cover: *Diplomatic wife, Lyn Corner, off to a garden party at Buckingham Palace. London 1953.* (By kind permission of Lyn Corner)

Back cover: *New Zealand diplomatic wives outside the Shrine of Imam Reza, Iran 1987. Judith Paulin (left) and Lou Ormsby (right).* (By kind permission of Irvine and Judith Paulin)

Frontispiece: *Embassy wives and secretaries modelling New Zealand fashions for First Lady, Jacqueline Kennedy. Washington 1962. From left: Mrs Wilson, Pam Miller, Anne McLean, Janine Hunn.* (By kind permission of Don and Janine Hunn)

Publisher: Wendy Harrex
Designer: Fiona Moffat
Indexer: Diane Lowther
Printed in New Zealand by Printlink Ltd, Wellington

CONTENTS

Foreword

For nine years as Foreign Minister, I sent New Zealand diplomats abroad to challenging new posts as Ambassadors or High Commissioners. Every time they came to see me before leaving to take up their posts, we would discuss priorities in terms of the bilateral relationship and the challenges that lay ahead. Establishing new contacts, working existing relationships and pressing New Zealand's case for access or mutual cooperation, or whatever the relationship demanded, lay ahead of these career diplomats. They were among the brightest and best of New Zealand's public servants, well educated and usually impatient to start their three or four years representing our country.

Behind the scenes, the lives of others were inevitably thrown up in the air as these appointments were made. Spouses, partners and children had to pack up and start over in a foreign country. I know that some relished the move, while, for others, news of the new posting came as a huge blow. The political arena is not dissimilar, in that the politician gets all the adrenaline rushes and the spouse, often at home, is left out in the cold.

Only those in these relationships can ever really know the benefits and sacrifices involved. Some spouses have to forgo careers for one or even two decades, knowing their chances of catching up with their contemporaries on their return to New Zealand will be slim. Others have opportunities that might never otherwise have come their way. For most, I suspect, there is a predictable mix of angst and excitement. Ageing parents and lifelong friends are left behind, and a new country is embraced. Children are settled at new schools, a local language is mastered to varying levels, and new friendships are made via children and the diplomatic set. These sorts of adjustments face all spouses who follow their partners overseas.

In the case of diplomatic spouses, usually wives, there is another dimension – that of unpaid and often unsung diplomat. Joanna Woods is one of those wives and exemplifies the partnerships that have added so much value to New Zealand's international representation over the years. She and Richard made their mark in world capitals as a team. One without the other would not have flourished, I suspect, and New Zealand Inc. has benefited from their love story that started in Rome in 1970.

At diplomatic dinner tables all over the world, every second place is often taken by the spouse or partner of a prime minister, president, or ambassador. At ambassadorial level, such dinners afford opportunities to mix more informally with the power brokers of the host country. I know from my own experience that some of the more interesting stories about the individuals concerned come from the partners or wives. There is no deliberate or artificial attempt to gather background intelligence. Rather, conversation inevitably turns at some point to families, the stresses, the celebrations that are happening in the private lives of some of the world's most influential players, and sometimes genuine and long-lasting friendships are forged.

No politician or diplomat is perfect and nor are their partners, spouses, or wives. But, as Joanna herself points out, in New Zealand we have been remarkably fortunate to have had a supplementary diplomatic representation in the form of the spouses that has shown the best qualities of New Zealanders – tolerance, an ability to compromise and a helping hand where needed.

In recent years, the expectations of diplomatic spouses have changed. No longer is it necessarily a 'two for the price of one' team, although the majority of diplomatic couples still work together to some extent. Restructuring of the Ministry of Foreign Affairs and Trade was inevitable, but the reaction from MFAT spouses to some of the changes mooted earlier this year, and the subsequent reconsideration of some aspects of those reforms, has shown that they remain a force to be reckoned with. That comes as no surprise to those of us who have seen these women – and some men – hold their own with political and diplomatic leaders throughout the world.

Everything between these covers displays Joanna's great talent for writing and many readers, including diplomats, spouses and even former Foreign Ministers, will nod in agreement. They will also get a lot of laughs from this timely and entertaining book.

Rt Hon Sir Don McKinnon, ONZ GCVD

Acknowledgements

By far my greatest debt is to all those who have shared their stories with me. Without their collaboration, this book could never have been written and I am eternally grateful to them for responding so generously not only with their time and their memories, but also with their family photographs and letters. For me, one of the greatest pleasures of collecting these stories has been the warm friendships that I have made with so many of their subjects. They are the heroines of my book and I trust that they will be happy with their portrayal.

Spouses and descendants have also played a crucial role. In particular, I would like to thank Adrian Simcock for giving me such unfettered access to the letters of his late wife, Moina; Guy and Michael Powles for allowing me to read their parents' papers; and John Fry, husband of the late Ruth Fry, whose book *Maud & Amber* was an invaluable resource for my first chapter.

In addition I would like to acknowledge the many others who have patiently submitted to my questioning. Foremost among these are Robert Wade and Judy Zavos, whose input has made a significant contribution to the whole; Rod Gates, from whom I learnt a great deal about Tonga; and Sally Edmonds, who helped me to piece together the life of her late husband, Paul.

For much of my archival research, I am indebted to the staff at the Ministry of Foreign Affairs and Trade and especially to Deputy Secretary, Peter Hamilton, to whom I made my original approach for access to the Ministry's files. Thanks to his support and the prompt follow-up by the then Acting Director for Human Resources, Winton Holmes, I have received every possible assistance from Family Liaison Officer, Prue Isaacs, and from

Neil Robertson, Adviser Historical Research, both of whom have responded to my many requests with unfailing efficiency and good humour. Other staff, especially MFAT Librarian, Mary Laking, could not have been more helpful. I also greatly appreciated the opportunity to meet Bernice Anderson, Executive Secretary of the Foreign Service Association, and Rosie Walsh, co-ordinator of MFAT's gay and lesbian network.

No acknowledgements of mine would be complete without a short paean of praise to the staff and resources of the Alexander Turnbull and National Libraries. The selection in my bibliography gives only the barest outline of the wealth of information that these two libraries have afforded me, ranging from family papers and unpublished letters to books, microfilms and videos. Despite the disruption of moving out of the Library building, the service to readers has never missed a beat and I would like to express my heartfelt gratitude to the staff of both libraries for their courtesy and professionalism.

Another significant resource has been the Alexander Turnbull Library's Oral History Centre, with its astounding range of interviews, including quite a number with 'diplomatic ladies', long since departed. The opportunity to listen to these interviews has enabled me to 'meet' my subjects in a way that I never dreamt would be possible and I am infinitely grateful to Curator, Linda Evans, and Oral History Adviser, Lynette Shum, for their meticulous stewardship of the collection.

I have also made extensive use of images from the Turnbull's photographic and newspaper archives where I have been ably assisted by Joan McCracken (formerly Team Leader, Pictures Online), Heather Mathie, and most notably by Research Librarian, Peter Attwell.

The most important figure of all, however, is Wendy Harrex of Otago University Press. I am honoured and delighted that she is publishing my book and I know from experience that the result will be beautiful.

My final words of thanks are for my husband Richard, who has acted as my diplomatic adviser throughout, and whose patience with my anti-social hours and the weeks that I have spent buried in my writing has been nothing short of angelic.

Joanna Woods
SEPTEMBER 2012

Introduction

It was love at first sight. I wound up the narrow staircase, past the slit of a bedroom, to the only real room in the apartment. The landlord strode ahead, flinging open the shutters. *'Ecco San Pietro,'* he cried, as the light flooded in, revealing wooden beams and white-washed walls and a fireplace stacked with logs. I ran to the window and looked out. Across the rooftops, the great dome of St Peter's was clearly visible, gleaming in the morning sun. *'Ed ecco la terrazza,'* the landlord continued, pushing open the double doors onto a tiny terrace. I stepped out into the sunshine. From far below, the sounds of the street drifted upwards and over the neighbouring houses I could see the curve of the Tiber. 'I'll take it,' I said. The street was named Via Benedetta – the blessed street – and I knew at once that I would be happy there.

The landlord beamed. 'And your neighbour,' he said triumphantly, indicating the low wall that separated the adjoining terrace, 'is a diplomat from New Zealand.' My face fell. 'But I want to meet Italians,' I said, 'and the last thing I want is to spend my time with other foreigners.' 'In that case we will put up a screen,' said the landlord. By the time I moved in a few days later, a six-foot fence had been erected between the terraces to banish my unwelcome neighbour. But the Almighty had ordained otherwise and within three months of renting the apartment, I was seeking to break the lease. 'I'm getting married,' I explained to the landlord. 'So love is to blame,' he replied with a rueful smile, 'and who is the lucky fellow?' Recalling our earlier conversation, I hesitated, abashed. 'It's the neighbour,' I said.

So began my twenty-two years as a diplomatic representative of New Zealand. Although unpaid (and usually unsung), diplomatic wives represent their country for the citizens of a host nation quite as much as their husbands.

As hostesses to prime ministers and princes, and witnesses to revolutions and war, diplomatic wives can also find themselves in the front line of international politics. Yet their role has been ignored by historians and their stories have never been told. The realisation that unless somebody wrote them down, many of these stories would be lost, was a powerful incentive to write this book.

But they portray a world that is changing. In recent years the gender ratio within the Ministry of Foreign Affairs and Trade has altered and currently 35 per cent of New Zealand's diplomatic partners overseas are men, who can never replicate the unique role played by diplomatic wives in the past. Nor do couples necessarily work as a team. Many wives pursue their own careers and increasingly few are opting, as I did, to become full-time diplomatic accomplices.

The Ministry of Foreign Affairs and Trade has had no hand in writing this book, but in the interests of New Zealand's external relations, I have tried to avoid any comments that might give offence to other nations. On the other hand, I have not minced my words on the downsides of a career in diplomacy – or on the perils of living on 'the cocktail party circuit'. My overriding objective, however, has been to record the contribution of the wives so that all those able and intelligent women who have devoted years to serving their country may finally be given their due.

CHAPTER I.

Maud & Amber

Maud Pember Reeves was having the time of her life. Ever since her arrival in London in 1896 as the wife of the New Zealand Agent General, she had been lionised in women's suffrage circles as the representative of the first country in the world to give the vote to women. Already a veteran campaigner, who had been 'in the thick of the fight'[1] for women's franchise in New Zealand, she was more than a match for the gang of medical students who had marched from the nearby hospital of St Mary's Paddington to disrupt a women's suffrage meeting. As the students loosed a couple of fireworks over the heads of the terrified audience, she stepped forward and addressed the troublemakers: 'You wanted to hear a suffragette,' she said, 'I am the nearest approach to one on this platform.'[2] She gained their attention immediately and, according to the report which appeared in the *Times* the following morning, she went on to make the most coherent speech of the evening.

When William Pember Reeves became a member of the New Zealand Cabinet in 1891, Maud soon demonstrated that she was a force to be reckoned with. Although an article in the *New Zealand Graphic* innocently describes her simply as 'a pretty, girlish figure',[3] a letter she wrote to Sir John Hall at the height of the debate on women's suffrage reveals the extent of her influence: 'We are going to have our franchise after all. Isn't it glorious? … My husband is to be relied on. I have seen to that.'[4] Similarly, in 1895, when the working relationship between William and Prime Minister Richard Seddon had become untenable, it was Maud who lobbied the influential Minister of Agriculture, John McKenzie, to ensure that her husband was offered the position of Agent General in London. Fearing that William might demur, she told McKenzie 'to ignore his views'; she would see that he took it. Maud prevailed and McKenzie (who was not immune to her charms), later described her as 'the pluckiest little woman in New Zealand'.[5]

Maud certainly kept her head when the mood at the meeting in Paddington turned ugly, remarking tartly: 'These gentlemen are doing us a lot of good tonight',[6] before she and the other women beat a dignified retreat. Minutes later the protesters rushed the platform, smashing the furniture and dragging posters from the walls, and were evicted only with difficulty by the police.

Today the participation of the wife of New Zealand's senior diplomatic representative to Britain in a stormy political meeting in London could well lead to a serious diplomatic incident. But in 1907, when the meeting took place, New Zealand had neither a foreign ministry nor a diplomatic service, and still left the conduct of its foreign policy to Britain. Thus Maud did not regard her husband's posting to London as a diplomatic assignment, but rather as an extended visit 'home' during which she might pursue her political interests as she pleased.

When William accepted the post of Agent General, it was the New Zealand government's only senior position overseas. The first appointment in 1870 had originated in the need for a high-ranking officer to administer the immigration programme and raise money for public works. But by 1880 the role had begun to change and Hall, who was then Prime Minister, argued that the Agent General should not be 'a mere clerk or agent, but a gentleman of position and influence' who would be able 'to communicate with effect with the Imperial Government'.[7]

A year earlier, Julius Vogel had also pressed for the Agent General's position to 'be analogous to that of an ambassador', even though he was representing 'a portion of the same Empire'.[8] Despite these interventions, however, it was not until 1905 that the Agent General's title was changed to the diplomatic rank of High Commissioner,* thereby acknowledging New Zealand's need for an independent representative in Britain and transforming Maud into New Zealand's first diplomatic wife.

Although she was now on an equal footing with the wives of other senior diplomats, Maud had no desire to embark on the traditional round of formal dinners and receptions. Nor had she any intention of abandoning her busy programme of writing and speaking in support of women's suffrage. But

---

* The title used by former British colonies for Commonwealth ambassadors within each other's countries.

*New Zealand's first
diplomatic couple. Maud
and William Pember Reeves,
London c. 1909.*

(Blanco White Family Collection)

she still did her fair share of entertaining and charity work. When Prime
Minister Seddon and his wife arrived in London for Queen Victoria's
Diamond Jubilee in 1897, both the Reeves were at the station to meet them
and later hosted a large party in their honour. Similarly, during the Boer
War, Maud served dutifully on a committee of women who were raising
money for 'parcels of comforts'[9] to be sent to the New Zealand contingent.

Part of Maud's reluctance to play the diplomatic hostess may have
sprung from the absence of an official Residence. Unlike some later New
Zealand High Commissioners, for whom splendid homes were acquired
and furnished in London, the Reeves lived modestly in an inexpensive part
of Kensington. But thanks to William's high reputation in Liberal circles,
he and Maud enjoyed enviably close relationships with many of the leading
figures of Britain's socialist intelligentsia – including the high priests of the
Fabian Society, Beatrice and Sidney Webb.

The early socialism of the Fabians had exerted a formative influence on
William's political thinking. Indeed both he and Maud were so enamoured of
the Fabians that they christened their only son Fabian. William's admiration
for their ideas also helped to shape the groundbreaking social legislation

enacted by the New Zealand Liberals in the 1890s, which earned New Zealand the title of 'social laboratory of the world'. Later, many Fabian beliefs found their way into law in Britain, not least because the newly formed British Labour Party drew heavily on their intellectual arguments. But the trail had been blazed by New Zealand.

Against this background, it is hardly surprising that the Fabians received William and Maud with open arms. Within a few weeks of his arrival in London, William was asked to address the Society and later he received a flattering invitation to join an exclusive Fabian dining club. More significantly, he and Maud rapidly became members of the Webbs' inner circle, joining them for country weekends and dining together in London.

In 1898, the Webbs paid a visit to New Zealand. They loved the 'beautiful, fertile and wonderfully varied' landscape and found the people delightful. In her diary, Beatrice recorded her 'agreeable impression' of a country 'where there are no millionaires and hardly any slums' before concluding: 'All in all, if I had to bring up a family outside Great Britain, I would choose New Zealand.'[10] Although there is no suggestion that Beatrice's enthusiasm for New Zealand was influenced by her friendship with the Reeves, she certainly had hardly a good word for the Australians, especially the women who, she claimed, 'lack culture, charm and any kind of grace.' Worse still, 'they apparently think it is "unwomanly" to take an active part in public affairs',[11] which was not an accusation that could ever have been levelled at Maud.

Once back in London, Beatrice continued to preside over her *salon*, at which she charmed and cajoled guests of every political hue to further the interests of Socialism. For any diplomatic couple seeking access to influential figures, the company that the Webbs kept was the stuff of dreams. An extract from Beatrice's 1904 diary (when Balfour was Prime Minister), reveals the circles in which she and husband moved:

> *For the Wells's we had a little dinner – carefully selected – Mr Balfour, the Bishop of Stepney, the Bernard Shaws, Mrs Reeves and a Mr Thesiger, the new L.C.C. Moderate. The P.M. finding himself in a little party of intimates ... let himself go and, I think, thoroughly enjoyed the mixture of chaff and dialectic which flew from GBS to Wells and round the table.*[12]

William was not there, perhaps laid low by one of his wracking headaches. But Maud would have been more than able to hold her own without him.

Disappointingly few details have survived of the confrontation that took place on 14 December 1906 between the wife of the New Zealand High Commissioner and Mr George Bernard Shaw. But the scene is not difficult to reconstruct and according to those who witnessed it, there was no doubt that Shaw came off 'distinctly the worse.'[13] At fifty, Shaw was at the height of his powers, a brilliant platform speaker and Britain's leading dramatist. He had an athletic physique with barely a grey hair, and cut a far more impressive figure than the eccentric-looking scarecrow who visited New Zealand in 1934. Moreover he was in his home territory, in front of a large gathering of adoring Fabians, whose Society he had helped to establish.

Maud, by comparison, was a relative newcomer who had only recently joined the Society. But since her days as the wife of a cabinet minister, she had lost none of her political canniness – or her good looks. According to H.G. Wells' autobiography, she was an 'extremely pretty' woman, 'with a dash of Hungarian blood', whom people in London found 'charming'. Further on, he describes her as 'a very subtle and interesting person … full of humour' and 'a very bright talker.'[14] Maud was equally taken with Wells and it was partly her staunch support for his radical proposals to reform the Fabian Society that had led to her confrontation with Shaw.

But Maud also had an agenda of her own. Ever since joining the Society, she had been determined to harness its influence for the women's cause – and she never doubted that she would succeed. The tone of a letter that she wrote to one of the women's suffrage societies shortly before her showdown with Shaw has a familiar ring: 'I am organising the women who are very much [roused] and we will win.'[15] As usual she had been working behind the scenes.

When Maud rose to her feet, just after Shaw had completely demolished Wells in a dazzling display of oratory, and informed him that unless the Executive Committee agreed to an amendment in support of equal citizenship for women the entire female membership of the Fabian Society would vote in favour of Wells, Shaw didn't stand a chance. There was considerable opposition from the Committee, but after further 'negotiations' with Maud, Shaw capitulated completely. Her amendment was passed and became the only addition made to the iconic 'Fabian Basis' from its inception in 1887 until the end of World War I.

Shortly afterwards both Maud and Wells were elected to the Fabian Executive, but suspecting that the men were still lukewarm about the women's cause, Maud promptly called a meeting of the Fabian women at her house. There they formed themselves into a hard-working group that subsequently did much of the spadework for the welfare policies relating to women and children today.

For Maud's own children, the sight of their mother at home must have been a rare treat. Although none were sent to boarding school, from all accounts the three Reeves children suffered the fate of many diplomatic children, namely a blend of extraordinary opportunities to mix with the cultural and political elite of the host country coupled with parental neglect. If Maud ever drew breath to think about her maternal responsibilities, she may even have congratulated herself on the success of the joint family holidays that she had organised with the Wells, not to mention the many happy weekends that the two families spent together playing charades and racing demon. But by the middle of 1907 she was so immersed in what Wells calls 'her own bright life'[16] that she seems to have been quite unaware of the unruly passions that were raging in her elder daughter's heart.

In the autumn of 1905, Amber Reeves had gone to Newnham College, Cambridge, at the age of eighteen. William wanted her to stay in London to be presented at Court, but Amber had other ideas and she soon overcame her father's objections. As Maud's daughter, she believed fervently in equality of the sexes and with her 'quick greedy mind'[17] and her mass of unruly hair, she was already very much the prototype of the fashionable 'New Woman'. Within a few months of arriving at Cambridge, she was making waves. A brilliant student, she participated vigorously in the Newnham Debating Society and spoke daringly to the Philosophical Society on 'the relativity of morals'.[18] During 1906 she became a founder member of the Fabian Nursery, which was a youthful branch of the Society whose members spent much of their time debating and dancing, and falling in love with each other.

For the young Fabians by far the most attractive figure among the Fabian leadership was Wells, who had already captivated millions of readers with his visionary *Time Machine* and *War of the Worlds*. What interested the young Fabians, however, was not Wells' science fiction, but rather the revolutionary social theories that he expounds in *A Modern Utopia* and *In the Days of the Comet*. At the unchaperoned rambles and reading parties of the Cambridge University Fabian Society his ideas were endlessly debated, especially by Amber who was their most ardent advocate.

From Wells' autobiography, it is easy to see why the clever (and doubtless lusty) young Fabians might have found him more fun than the earnest Webbs:

I spoke out for 'Free Love'. ... I did my best to maintain that love-making was a thing in itself, a thing to thank the gods for, but not to be taken too seriously …. The spreading knowledge of birth-control … seemed to justify my contention that love was now to be taken more lightly than it had been in the past. It was to be refreshment and invigoration, as I set out quite plainly in my 'Modern Utopia'.[19]

At least he had the courage of his convictions. Further on in his autobiography Wells unblushingly describes the 'compromise' on sexual fidelity that he and his wife, Jane, had reached – namely that 'she suppressed any jealous impulse and gave me whatever freedom I desired.'[20] He even claims that Jane regarded his 'sexual imaginativeness as a sort of constitutional disease', adding wistfully: 'Perhaps if she had not been immune to such fevers I should not have gone astray.'[21]

Later it was suggested that by voicing her approval of *In the Days of the Comet*, Maud had implicitly condoned Wells' notions of free love and group marriage. But the book was a futuristic work of fiction and it is far more likely that she never took it seriously. Nor would she have known anything about Wells' pact with his wife. From her letters it is clear that Maud trusted him completely and during the long Cambridge vacations, she allowed Amber to stay with the Wells for weeks on end. In August 1907, she wrote a letter to Jane telling her that Amber was 'panting' to be with them. The following April, after another lengthy visit by Amber, Maud wrote again: 'Thank you so much for your goodness to Amber … She adores you both … You are good fairies to all these young people.'[22] Some months later, she echoes the same sentiments: 'You are being angels to Amber who seems to be having the best sort of time.'[23]

At Cambridge, as an old family friend, Wells was able to circumvent Newnham's draconian regulations and visit Amber in her room. The sight of his 'loud checks disappearing round the corners of Newnham corridors' raised Amber's social status sky high. According to one of her contemporaries, 'she became more dashing than anyone else we knew.'[24] Quite how 'dashing' she was is recounted in minute detail by Wells:

Of necessity our talks grew more and more intimate and she conceived the pretty fancy of calling me by the flattering title of 'Master' … One day she broke the thin ice over my suppressions by telling me she was in love, and when I asked 'with whom?' throwing herself into my by no means unwilling arms … We set about the business of making love with the greatest energy. We lay together naked in bed as a sort of betrothal; we contrived a meeting in Soho, when we became lovers in the fullest sense of the word.

> *Before she went back to Cambridge for her examination ... she went off*
> *ostensibly to read by herself in an imaginary cottage in Epping Forest,*
> *but actually to join me in a lodging in Southend. There we had some*
> *days of insatiable mutual appreciation ... And I remember also that,*
> *after our luggage had gone down to the waiting cab, we hesitated on the*
> *landing lifting our eyebrows and went back gleefully for a last cheerful*
> *encounter in the room we were leaving.*[25]

On her return to Cambridge, Amber took her finals and got a double first.

Soon thereafter Amber and a group of young Fabians, which included Rupert Brooke, went to stay with the Webbs. Beatrice immediately spotted the danger signals:

> *I also had the brilliant Amber Reeves, the double first Moral Tripos, an*
> *amazingly vital person and I suppose very clever, but a terrible little*
> *pagan – vain, egoistical, and careless of other people's happiness ... A*
> *somewhat dangerous friendship is springing up between her and H.G.*
> *Wells. I think they are both too soundly self-interested to do more than*
> *cause poor Jane Wells some fearful feelings – but if Amber were my*
> *child I should be anxious.*[26]

Beatrice's perceptive comments came far closer to the truth than Jane would ever have admitted. Throughout the affair, according to Wells, 'Jane was invincibly the wife, and Amber the young mistress; we all understood each other, we asserted, beautifully.'[27] He chose to ignore the anguish which later led Jane to retreat to a secret flat in Bloomsbury, where she poured her unhappiness into an unsuccessful novel.

Even for Wells not everything went according to plan. Amber's 'erotic adventurousness' combined with her 'slender nimble body' and 'fuzz of soft black hair' was turning his theories on free love on their head.[28] At forty-one, he found himself in the grip of an intense sexual passion and 'a jealous fixation' which made the thought of relinquishing Amber to any other man unbearable. Matters were made worse by her throng of admirers, which included a young barrister named Rivers Blanco White with whom she spent much of her time when she and Wells were not romping in their love nest in Eccleston Square.

Typically, Maud and William were the last to know. Perhaps unwisely they had given Amber an extraordinarily free rein and she in turn had become adept at deceiving them. But given the code of conduct at the time, Maud's blind trust in Wells was not as naïve as it appears today. As a member of London society, she would have been well aware that the Edwardian

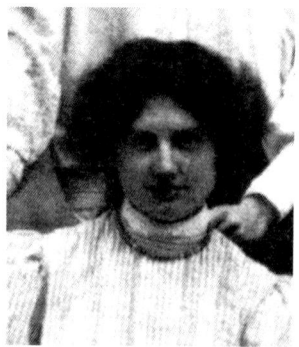

Left: Amber Reeves as an undergraduate at Newnham College, Cambridge, 1908. (Principal and Fellows of Newnham College, Cambridge) *Right: The culprit. H.G. Wells in his 40s, c. 1909.*

upper classes – with the King leading the charge – were notorious for their extramarital activities. Tip-toeing between bedrooms, however, was a pastime for married women whose reputations were shielded by their wedding rings. In the circles in which Maud and William moved it was almost inconceivable that a 'gentleman' would seduce the innocent daughter of a friend.

Maud also had other things to worry about, which could explain why she never picked up on the rampant gossip about Amber and Wells that was circulating among the Fabians. In 1908, William discovered that he was about to lose his job. Seddon's successor, Joseph Ward, wanted to reward a Cabinet colleague with the prestigious post of High Commissioner – a situation with which later New Zealand diplomats would also become familiar.

After serving his country outstandingly for over twelve years, William must have found his arbitrary removal to make way for a political crony of Ward's a bitter pill to swallow. The knowledge that he had once been a 'crony' himself would not have lessened the pain of being usurped by a new favourite, whose skills were not a patch on his. Faced with imminent unemployment, he put out feelers in New Zealand. But his political star had set and friends advised him to remain in London, where at least he had a job offer – the post of Director of the London School of Economics (LSE),* which was in the gift of the Webbs. As an additional inducement to resign, Ward helped him onto the board of the National Bank of New Zealand.

---

* The LSE was founded in 1895 with the money from a bequest to the Fabians.

Around April 1909, when he was still smarting from his demotion, William received a letter from Rivers Blanco White. He reacted to its contents with fury and according to the novelist, Compton Mackenzie, declared that he was going to shoot Wells at the first opportunity. In an anecdote that has a strong whiff of Wellsian mischief, Mackenzie claims that William used to sit in a bow window of the Savile Club in Piccadilly, to which both he and Wells belonged, with a pistol beside him waiting to take a shot at Wells. Whatever the truth of this story, the committee of the Club sided with 'the outraged father' and Wells was asked to resign.[29]

Rivers' letter was the first intimation William had had of Amber's affair, revealing that she had been 'ruined' by Wells and was expecting his baby. It concluded in the most remarkable act of chivalry because Rivers was offering to marry her.

Several versions exist of the tangled tale of Amber's pregnancy and her shot-gun marriage to Rivers. Wells claims that the baby was her idea and that she asked him to give her a child 'whatever happens'. With his customary frankness, he adds: 'I made no attempt to question this sudden philo-progenitiveness in her, and we set about the business there and then.'[30]

Amber Blanco White with her daughter, Anna Jane, 1910.
(Blanco White Family Collection)

An elopement to France followed, which ended in fiasco when it became evident that Wells was never going to leave Jane. In May, Amber was hastily married to Rivers.

For William and Maud, one of the most distressing aspects of the whole affair was Amber's continuing relationship with her lover. From her Fabian pinnacle, Beatrice observed the unfolding drama:

> The plot thickens around the tragic Wells–Blanco White–Reeves affair; and the Reeves are coming in their misery to us for counsel and sympathy. The blackguardism of Wells is every day more apparent … The position now is that Amber is living in a cottage taken by Wells, and is receiving frequent visits from him while her husband lives in his chambers in London. And poor Reeves is contributing £300 a year to keep up this extraordinary ménage.[31]

In October, Wells added insult to injury by publishing a scandalous novel called *Ann Veronica* in which he fictionalises his relationship with Amber and pillories William as the tyrannical and small-minded father. At the LSE, where every student was reading *Ann Veronica,* William's sufferings reached their apogee and his appearances there became a daily crucifixion. Over the following months, the Webbs watched the public humiliation of their new Director with concern and castigated themselves for having introduced Wells to the Reeves. In late December, Beatrice noted in her diary that 'both of them were shrivelled up with the pain of their daughter's past (?) relations with Wells.'[32]

Although Maud escaped *Ann Veronica* (Wells considerately kills her off before the story starts), she did not escape Wells' pen. But his letter accusing her of collusion over his affair with Amber was as unfounded as his later suggestions that she had sought to conceal the situation from her husband. Similar rumours were gleefully peddled by others and even Beatrice, who was a loyal friend, suggested that Maud had paid the price for being so 'advanced' in her views.

Far more pragmatic than her highly strung husband, Maud worked out her redemption – if indeed she needed to – by embarking on an astonishing self-imposed task among the poor families of Lambeth. Four years later, the fruit of her meticulous social investigations emerged as a substantial pamphlet, published by the Fabian Women's Group, followed by a book entitled *Round about a pound a week.* Maud's humanity and common sense resound through its pages and her thunderous indictment of Britain's 'masculine state, representing only male voters, and until lately chiefly those

A meticulous researcher.
Maud Pember Reeves
immersed in her reading,
1914. (Blanco White Family Collection)

of the richer classes',[33] demonstrates how faithfully she still adhered to New Zealand's Liberal philosophy. The book was an instant best-seller and many of Maud's suggestions, such as maternity clinics, school meals and a central authority responsible for children's welfare, have entered the statute books.

Amber gained a rather different sort of distinction. After Wells had portrayed her in *Ann Veronica*, she enjoyed a vogue as the poster-girl for the adherents of the 'New Woman'. In 1910, Shaw depicted her as the turbulent heroine of his drawing-room comedy, *Misalliance*. She is also clearly Wells' model for Isobel Rivers in *The New Machiavelli* (although he denies it), as well as for the character of Amanda in his *The Research Magnificent*.

A sketch of Amber in 1912 shows a reflective young woman with a wistful expression in her eyes. She and her child by Wells had long since settled down with Rivers and little came of her 'precocious promise'.[34] Like many diplomatic daughters, she had been exposed to a heady world in her youth – only to discover that real life was very different.

In 1920 New Zealand became a founding member of the League of Nations, affirming the new sense of nationhood that was born of the bloody conflicts of World War I. But it would take another war to persuade New Zealanders that the time had come to cut the umbilical cord with Britain and form a diplomatic service of their own.

CHAPTER 2

Moscow Wives

On the morning of 2 November 1944, Jean Boswell was on the last leg of the journey to join her husband at the recently established New Zealand Legation in Moscow. It had taken her three months to travel to Russia, on blacked-out ships to Bombay and Karachi and then on up the Persian Gulf to the Iranian port of Khorramshahr. From there, she and her travelling companion, Ruth Macky, had taken a taxi through the desert to the oil town of Ahwaz where they caught the train to Tehran.

For most of the journey, they had been escorted by the reassuring figure of R.T. Patrick, a chubby bachelor in his fifties who had been appointed First Secretary at the new Legation, and a young lawyer named Ray Perry, who was to act as Second Secretary. In Iran, the men had stayed behind to deal with the shipment of supplies that had travelled with them from New Zealand, leaving the two women to take the flight to Russia alone.

The aisle of the Soviet-built Dakota, which the New Zealand government had chartered, was piled high with their luggage. There was nothing to eat or drink and the noise was deafening. But after the suffocating drive across the desert, and the thirty-six hour train journey to Tehran, it seemed like the lap of luxury. The only other passengers were a young Russian journalist and a gigantic Czech, both of whom had hitched a ride.

Since their overnight stop in Baku, the pilot had been hedge-hopping, swooping low over the countryside so that his diplomatic passengers could enjoy the view. From her seat beside the window, Jean stared down at the devastation. More than two years had passed since the German armies had swept across Russia, but their path of destruction was still marked by blackened forests and charred tree-tops neatly sliced off by artillery fire.

The landscape was pock-marked with bomb-craters; whole villages lay in ruins, and in the burnt-out railway stations she could see overturned trains with their trucks and carriages scattered like children's toys. With her countrywoman's eye Jean noted the acres of grassland. There was not a herd to be seen, yet in New Zealand the land would have been dotted with sheep and cattle.

In a few minutes the plane would be landing at Stalingrad. It was only a short refuelling stop, but both women had set their hearts on visiting the legendary Soviet city whose heroic defence had changed the course of the War. At the airport the Russian Commandant listened to them politely. Unfortunately the city was too far away, he said, and in any case he had no transport. 'Couldn't we get a taxi?' pleaded Jean.[1] He shook his head firmly and directed them towards the makeshift structure that served as a terminal building.

Many hours later, Jean and Ruth found themselves contemplating a row of five beds. In Moscow, the weather had closed in and their flight had been postponed until the morning, but Jean's suggestion that they might find a hotel in Stalingrad had been laughed to scorn. Instead, all four passengers were spending the night in a single bedroom at the airport. The giant Czech, who was still recovering from the bottle of vodka he had downed the previous evening, remained silent, but the young journalist shifted awkwardly. 'Does that mean we have to sleep in our clothes?' he asked. Glancing at Ruth's trim figure, with her smudge of red lipstick and dark, wavy hair, Jean took command: 'We are sleeping in our nighties,' she said, 'and you two boys are making yourselves scarce while we get into them.'[2] They obeyed like lambs and, in the morning, Jean had them both running back and forth with a bowl of water so that she and Ruth could brush their teeth.

The two women could not have been more different. At fifty-three, Jean cut a small, determined figure, dressed in the muted fashions of wartime New Zealand, with a pair of unbecoming black-rimmed spectacles permanently perched on her nose. Before this trip she had travelled very little, and nothing that she had seen during her three-month odyssey across Asia and the Pacific had altered her conviction that the best place in the world was New Zealand.

In her account of her experiences, Jean rails at the 'stark crudity and filth' of the airport toilets, which lay on the far side of a muddy quagmire, and 'the utter indifference of the people to what we consider the ordinary decencies.'[3] She had been raised in a pioneer settlement in Northland and, having spent

New Zealand's first envoys to Russia. Jean and Charles Boswell, c. 1945.

her early years in a hut made of nikau palms, she knew all about filth and mud. But she came from stock that placed cleanliness close to godliness and still managed, against overwhelming odds, to maintain the proprieties of Victorian life in the middle of the bush.

When Charles Boswell was offered the position of New Zealand Minister in Moscow, it never occurred to Jean not to accompany him. From his earliest days as a schoolteacher in a remote area of Northland, she had always supported him. Similarly, when his interests turned to politics, she had busied herself with the local Fabian Society and shared in his glory and his disappointment when his brief tenure as Labour member for the Bay of Islands ended in defeat. Although the title of Minister had a distinctly pleasing ring to it, Jean had no desire to go to Russia. Their first grandchild had just been born in Auckland and she would far rather have stayed at home.

For Ruth, on the other hand, this was the adventure of a lifetime. She had been learning Russian for months and when she heard that her application for the post of Archivist at the Moscow Legation had been successful, she was overjoyed. Aged thirty and single, she dressed well and, after working in Britain and Europe for nearly a decade, spoke fluent French and German. Moreover, unlike Jean, she was a city girl, raised comfortably in suburban Auckland where her parents owned a business. As they traversed the world, however, the two women buried their differences. In the streets of Karachi and Khorramshahr, their shared gender and nationality counted for far more than any disparities of background and education, and during their enforced stopover in Stalingrad they were yet further united by their determination to visit the city.

The following day any hopes of flying were once again dashed by fog in Moscow. But during the afternoon the Commandant relented and offered to take his diplomatic visitors on a tour of Stalingrad. The story of its defence had caught the imagination of the world, but despite the copious media coverage, nothing had prepared Jean and Ruth for what awaited them. It was a scene of utter destruction. All that remained of the city was a shattered, blasted shell. Most of the buildings were completely flattened and the gaping windows in the few walls still standing reminded Jean of the empty eye-sockets of a skull. To her horrified gaze, it was not a town at all. It looked like 'the devil's brickyard' through which some demonic force had swept in fury.[4]

The battle had begun in September 1942, in the wake of the Germans' lightning advance across Russia. With massive air support, they expected to take Stalingrad in a matter of days. Forty thousand civilians died in the carpet bombing, but throughout the worst of the Russian winter the local garrison continued to fight tooth and nail, often in hand-to-hand combat on streets that changed sides several times a day. Even after the Germans had occupied the city its defenders fought on, from sewers and cellars or from dug-outs scooped out of the rubble.

Cringing at her foolish talk of hotels and taxis, Jean listened mutely as the Commandant described the final days. Drawing in the dust with his cane, he indicated the positions of the relieving Russian armies that had gradually encircled the city and forced the Germans to surrender. At the end of the tour, the two women were shown the underground room occupied by the hapless German Commander, von Paulus. His office was untouched, with his desk and chair neatly in place and his papers lying on the table.

To Ruth, who had seen the ravages of the London blitz, it seemed almost unimaginable that people could still be living there. But among the ruins they had come across a wretched market where women were selling vegetables and nearby she had glimpsed the fresh wood of a brand new swing 'working overtime for a crowd of squealing children'.[5] On the third morning, the weather cleared and Jean and Ruth were able to continue their journey. They landed in Moscow where Charles and his two staff were due to meet them, just as the first snow was falling. It was 4 November and they had set sail from New Zealand on 28 July.

Moscow was one of New Zealand's earliest diplomatic posts, preceded only by Washington, Ottawa and Canberra. All were opened during World War II, when it became evident that New Zealand needed to co-ordinate more closely with its wartime allies. This need was further emphasised by the fall of Singapore, which demonstrated all too clearly that New Zealand could no longer count on Britain for protection. Thus in 1943, after many years of denying the need for an independent foreign policy, the New Zealand government was at last persuaded to widen its circle of friends and form a diplomatic service.

The man appointed to direct the newly created Department of External Affairs was a librarian named Alister McIntosh, who ran the fledgling diplomatic service from a warren of rooms that had been constructed on the roof of Parliament. With his brilliant and subtle mind, McIntosh was ideally suited to his role. He cared lovingly for his hand-picked staff, who later likened the intellectual atmosphere of the department to that of 'a good university'.[6] But he was also capable of Machiavellian malice against those he disliked – one of whom was Charles Boswell.

From the outset, the Moscow Legation had been a political football, not least because the New Zealand public had little affection for the Soviet Union – even if it had become a wartime ally. Then, much to McIntosh's disgust, Prime Minister Peter Fraser had decided to compensate his old mate, Boswell, for the loss of his Bay of Islands seat with the prize of Minister in Moscow. The appointment was greeted with widespread scepticism and the Auckland *Herald*'s comment that 'it is difficult to discern a single qualification which Mr Boswell possesses for his task' echoes McIntosh's views so closely that one is tempted to see his hand in it.[7]

Worse still, in a desperate stab at the unfamiliar task of furnishing a diplomatic establishment, R.T. Patrick had consulted the Public Works Department and had come up with a list for the Minister's Residence that included '10 Chesterfields, 20 easy chairs and 12 fireside chairs' plus fifteen card tables and a billiard table with all 'the necessary appurtenances'. In July 1944 the entire inventory, complete with palm stands and cocktail cabinets, appeared in the Christchurch *Press* and was seized on gleefully by the Opposition as a 'wicked waste of public money'.[8] McIntosh bore the brunt of the Prime Minister's wrath and the order was cancelled.

Staffing the Legation had proved a further challenge. In McIntosh's view, Boswell was a loose cannon, who had to be well fenced in with public servants. But with a Department that was not even a year old, he had no pool of diplomatic officers or linguists on which to draw. In the end, he cobbled together a team of four men and one woman, of which the outstanding star was a Cambridge-educated, Russian-speaking New Zealander named Paddy Costello.

The task of accompanying the Minister to the airport to meet his wife was, of course, a command performance. But Paddy Costello, who had travelled to Moscow with Charles in August, and his younger colleague, Doug Lake, would also have been keen to take a look at Ruth. As yet the Legation had neither an office nor a Residence and they would all be working together at close quarters from their bedrooms in the hotel.

When Jean saw the two tiny rooms that had been allocated to the New Zealand Minister at Moscow's National Hotel, her joy at being reunited with her husband evaporated rapidly. The rooms were at the back of the building, with little natural light and a bathroom that was so small that Charles had to stand with one foot in the bedroom when he wanted to shave. For weeks the Soviet government had been promising to allocate them a suitable building, but for a nation that was still fighting a bloody war with Germany, the demands of a small Commonwealth country were not a top priority.

Battling with depression, Jean tried to settle into a daily routine. But without a household to manage and nowhere to entertain, she had nothing to do. Outside the temperature hovered around 20° below and apart from the walk that she and Charles took every afternoon, she spent most of her day in her room. The hotel's wartime fare of reconstituted eggs and cabbage soup only added to her gloom and in the copious letters that she wrote to pass the time, she describes cooking their New Zealand supplies in tins on a hot plate in their room.

During her daily walks Jean observed the misery of the ordinary people from the perspective of her own tough childhood. She was disgusted by the preferential treatment given to 'the Bolshoy [sic] artists, high ranking officers … and the big Party-men'. 'I don't want to see this brand of "equality" in our country, I can tell you', she wrote to her friend, Mrs Dodd. Instead of trying to 'inculcate culture', the Soviets should first 'give all the people warm houses' and 'good warm clothes'. She was equally outraged by the sight of women shovelling snow off the icy streets, while a man stood by directing them. But what shocked her most of all was 'the apparent carelessness to human suffering' in a city where thousands of people could walk past a dying man without giving him a second glance.[9]

The staff of the New Zealand Legation in Moscow. 1946. Front row: R.T.G. Patrick, Charles Boswell, Paddy Costello. Back Row: Ray Perry (with pipe), Ruth Macky, Douglas Lake. (By kind permission of Sir James McNeish, Giraffe Publishing House, Moscow)

Ruth's Moscow was another planet. The cosy 'happy-go-lucky bedroom-to-bedroom set-up' of the office hardly felt like a job, and she had fallen hopelessly in love with the city. Everything about it captivated her, from the glorious concert programmes to the 'little round rosy-cheeked woman' who walked three streets with her to help her to buy theatre tickets. In a long letter to her family in January 1945, her happiness leaps from the page: 'There is so much to tell ... so much to do and see ... I hope to God I'm here for years'.[10] But Ruth's passions were not only aroused by the culture and the people; according to the historian Michael King, she was also having an affair with Paddy.[11]

At six foot two with more than his fair share of Irish charm, Paddy had a way with women. His wife had stayed in England, but in any case his occasional infidelities – including a mistress in Cairo with whom he had practised his Russian – never troubled her. Bella, or 'Bil' as she preferred to be called, had long ago captured Paddy's mind and soul and she knew that she had little to fear from passing fancies such as Ruth.

Bil Costello was the child of Russian Jewish immigrants who had come to Britain from the Ukraine before she was born. She was raised in one of the toughest areas of London's East End, in a hotbed of Communism, and she was a committed Marxist. She was also an ardent evangelist and Paddy's short-lived membership of the Communist Party dates from the time of their first meeting. They married in September 1935 and the first of their five children arrived nine months later. But marriage and motherhood did nothing to dampen Bil's crusading zeal. In October 1943 (when Paddy was attached to General Freyberg's staff as an intelligence officer) his close friend, Dan Davin, recalls a disturbing visit to Bil during which she spent an entire weekend trying to convert him to Communism. She failed, but as his diary records, 'It was a close thing … leaving me shaken.'[12]

In his biography *The Sixth Man*, James McNeish claims that Paddy was also 'a compulsive teacher and proselytiser'.[13] If so, he would have found Ruth easy game. Emotionally vulnerable and dazzled by his intellect, she would have embraced his Communist beliefs as part and parcel of the magical Russian world to which he had introduced her. Whoever was responsible – and Paddy has to be a prime suspect – within a few months of her arrival in Moscow, Ruth had made an unshakeable commitment to Communism, which gave a rose-tinted glow to the rest of her posting.

She was not an isolated case. During the grim years of the 1930s depression, the Marxist-Leninist doctrines of the Soviet Union had gained thousands of adherents amongst middle-class intellectuals in Britain and Europe, who knew nothing of the horrors of the Gulag or Stalin's brutal purges. Combined with the stirring music of Tchaikovsky and the golden domes of the Kremlin, it was a powerful mix which seduced, among others, the notorious 'Cambridge spies' Burgess, Philby, Blunt and Maclean. Even the ageing Webbs succumbed, becoming staunch supporters of Communism for the rest of their lives.

But while Ruth was sampling the delights of the Bolshoi and exploring the bookshops with Paddy, a Red Army officer named Alexander Solzhenitsyn was being viciously beaten and interrogated in the Lubyanka prison for daring to criticise Stalin. For a few frank comments in a letter, he was condemned to an eight-year sentence in a labour camp and exile for life in Kazakhstan. His horrific experiences are immortalised in his novel *One Day in the Life of Ivan Denisovich* and in his epoch-making *Gulag Archipelago*, which is now compulsory reading for Russian schoolchildren.

After their arrival in Moscow, Jean and Ruth went their separate ways. As the Minister's wife, Jean would not normally have consorted with the Archivist, which, as she explains in a letter to Mrs Dodd, was simply 'a snobbish rendition of typist & stenographer'.[14] With an MA in French, Ruth's abilities went far beyond typing, but in the rank-conscious world of diplomacy, the differing status of the two women precluded an ongoing friendship. Nevertheless, after their many weeks of intimacy, Jean could not have failed to observe the starry-eyed state of her former travelling companion – nor the amount of time that she was spending with Paddy. In a top secret telegram from Charles, marked 'Personal for McIntosh', he refers to having to 'expedite the arrival of the Costello family in order to terminate certain gossip.'[15] It seems likely, however, that the whistle-blower was Jean.

The suggestion that Bil Costello should join her husband presented McIntosh with a delicate problem. When he interviewed Paddy in London, he had chosen to regard his leftwing views as 'no more radically-minded than they should be'. But Bil was quite another matter. She had a dossier with the British security authorities and a condition of Paddy's recruitment had been that his wife should not accompany him. Much to his discomfiture, however, McIntosh had recently learnt from the British High Commissioner in Wellington that Paddy's earlier employment at Exeter University had been terminated for 'undesirable Communist activities' and that his wife still had a close association with the local Communist Party.[16]

McIntosh agonised over it for days, unable to bear the thought of losing the man whom he regarded as his most brilliant recruit. In the end he decided to accept Paddy's assurances that his dismissal from Exeter University was due 'more to the atmosphere of semi-hysteria … than to any particular activities of mine'. On Bil's activities, Paddy was rather less than convincing, claiming that 'to the best of my knowledge' she had ceased to have any connection with the Communist Party for over a year.[17] But that was good enough for McIntosh, who heaved a sigh of relief and approved her travel forthwith.

When Bil arrived in Moscow in September 1945, the deadly race to acquire the atom bomb was at its height. The Americans believed they had a head start, but within a few days of the US bombings of Hiroshima and Nagasaki, an American Communist named Lona Cohen had delivered a sheaf of highly classified papers from the atomic project at Los Alamos to the

Soviet Consulate in New York. En route, her train was searched by military police, but according to the *Mitrokhin Archive*, she tucked the atomic secrets inside a newspaper and asked a policeman to hold them while she opened her bags for inspection.

Much of Paddy's finest reporting was on the atomic arms race. In diplomatic circles most people thought that the Soviets were playing a game of bluff, but at an early stage Paddy assured McIntosh that the Russians had the bomb. 'He showed us this conclusively, and so accurately you'd have thought he had inside information', McIntosh remarked later.[18] Convinced of Paddy's loyalty, however, McIntosh attributed his uncanny foresight to his skill as a political reporter.

Ruth seems to have accepted Bil's arrival with good grace. In a letter to McIntosh, she refers charitably to her 'excellent cooking' and to the great improvement in Paddy's health since he had moved to a flat with his family. Doubtless well aware that she was on probation, Bil was the soul of discretion and kept her distance from the Legation, whose members were still languishing in the hotel. As diplomatic wives, she and Jean would have had nothing in common and in a later interview Jean confirms that 'Mrs Costello kept very much to herself'.[19] Their only recorded conversation was about food.

Living in their comfortable Moscow flat, complete with maid, the Costellos rapidly went native. All their neighbours were Russian and their children attended the local school. A photograph taken of the family in 1948 shows Bil demurely clad in a white blouse with her large dark eyes fixed steadily on the camera. With Paddy's air of high seriousness and her own central European features, they look like model members of the Soviet 'Nomenklatura'.

Meanwhile the long months in the hotel were taking their toll on Ruth. She was desperately thin and seemed to get cold after cold. Jean thought she should go home, 'but it would just about break her heart'.[20] More discerningly, Paddy noted her 'overstrung nerves'.[21] For several months, he had been urging McIntosh to promote her from her clerical status to a diplomat. In his view Doug Lake, who was listed as the Legation's office assistant and typist, would also make 'an excellent attaché'.[22] Furthermore, as diplomats, both would receive better rations of food and clothing.

Even for those with diplomatic privileges, food was a major problem. In their hotel room, the Boswells' dinner often consisted of a tin of beans or herrings, which was all they could buy at the local 'diplomatic' shop.

Model members of the Soviet 'nomenklatura'. Bil and Paddy Costello with their children in Moscow, 1948. (By kind permission of Sir James McNeish, Josephine Proctor)

During her first six months in Moscow, Jean lost a stone and, as the weeks in the hotel stretched into months, her homesickness for New Zealand only seemed to increase. The one bright spot was their mounting bank balance. She and Charles were living on the sniff of an oil rag and at the rate they were saving his generous entertainment allowance, Charles calculated they might even be able to pay off their mortgage. But the slow-moving wheels of the Soviet bureaucracy had finally begun to turn and in May 1946, after twenty-one months in the National Hotel, the New Zealand Legation moved to a home of its own.

The Kekushev Mansion was a curious mixture of fantasy and Art Nouveau. Compared with the enormous palace overlooking the Kremlin occupied by the British, or the American Ambassador's vast Residence with its eighty-two foot long reception room and a chandelier the size of a Christmas tree, it was quite modest. But with a five-room office and a staff flat on the ground floor, and a ten-room apartment for the Boswells upstairs, it was a great improvement on the National Hotel. The furnishing, naturally, was Jean's department and in an exhausting two weeks she, Charles and Paddy bought everything, 'down to the last salt spoon', in Stockholm.[23]

On the way to Sweden, they stopped in Leningrad. Jean gazed dutifully at the Winter Palace and plodded down Nevsky Prospekt. Some of the vistas were undoubtedly very fine, but as far as she was concerned 'even such a lovely city as Leningrad' could not compare 'in beauty, nor in comfort or convenience' to the cities at home.[24] With the prospect of a house of her own, however, Jean's letters become more cheerful. She writes gaily of the 'peacocks' parade' at state receptions, when the members of the Diplomatic Corps emerged resplendent in their uniforms and decorations, and of feasting her eyes on the beautiful wife of the British Air Attaché – 'I could never tire of looking at her' – and the handsome Netherlands Ambassador.[25]

In October 1946, Ruth's life also took a dramatic turn for the better. Concerned by the reports of her ill-health, McIntosh arranged for her to be attached for twelve weeks to the New Zealand Delegation at the Paris Peace Conference. Paddy went too, but by this time Ruth had transferred her affections elsewhere. She had found another soulmate in the office and at the end of the Conference she took three weeks' leave, during which she and Doug Lake were married.

They broke the news to their colleagues in Moscow by telegram. Paddy's reactions were mixed and in a letter to McIntosh he questions Doug's wisdom in marrying 'a girl 5 years older and better educated than himself'. On Ruth, whose biological clock had been ticking for some time, he adopts a rather different tone: marriage was just what she needed and 'if she has the sense to let her job go and to have a baby, I believe she'll get some of the emotional stability that she lacks now'.[26] While these comments may well reflect his pique at not being in on the secret, in the light of future events Paddy's observations seem to have been remarkably shrewd.

Unlike other female employees of the Department of External Affairs, Ruth was not made to resign on marriage. Ray Perry and R.T. Patrick had long since returned to New Zealand and, with her fluent Russian, she had become a key member of the team. When her first baby arrived in July 1948, she gave birth in a Moscow maternity home and predictably wrote an ecstatic report on the Soviet approach to childbirth – which according to Doug included an instruction to massage her breasts with vodka. By this time he, too, had become an ardent convert to Communism, thereby creating an insuperable ideological gulf between the Legation's three remaining staff and the Boswells. To the Boswells' faces, Paddy was as charming as ever. Indeed, both Charles and Jean came to regard him with great affection. But his letters to Wellington are full of sly asides on their social ineptitude and penny-pinching ways, which were relished by McIntosh.

After his return to New Zealand in September 1949, Charles delivered a resounding condemnation of Communism to the Prime Minister. He also had a painful interview with McIntosh who, with the help of the Commissioner of Police, had obtained a copy of his bank account. During his five years in Moscow Charles had saved over £5,000 which, according to McIntosh's calculations, was most of the allowance that he should have spent on entertaining. After his twenty-one months in the National Hotel, Charles reckoned he deserved every penny of it. Furious and humiliated, he went home to Jean and together they plotted their revenge.

On 3 December 1949, the first of Jean's nine articles on her experiences in Moscow appeared in the Auckland *Herald*. In them she gives a damning picture of life in Stalinist Russia, with a blow-by-blow account of the many vicissitudes that she and Charles endured there. The articles were written with pace and drama and the *Herald*'s readers loved them. Moreover, Jean's timing could not have been more perfect. In New Zealand, anti-Communist sentiment was running high and the new National government had just announced its intention to close the Legation.

Seated at his desk, McIntosh skimmed Jean's articles with irritation. Quite apart from their content, she had no right to publish them without his permission. Then he turned wearily to the lengthy typescript that had been handed to him by Doug, who had also returned to Wellington. It was a scathing article by Ruth rebutting Jean's 'one-eyed' view of the Soviet Union – and an uncompromising defence of Marxism.[27] In a post-war world, in which an 'iron curtain' had descended on Europe and Senator McCarthy was baying for Communist blood, Ruth's article was an act of folly. Worse still, it was destined for publication by the highly suspect New Zealand Society for Closer Relations with the USSR.

When he had finished reading, McIntosh called in his secretary and dictated a stern letter to Ruth, pointing out that 'as an ex Diplomatic Officer and the wife of a Diplomatic Officer you are not as free as the private citizen to express your views in public'. Sensing that she had the bit between her teeth, McIntosh did not mince his words: if she published 'the majority … will have no doubt that you are a Communist … It will be impossible to send Doug overseas again … and here in the Department his position may well be rendered untenable … He has every chance of making an outstanding career in this Service. All I am saying, as brutally as I can, is that you are going the right way to ruin it'.[28]

Ruth, who had resigned her job not long after the birth of her first child, wrote him a dignified reply thanking him his advice, which she completely disregarded. Younger and far less strong-minded than his wife, Doug ducked for cover by claiming that he had too much respect for Ruth 'to attempt to over-rule her or to persuade her to act against her conscience'.[29] A few months later, the article appeared in a quaint booklet illustrated with photographs of smiling Soviet schoolchildren and shops overflowing with food. But Ruth did not have Jean's journalistic flair and her article makes wearisome reading. Meanwhile, as predicted, Doug's career was ruined and he was subsequently forced to resign from the Department under suspicion of being a Communist.

The story of the Lakes' commitment to Marxism does not finish here. In 1962, they went to live in Communist China where, at Ruth's instigation, their three young daughters joined the Red Guards. On her return to New Zealand, Ruth continued with her political activism. But with his questionable credentials, no one would employ Doug and he ended up working as a storeman.

Jean's story has a happier ending. On the strength of her articles in the *Herald*, she became a popular speaker on 'Life behind the Curtain'. She played croquet and went to church and in her sixties she wrote two charming books, which give a vivid picture of her childhood in Northland and have become classics of their kind.

Unlike Jean and Ruth, Bil remains a shadowy figure. She left no memoirs or letters and all that survives in the public domain is a few scribbled cards and some family photographs. But although we never hear her voice, it is clear from the testimonies of others that she was the dominant partner in the marriage, who hovered behind her husband like a puppet-master pulling the strings.

When the post in Moscow was closed, the Costellos were transferred to the newly opened Legation in Paris. But Western intelligence agencies had been watching Paddy and when the American Ambassador in Wellington called on the Prime Minister, Sidney Holland, demanding Paddy's dismissal, McIntosh bowed to the inevitable and asked him to resign.

Paddy's letter of resignation is dated 2 July 1954. Shortly beforehand, however, New Zealand passports were wrongly issued by the New Zealand

Legation in Paris to the quick-witted Lona Cohen and her spymaster husband, Morris. Using the names of Helen and Peter Kroger, the Cohens moved to England, where they became leading members of the notorious Portland spy-ring. After their arrest, no conclusive evidence linking them to the Costellos was ever found, but the case earned Paddy the dubious accolade of being 'one of the KGB's top 10 agents' and a permanent place in the Cold War hall of fame.[30] Since then, pages of investigative journalism have been devoted to him. Yet despite the comment by the eminent journalist Geoffrey Cox that much of Paddy's ruthlessness was fuelled by his determination to 'out-do' his wife in her 'intellectual toughness as a Communist', scarcely a line has been written about Bil.[31]

Perhaps the most telling evidence comes from McIntosh. A few months before he died, he gave an interview to Michael King in which he openly acknowledges, for the first time, that Paddy had indeed been working for the Russians. But until the full story is released by the intelligence services, Bil's true role will never be known.

CHAPTER 3.

The Mistress of Vailima

When Robert Louis Stevenson sailed into Apia Harbour on 7 December 1889, he had no intention of settling there. But the beauty of Samoa captivated him and within a few weeks he had purchased an estate of three hundred acres to which he gave the picturesque name of 'Vailima' – meaning five waters. The world-famous author of *Treasure Island* spent lavishly on his new house, which took barely a year to build. Once its floors had been waxed and its rooms filled with antique furniture and works of art, it became known as one of the great stately homes of the Pacific. In a bohemian household of in-laws and stepchildren, Stevenson's domestic arrangements were a blend of the feudal and the exotic. His barefoot houseboys wore flowers in their hair and, in deference to their employer's Scottish origins, changed into Royal Stuart *lava-lavas* on Sundays.

After Stevenson's death in 1894, Vailima was purchased by a German businessman, who completed the original plan by adding another wing with an open-sided ballroom. When the Germans colonised Samoa in 1900, it became the Governor's Residence. But for literary travellers such as 26-year-old Rupert Brooke, who arrived in Apia in November 1913, it remained a place of pilgrimage. Brooke felt a close kinship with Stevenson and his main objective was to visit Vailima and climb the rugged path to the writer's grave on the summit of nearby Mount Vaea.

Like Stevenson, Brooke instantly fell under the spell of Samoa. In a long letter to Violet Asquith, he writes of the 'sheer loveliness' of 'the white sand under the high palms' and 'the black line of the reef a mile out'. Further on in his letter he describes the Samoans as 'the loveliest people in the world, moving and running and dancing like gods and goddesses.'[1] He stayed in

Samoa for less than two weeks, but he spent another three months in the Pacific before reluctantly returning home.

Shortly after the outbreak of World War I, Brooke wrote an article for the *New Statesman*. In it he muses over the recent New Zealand occupation of Samoa, which established an administration that lasted for nearly fifty years. 'A New Zealand Expeditionary Force took it', he writes, 'I suppose they left a garrison, and went away. I can very vividly see them steaming out in the evening; and the crowd on shore would be singing them that sweetest and best-known of South Sea songs, which begins "Good-bye, my Flenni" … I hope they'll rule Samoa well.'[2]

Despite Samoa's well-known charms, Eileen Powles was far from pleased when her husband was offered the position of High Commissioner of Samoa. It was August 1948 and for the first time since the outbreak of World War II she was enjoying a settled existence. Her husband, Dick, was Counsellor at the New Zealand Legation in Washington, but throughout the war he had been in uniform, travelling constantly and leaving Eileen to hold the fort with their two small children in Wellington. Now the family was finally together again; Washington was a delightful place to live, and the last thing she wanted was to move.

Dick's feelings were more mixed. His plain-speaking boss, Carl Berendsen, had warned him that no one had ever emerged from the administration of Samoa with his reputation unsullied. But in career terms it would be an exciting challenge and the rank of High Commissioner would be a significant promotion. Strictly speaking, however, he would no longer be a diplomat because, confusingly, the High Commissioner of Samoa was not a diplomatic envoy, but in effect the Governor who would reside at Vailima.*

Although the letter from the Prime Minister, Peter Fraser, had come like a bolt from the blue, Dick's name had been on the table for some time. Fraser was looking for someone to oversee the delicate task of handing over the reins of government to the Samoans and, with his combination of discipline and liberalism, Dick seemed tailor-made for the job. Not everyone appreciated his qualities; McIntosh complained that he never knew whether he was speaking to Colonel Powles the military stickler, or to Mr Powles the reader of the *Guardian Weekly*. But Eileen understood her husband perfectly and as she and Dick weighed up the merits of the offer, she knew at once that

---

* Until its independence in 1962, Samoa was a United Nations Trust Territory administered by New Zealand.

he wanted to accept it – and that she would go with him. A sense of duty and the desire for adventure would certainly have influenced her thinking, but the overriding factor was her unswerving devotion to the clever, complicated man she had married.

Buried in a boxful of despatches to the Department of Island Territories is a collection of love letters. The earliest ones are written with all the ardour of youth by a girl barely out of her teens to her future husband. More revealing, however, are Eileen's later letters, which date from fifteen years after her marriage when she was finding the ongoing separations from Dick hard to bear. In a stream of letters written in early 1946, she pours out her feelings for him: 'I love you and long for you every day. You are so much part of my life that I feel I am only running on one cylinder when you are away. It is an extraordinary feeling – I think you have had it too.' Twelve days later, she writes again: 'I will be such a happy woman when I have in you my arms once more … It is such a waste of time to be apart, but … we are lucky that we know each other so well that we can come together again just where we parted'. Another equally passionate letter follows: 'I love you with all my heart – and some – and to be with you through your life, and to have your wonderful love, are privileges to cherish most in all the world.'[3] Dick was the mainstay of her existence and, although she confesses to him that their children also have 'a little part'[4] of her love, her deepest affections were for her husband.

For the Powles' two sons, their parents' decision to go to Samoa had far-reaching repercussions. From their pleasant day schools in Washington, they were sent to board in New Zealand with just one paid visit to their parents in three years. In response to Dick's request for annual air fares, an official at the Department of External Affairs tried to soften the blow: 'It is unlikely that the Administration would agree to any additional trips … but on past experience you would probably be required to come to New Zealand at least once a year for consultation.'[5] Nine-year-old Michael, who for nearly a decade spent most of his school holidays staying with cousins, never felt close to his parents again. Later, when the implications of their decision began to sink in, Dick and Eileen suffered too. Shortly after his arrival in Samoa, Dick wrote plaintively to a friend: 'It is a sad and empty existence for parents to live without their children, and I sometimes wonder how we rushed into this so blithely.'[6]

In the meantime Dick and his predecessor, Colonel Voelcker, were busily exchanging letters on the vital matter of dress: 'For evening I wear

Dressed to kill: diplomatic ladies at an unidentified occasion in Washington c. 1948. Eileen Powles is in the front row sporting an ostrich feather. (Powles Family Collection, Reni Photo News Service, Alexander Turnbull Library, Wellington, PAColl-5268-2-1-01)

a white dinner jacket, with a soft white shirt, black trousers and tie, and for formal occasions a white shell jacket, cummerbund and miniatures with black trousers, stiff shirt and collar', explains Voelcker. A sola topi would not be necessary, but in a country where 'considerable store is set by the preservation of what they call dignity', he strongly recommended an official uniform as worn by the British Governor of Fiji.[7] Swords and ostrich feathers were not Dick's style and he later claims to have been 'a complete failure' as a colourful gubernatorial figure.[8] Instead, he settled for a white suit to which he added some minor military touches. Eileen's requirements were far simpler. According to the bachelor Voelcker, all she needed were 'cottony things'.[9] Hats were rarely worn and the most important garment to remember was her bathing dress.

In the Prime Minister's Department preparations were also steaming ahead. Fraser was anxious for his hand-picked appointee to arrive in style and he had arranged for Dick and Eileen to travel to Samoa aboard the Royal

New Zealand Navy's recently purchased frigate, *Hawea*, which boasted an impressive armament. Their arrival on 1 March 1949 was a moving occasion. A huge crowd had gathered to welcome them and as they sailed into the harbour at Apia, the wharf and its adjoining streets were lined with smiling faces. It was their first sight of Samoa and Dick would never forget the beauty of that 'first bright day' – or the emotions that the warmth of the welcome aroused in him.[10]

From the waterfront they were driven to their new home between banks of hibiscus and up a long avenue of teak trees. Many years later, Eileen described her first impressions of Vailima: she found the setting glorious and the house was magnificent, but it seemed enormous and she was shocked by its shabbiness. As the car drew into the porch, Eileen saw a line of figures waiting to greet them. It was the household staff, the men resplendent in gleaming white *lava-lavas* with scarlet sashes and the women in brightly coloured dresses with flowers in their hair.

Down in the town the official welcoming party awaited them and, with little time to spare, Eileen hurried up to the bedroom. Outside the air was like a warm bath, but the interior of the house with its high ceilings and white walls felt deliciously cool. The inside was badly run down and she could see at a glance that she was going to need every inch of the bolt of blue cotton that she had brought from New Zealand. Only a few pretty vases and the odd piece of furniture dating from the time of Stevenson bore witness to its former splendour.

Seated on a flower-decked dais with a group of dignitaries, Eileen began to wilt. There was no shade and the excitements of the day were beginning to catch up on her. As she battled with the unaccustomed heat, an older woman with a gentle smile stepped forward and handed her a fan. Eileen took it thankfully. 'Who was that?' she whispered to the official beside her. 'That's the widow of Mata'afa,' he said. She looked at the older woman with renewed interest. Mata'afa was one of the paramount chiefs, who had been President of Samoa's ill-fated independence movement, the Mau. Eileen knew all about the Mau and as Dick's wife she would have been well briefed on the tragic blunders of 'Black Saturday', which continued to cast a dark shadow over Samoa's relationship with New Zealand.[11]

A few days later, Dick and Eileen accepted their first invitation to dinner. It came from another widow whose late husband, the fiery nationalist Olaf Nelson, was quite as well known as Mata'afa. The Powles' decision to attend was quite contrary to the advice that they had been given in New Zealand,

Reluctant grandees:
Dick and Eileen Powles
at Vailima, c. 1956.

(Powles Family Collection, Alexander
Turnbull Library, PA1-o-821-11)

which was to keep a lofty distance from local society. But it was an important breakthrough with the Samoans, and the news soon went around the town that the new High Commissioner and his wife were very different from the starchy, colonial administrators who had preceded them.

That evening, the Powles met many of the leading Samoans. Foremost among these was the tall imposing Tupua Tamasese Mea'ole, who was a paramount chief and a serious political figure. But he also had a fun-loving side and enjoyed nothing more than launching his twenty-stone frame down the five-metre waterfall at Papasee'a, landing with a huge splash in the pool below. The surrounding forest was said to be full of spirits and before their first slide, Dick and Eileen were taken aside by Tamasese and warned against making any noise that might disturb the resident *aitu*. The Powles became close friends with Tamasese – a relationship that was made all the more remarkable by the shameful death of his elder brother at the hands of New Zealanders. But his wife, Irene, was more wary and her feelings were further complicated by her bitterness over New Zealand's treatment of her father, Olaf Nelson.

'Black Saturday' stands out as one of the most bungled police operations in New Zealand's history. On 28 December 1929 eleven people died when New Zealand military police opened fire on the members of the Mau, who were processing peacefully in Apia. As the situation erupted, Tupua Tamasese Lealofi (who like his brother was an enormous man) went to the front of the crowd to try to halt the violence. An easy target, he was fatally wounded and died a few hours later. In the aftermath hundreds of Mau members took to the hills, where they were later hunted down by New Zealand Marines who had been called in by the Governor.

Any hopes that New Zealand would 'rule Samoa well' were sadly misplaced and this unhappy episode marks the culmination of many years of inept administration. The first blunder came in 1919 when the SS *Talune* was allowed to dock in Apia without quarantine, introducing an influenza epidemic that killed thousands of Samoans. Worse still, when the Governor of neighbouring American Samoa (where there had been no deaths) offered medical aid, it was turned down by the officer in charge. The non-violent Mau movement was equally mishandled and throughout the 1920s harsh sentences of exile and imprisonment were meted out to its leaders – especially to Olaf Nelson. By March 1930 the male members of the Mau had agreed to disperse, but thanks to the Women's Mau, the movement survived for several more years and the desire for independence had never died.

Fortunately for the Powles, the other leading couple whom they met on this occasion had suffered no similar wrongs. Malietoa Tanumafili II, who came from a long line of Samoan kings, was also a paramount chief and his wife, Lili, was a beauty who, according to Dick, possessed both grace and intelligence. In such company, the Powles enjoyed a lively evening. Nevertheless, as they drove home from this first foray into local high society, both of them must have realised that living in Samoa was going to be far more complicated than they had ever imagined.

Eileen's first task at Vailima was to get rid of the jailbirds. Under their predecessor, the sixty acres of grounds had been tended by a team of prisoners who worked under the eye of a warder. Voelcker, it seemed, had been on cosy terms with both the judge and the gaoler to ensure a regular supply. In Samoa, where a 'three-sided' cell had notoriously allowed prisoners to swim home to see their families, it seems unlikely that the gardeners were in chains. But the thought of convict labour appalled Eileen and in any case she was longing to get into the garden herself. Voelcker's cook (who stole the sugar) lasted a little longer. Later, however, Eileen employed the Head Boy's

The household staff at Vailima, 1950s. (Powles Family Collection, Alexander Turnbull Library, Wellington, PAColl-5268-2-2-28)

wife, Sanini, who could memorise a recipe instantly and then repeat it back to her.

Eileen's box of recipe cards is another treasure that is lurking in the official files. Among the more sophisticated dishes are a Mint and Pea Aspic 'set in a mould' and an exotic-sounding Hot Prune Soufflé. Old favourites like Apple Charlotte and Irish Stew also feature prominently and tucked between the recipes for Ginger Fudge and Minted Sugar Fingers is one for the inevitable Pavlova. But what evokes the long summer days and the garden parties most vividly is the 'Buffet Punch' made of ginger ale and pineapple, which, together with bananas, coconuts and taro, grew in abundance at Vailima.

After years of neglect, there was an overwhelming amount of work to be done on the house and garden. Yet in Dick's downtown office the five hundred-strong guest list for the annual King's Birthday garden party was already being prepared and, although she had barely arrived, Eileen could see from the diary that a steady stream of politicians and officials were expected from New Zealand and the UN Trusteeship Council in New York. Apart from Aggie Grey's well-known establishment on the waterfront, Apia had no hotels, and all these visiting dignitaries would stay at Vailima, leaving their shoes outside the bedroom doors nightly to be cleaned by the household staff. But much as Eileen longed to roll up her sleeves and start pruning the roses, there was something far more important on the agenda. She and Dick were going on their first *malaga*.

Going on *malaga* is a time-honoured Samoan occupation and consists of walking from village to village, partaking of the local hospitality. The Powles' first *malaga* was an ambitious one involving an almost complete circuit of the main island, Savai'i, which took them nearly two weeks. They travelled in a small group, mostly on beautiful beachside paths along which arches of flowers and greenery had been erected in their honour. Every night they stopped at a different village, where they were accommodated in a traditional thatched *fale* reserved for guests. While Dick was entertained by the local chiefs, Eileen was looked after by the members of the Women's Committee, who seemed to run everything in the village from hospitality to health. Apart from a few contacts in Apia, this was her first real encounter with the local women. She found them supremely well organised and, although tradition dictated that they should walk behind their husbands, there was no mistaking their self-assurance – or their influence within the community.

To a newcomer, social relations in Samoa can be baffling. The paramount chiefs enjoy the status of royalty and the rest of society is rigidly stratified between the *matai* – the nobles – and everyone else. Yet, as Eileen soon observed, there were no tensions between the classes. Instead, they all seemed to live together like a family. With her household staff, she enjoyed the same easy informality, often working alongside the men in the garden or chatting with the women in the kitchen. For them, like Tamasese, the spirit world was very much in evidence and on one occasion Eileen was called into the kitchen to watch three *aitu* floating across the lawn. The staff could see them quite clearly, but to her they were invisible.

She also realised that Vailima belonged quite as much to the staff as it did to her. On the day that she gave her first ball, she came downstairs early in the morning to find the whole ballroom decked with flowers. The staff had been up since dawn, picking hundreds of hibiscus from the hedgerows and entwining the pillars with ferns. It was their own initiative and they did it for love. But with the local Europeans, Eileen's experiences were less happy. They regarded Vailima as European territory and at the King's Birthday garden party several of them turned on their heels and walked out when they saw the number of Samoans present. For her part, Eileen was shocked to discover how few of her new Samoan friends had ever been invited to Vailima.

Once the novelty of their arrival had worn off, Dick and Eileen started to feel the pressure. In August 1949, Dick admitted to a friend that 'the shock of finding out what this job was really like' was causing him considerable nervous and physical strain.[12] Eileen, meanwhile, was working flat out on the house and garden and coping with endless visitors. When a United Nations mission arrived to inspect Dick's progress, she was in hospital with typhoid fever. But she still managed to stagger home and entertain them to tea at Vailima.

Over the following months, the pace continued remorselessly. In a letter to Berendsen the following year, Dick confesses to 'serious doubts as to whether Eileen or I have even the physical constitution necessary to stand up to the combined strain of the work and the activities of the position itself, and of the social responsibilities which are so clamorously expected of one.'[13] They were living in a goldfish bowl, in a community that Dick later describes as a 'small but seething hot-bed of personalities and intrigue', which it took all of Eileen's tact and charm to manage.[14] A photograph taken during these early years shows an unassuming couple, Dick slightly self-conscious in his semi-military uniform and Eileen with a shy smile. They both look tired, but there is also a touching closeness about them.

In a later interview, Eileen firmly dismisses any suggestion that she influenced her husband's political decisions. But there can be little doubt that she contributed a great deal to the success of their personal relationships – which in the hot-house atmosphere of Apia were quite as important as politics. Dick had no small talk and he could be prickly in social situations, whereas Eileen was a past master at putting others at their ease and, judging from her skilful handling of her interviewer, she was also a deft conversationalist.

As their three-year appointment extended into a second (and later third) term, life was not without its lighter moments. In 1953, Hollywood descended on Apia in the form of Gary Cooper and *Return to Paradise*, which was filmed in Samoa. According to their son, Michael, Eileen was sorely smitten, but she only managed to get her photograph taken with Cooper's sidekick, Barry Jones, who played the less romantic role of a missionary. One of Dick's staff, a dashing young diplomat named Paul Edmonds, did rather better. After unsuccessfully pursuing the Samoan leading lady, Moira Walker, he married her equally attractive younger sister, Sheila.

Under Eileen's careful stewardship, Vailima was gradually regaining some of its former glory. Their numerous guests were among the chief beneficiaries and after a ten-day visit in 1957 the wife of the distinguished historian J.C. Beaglehole was ecstatic: 'Such luxury and comfort I've never known … and the whole place just so beautiful.'[15] Another illustrious guest

Eileen Powles (left) and a friend collecting shellfish on the beach in Samoa, 1950s.

(Powles Family Collection, Alexander Turnbull Library, Wellington, PA1-o-821-23)

Dick and Eileen Powles aboard a launch with son, Michael, and future joint Head of State, Tupua Tamasese Meaʻole, in the background, Samoa 1950s.

(Powles Family Collection, photo Donald Ross, Alexander Turnbull Library, Wellington, PA1-o-822-24)

was the New Zealand Governor General, Lord Cobham, who came with his wife on a 'never-to-be-forgotten visit' to Samoa. But judging from the two-page letter which he sent afterwards, fulminating against an 'excrescent definite article' that he had discovered in the poem on Stevenson's tomb, he cannot always have been an easy guest.[16]

For the two boys, exotic holidays in Samoa were a considerable compensation for the long periods of separation from their parents. Eileen talks of 'glorious' days spent boating and swimming and of moonlight picnics on the beaches.[17] Moreover, despite the government's parsimony, Dick's letters show that both his sons visited Samoa far more frequently than every three years. The journey itself was an adventure. Originally they travelled by DC3, which took three days via Norfolk Island, Fiji and Tonga. Later they went by flying boat, which continued on to Aitutaki and Tahiti and often carried some attractive female passengers. But Michael remembers that when he announced on landing that he had invited one particularly beautiful Tahitian girl to join them for lunch at Vailima, Dick and Eileen were not amused.

Ever since her first *malaga* Eileen had been thinking hard and long about the Women's Committees. From her close friendship with Lili Malietoa and (in slower time) with Irene Tamasese, she now understood far more about the role of the Committees and the many benefits that they had brought to their communities since their formation in the 1920s. But in a nation composed of hundreds of villages, they worked as separate units, and it was Eileen who first grasped what a force they could become if they were united.

Her idea of a national forum caught on like wildfire. Before long the radio network between the villages was buzzing and a date was set for an all-day session in Apia. Nothing like this had ever happened before and as the women arrived in their hundreds on foot and by bus, or on boats from the outlying islands, the excitement was palpable. At that first great meeting, Eileen insisted that this was to be *Samoa Mo Samoa*, Samoa for Samoans, and Irene Tamasese, Lili Malietoa and her charismatic sister-in-law, Salamasina Malietoa, who was principal of the leading school for girls in Apia, were elected as Presidents. But although Eileen refused any starring role for herself, at the end of the session she suggested that all future meetings should take place at Vailima.

The second meeting of the Women's Committees was an unforgettable occasion. Once again, it was attended by hundreds of women, many of whom had travelled for several days. They arrived early in the morning pouring up the drive of Vailima in their best clothes, garlanded with *leis* and walking with the stately, slow walk of the Samoans that had reminded Rupert Brooke of the gods. The meeting took place in the ballroom, where Eileen had provided cold drinks and scattered mats for seating. Afterwards the women went out onto the lawns and sat in groups beneath the trees. They had all brought food, which they shared between them. As Eileen had foreseen, the unified Women's Committees went from strength to strength. Later, the members built a magnificent building of their own and changed their name to the National Council of Women. But for many years they continued to meet under Eileen's guidance at Vailima, filling the house with the babble of voices and the soft melodies of the Pacific.

Eileen and Dick stayed in Samoa for eleven years. Throughout their time, the mechanisms for parliamentary democracy were gradually evolving and when they left the preparations for self-government were all but completed. Tamasese and Malietoa became joint Heads of State and the son of Mata'afa was chosen as Prime Minister. All over the country, schools and hospitals had sprung up and many miles of new road had been built. More importantly, however, in the growing atmosphere of trust and friendship, the bitter memories of 'Black Saturday' had begun to fade.

Shortly before their departure in April 1960, Dick and Eileen went on a farewell *malaga*. Unlike their first expedition, they travelled mostly by boat and Land Rover. At every place, they were greeted with speeches and gifts and covered with *leis*. By this time they could speak Samoan and dance the *siva* with the best of them, and in many of the villages they ended up joining in the dancing to the strains of the local band and the singing of the Women's Committee. In the face of so much genuine regret at their departure, even the restrained Dick was occasionally overwhelmed by his feelings. In his farewell speech at Saleaula, he assured the assembled chiefs and orators with undisguised emotion that he and Eileen 'would never say goodbye' because they were taking part of Samoa with them in their hearts.[18]

As the village women gathered round her to pay tribute to her years of work with the Women's Committees, Eileen was equally moved. Like her Samoan sisters, she belonged to a generation of women who figuratively still walked behind their husbands and she expected no special recognition. Yet some would argue that her success in transforming the Women's Committees into a national body – thereby enabling half the population of Samoa to voice their aspirations – was a considerable achievement. She was,

Vailima as it looks today. (Robert Louis Stevenson Museum, Samoa)

as a Samoan friend tells her in a heart-warming farewell letter, 'the only First *Palagi* Lady in Vailima whose name is on every Samoan woman's lips.'[19]

Dick was knighted, but Eileen received no such personal honours. Her reward was her husband's happiness and the privilege of being the mistress of Vailima.

On 1 January 1962, Western Samoa became an independent nation and Vailima is now the Robert Louis Stevenson Museum.

CHAPTER 4.

Art Lovers

Lyn scrambled out of bed shivering. It was 4.00 a.m. and although the date had been carefully chosen as the sunniest day of the year, in traditional British style it had dawned grey and overcast with flurries of rain. With a house full of guests, she dressed noiselessly and tiptoed downstairs in her long silk ball gown and tiara to get her camera. Photography was her passion and before she and Frank left for Westminster Abbey, she set up her tripod in the dining-room and took their pictures.

As Deputy High Commissioner at New Zealand House in London, Frank Corner was one small cog in the huge machine that had been working for over a year to ensure that on Coronation Day everything – barring the weather – went perfectly. Resplendent in white tie and tails, and bearing a golden staff, he had been appointed a Gold Staff Officer at Westminster Abbey, where a seat had also been reserved for Lyn. Theoretically his role was that of an usher, but in practice he spent most of his time escorting foreign dignitaries and their wives to the specially installed loos.

In London, the excitement had reached fever pitch. Visitors had been pouring into the city for days and on the previous afternoon, when Lyn had taken her American guests on a tour of the street decorations, they had seen hundreds of people preparing to sleep out along the processional route. A few days earlier, as a special privilege, Lyn had attended the dress rehearsal at which she had witnessed the entire three-hour ceremony. A young woman had stood in for the Queen, silently enacting her every step except for the actual crowning, which was deemed too sacred even for rehearsal

By 6.00 a.m. on 2 June 1953, Lyn was sitting in her car outside Westminster Abbey. Frank had been invited to a sustaining breakfast by the

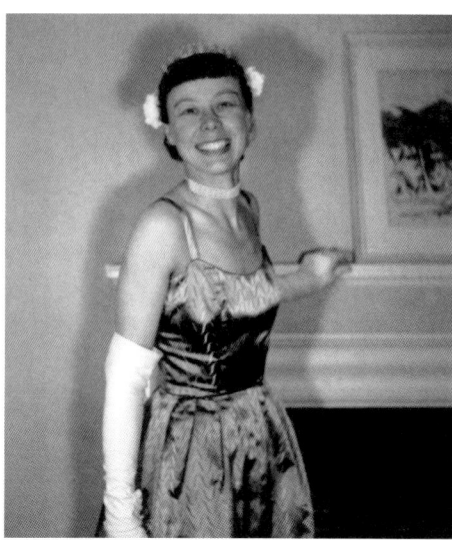

Lyn Corner in full court dress at 5.00 a.m. on Coronation Day, London, 2 June 1953. (By kind permission of Lyn Corner)

Coronation's chief organiser, the Duke of Norfolk, but Lyn was not included and to keep herself going for the next seven or eight hours, she had slipped a little supply of nuts and raisins into her evening bag. While she waited for Frank to emerge, she watched the splendidly attired guests streaming past to take their seats in the Abbey. It was a public holiday and without the usual roar of the traffic, the streets seemed strangely silent. All she could hear was the brisk patter of feet and the occasional clatter of a sword. As a trio of men approached, Lyn noticed that one had the morning's newspaper folded in his pocket. The big black headlines were clearly visible. 'EVEREST IS CLIMBED … HILLARY DOES IT'.[1] 'And that's how I learnt the news,' said Lyn, 'on Coronation morning.'[2]

The newly crowned Queen did not leave the Abbey until shortly before three o'clock. Her royal progress back to the Palace took over two hours, in a procession of 16,000 people that stretched for three kilometres. By this time it was pouring with rain. But nothing could dampen the spirits of the crowd and when Queen Salote of Tonga rolled by in an open landau, soaked to the skin and wreathed in smiles, she was cheered with almost as much enthusiasm as the Queen. After battling home through the crowds to change out of their finery, Lyn and Frank joined a flotilla of barges that sailed down the Thames to the strains of Handel's *Water Music*. Much later the Queen made a second appearance on the balcony of Buckingham Palace, and at midnight a magnificent display of fireworks illuminated the sky. It had been a long day.

Ten years into a brilliant diplomatic partnership, Lyn and Frank, like Ed Hillary, were headed for the top. But the origin of their alliance, at a rowdy student party in Wellington, could hardly have been further from diplomacy. It all began in 1941, when 20-year-old Frank asked 19-year-old Lyn to dance. At barely five foot two, with shining hair and a gamine charm that had already caught Frank's eye, the diminutive Lyn was an ideal match for his modest five foot eight and they made a perfect pair. Whether their first steps together were a waltz or a foxtrot (or even perhaps a jitterbug) is not recorded, but the encounter must have been a success because afterwards, according to Frank, Lyn accepted a banana split at the Rose Milk Bar downstairs. From then on they were inseparable and two years later they married.

Through Frank, who was doing an MA in history, Lyn joined the lively, intellectual circle that had formed around Victoria University's legendary historians, F.L.W. Wood and J.C. Beaglehole. Both men were champions of social justice and at their hospitable tables the political debate – together with talk of art and music – often lasted late into the night. Some considered them dangerously radical, including the Prime Minister, Peter Fraser, who reputedly regarded Victoria University as 'a hotbed of Communism'.[3] Of course it was nothing of the sort. But there can be little doubt that the influence of the left-leaning Wood and the LSE*-trained Beaglehole helped to form the liberal political outlook that Lyn and Frank espoused for the rest of their lives.

Whenever she visited the Beagleholes, Lyn could not take her eyes off the walls. The Beagleholes were serious collectors and they had an impressive array of paintings by contemporary New Zealand artists. Among them was a compelling portrait by a struggling orchardist named Toss Woollaston, a still life by T.A. McCormack and a series of works by the Auckland art teacher, John Weeks, who had studied Cubism in Paris. Elsewhere she became familiar with the stark canvases of Colin McCahon and the brooding landscapes of Eric Lee-Johnson, works that were at the cutting edge of New Zealand's art scene and to which she instantly responded. Before long, Lyn and Frank had acquired a small collection of their own and were eagerly snapping up any stray sketches by Weeks or T.A. McCormack that lay within their budget.

Alister McIntosh moved in the same intellectual circles and with his penchant for clever young men, he soon spotted Frank as a suitable recruit for the new Department of External Affairs. As Secretary of the War Cabinet

* London School of Economics, traditionally a bastion of socialism.

and de facto Head of the Prime Minister's Department, McIntosh was already overworked and he urgently needed a capable junior to whom he could delegate some of his responsibilities. By May 1943, he had wrested Frank from his wartime job in the Air Staff's Secret Registry and set him to work on the task of establishing New Zealand's Diplomatic Service. McIntosh was delighted with his catch and, in a letter to Berendsen a few months later, he describes Frank as 'easily the best youngster I've ever had any dealings with.'[4] But what he did not yet know was that he was getting two for the price of one.

One of Frank's first projects (prompted, so he claims, by a call on McIntosh by an outraged European diplomat proposing a duel) was a booklet on diplomatic protocol. Nobody in Wellington knew anything about it and, furthermore, Peter Fraser had no intention of kowtowing to such 'queer foreign practices'[5] as fussing over *placement* at dinner. But for Frank and Lyn, who were already being bombarded with invitations from Wellington's small band of foreign diplomats, the need for some instruction was becoming pressing.

Happily for them all the well-known manuals, including de Callières' classic *On the Manner of Negotiating with Princes* and Harold Nicolson's *Diplomacy*, were readily available in the adjoining General Assembly Library. As a modestly paid public servant, Frank would have found de Callières' stern injunction to clothe himself 'in magnificence' distinctly daunting. On the other hand, the useful tip that 'he should drink in such a manner as not to lose control of his own faculties while endeavouring to loosen the self-control of others' could have been quite helpful. Similarly, the advice that no aspiring diplomat should neglect the ladies of the court, 'for it is well known that the power of feminine charm often extends to cover the weightiest resolutions of state'[6] would certainly not have been lost on Lyn. Nor could she have failed to notice Nicolson's famous summary of diplomatic virtues:

> *These, then are the qualities of my ideal diplomatist. Truth, accuracy, calm, patience, good temper, modesty and loyalty … 'But,' the reader may object, 'you have forgotten intelligence, knowledge, discernment, prudence, hospitality, charm, industry, courage and even tact.' I have not forgotten them. I have taken them for granted.*[7]

Apart from Nicolson and de Callières, Lyn acquired much of her early education on what she calls 'the after hours requirements of a Foreign Service career'[8] at the houses of foreign diplomats. On the New Zealand side, her only role model was McIntosh's wife, Doris, and at the McIntoshes' elegant little dinner parties she observed everything from the careful mix of guests to the vases of magnolia or rhododendron that were arranged around the room. Behind the scenes she looked on admiringly as Doris 'performed some of those passes on the high wire that her cooking required',[9] noting that this too was something she needed to master. With an MA in Latin and French, as well as a teacher's training, she was well equipped to pursue a career of her own, but Frank's star was in the ascendant and her sights had already moved far beyond her junior position with the Country Library Service.

During these early years, Frank travelled constantly. But McIntosh had soon realised that Lyn was a valuable asset, and in July 1946 he arranged for her to join Frank at the Paris Peace Conference, where she would be a useful French-speaking addition to the staff. It was a hair-raising journey. The mode of transport was a converted Lancaster bomber, which was struck by lightning and forced to land in Iraq. There Lyn watched helplessly as the eight pounds of New Zealand butter that she was bringing to a friend in Paris melted away on the runway. The senior members of the delegation were flown on, but Lyn and the Minister's wife were left with the ailing aircraft, which took a further two weeks, with five unscheduled stops, to reach its destination.

Dining nightly at the Hotel Claridge on the Champs Elysées, Lyn soon forgot the discomforts of the trip. In Paris, food rationing was still in force, but the French government had pulled out the stops for the Peace Conference: wine and pâté de foie gras were in pre-war abundance. The Conference passed in a whirl of entertainments and cultural pursuits which left Lyn with an enduring love of Paris. It was also during this memorable ten weeks together that she and Frank formed their lifelong friendship with McIntosh.

Back in New Zealand, Frank was at the heart of the embryonic foreign policy that was gradually taking shape in Wellington. Imbued with the teaching of Wood and Beaglehole, he and Lyn belonged to the generation of New Zealanders who firmly believed that it was time for New Zealand to cut the colonial apron strings. In a memoir of his early career, Frank places a consciousness of 'New Zealand's geographical position in the South Pacific' and 'not off the coast of Western Europe'[10] at the top of the list of factors which should shape the government's foreign policy. But he had no illusions about the need for powerful allies and in July 1948 he wrote a paper that included the following:

It would seem, therefore, to be in our long-term interest to establish as soon as possible the most intimate relationship with the United States in order than she may develop the habit of thinking of New Zealand as a close associate and ally. It is not fanciful to suggest that the grand aim of New Zealand external policy and diplomacy might be to secure in some form an American guarantee of the security of New Zealand.[11]

Three months later, he and Lyn were on their way to Washington.

In Washington, Lyn's early apprenticeship in Wellington and Paris began to pay off. Unlike most wives on a first posting, she already understood the tools of the trade – not just Frank's, but also hers as the spouse of a junior diplomat representing a very small country in the capital of the world's greatest superpower. Her domain was not the corridors of the State Department or the conference table, yet for those who knew how the game was played the opportunities for winning friends and allies could be just as great around your own dining table.

At the Embassy her tasks were lowly. Wives were not permitted to work and at official parties she was expected to be part of the team looking after guests, moving chairs and making sure that no one was lonely. At home she took cooking lessons and entertained Frank's contacts. 'You knew it was your job,' said Lyn, 'and I just got on with it.'[12]

Many years later, she set out her credo:

A good table and a good setting may create warmth, but at the heart of any successful entertaining there must be the spark of genuine communication. The people met together are the vital core. Were they well chosen for likely interaction? Have they been given the chance to talk well? Have they established some mutual confidence and found reason to meet again? The person who underpins the complex function of inspiring warmth and enjoyment in social occasions has become recognised over the years as a true diplomatic partner ... a role which may now be seen as out-dated but which in many parts of the world has its use.[13]

Apart from her busy round of entertaining, Lyn also took advantage of the traditional network of spouses' activities to cultivate friendships with those who mattered. Thus a course in Spanish gained her a valuable entrée to a circle of Senators' wives who, like de Callières' court ladies, were women of considerable influence. Lyn made friends with them all and by the end of the course there was not one who did not know about New Zealand.

Frank and Lyn Corner with their beloved Studebaker, Bear Mountain, New York, c. 1950. (By kind permission of Lyn Corner)

Whenever she was off duty, Lyn haunted the museums and art galleries. Before leaving for Washington, she and Frank had bought one of their first serious paintings, a striking canvas by John Weeks which, together with their two pictures by Rita Angus, made an unequivocal statement about the quality of New Zealand art. For Lyn, art was an expression of national identity and displaying New Zealand art on her walls was as much part of representing her country as understanding the finer points of rugby or citing the numbers of sheep.

Meanwhile down at the Embassy, the 'grand aim' of which Frank had dreamed in 1948 was inching towards reality. On 1 September 1951, to the thunder of a 19-gun salute, New Zealand's veteran Ambassador, Carl Berendsen, signed the ANZUS treaty which pledged the United States, Australia and New Zealand to a military alliance and mutual support in the Pacific.

When Lyn and Frank eventually returned to New Zealand in 1958, they found that the Department of External Affairs had changed out of all recognition. It now boasted fifteen overseas posts, including half a dozen in Asia, and had a rapidly expanding workforce. For Lyn, who by this time had two small children, readjusting to life at home would become a familiar process. But once the marathon of unpacking and cleaning was completed, she went out to look at pictures. She was enthralled by what she saw. During her long absence, New Zealand's art scene had advanced by leaps and bounds and in the numerous newly opened galleries she found an abundance of works that could hold their own anywhere.

As McIntosh's deputy, Frank seems to have had no trouble in convincing his boss that the Department should put 'some decent art'[14] on the walls of its Embassies. New Zealand's economy was booming and during these prosperous post-war years the foundations were laid for a Departmental art collection that reads like a roll call of New Zealand's finest painters. Officially Frank was the prime mover but, with her unerring eye, Lyn was in the thick of things. Later others played a role, including another art-loving wife, Françoise Norrish, who in 1968 discovered a superb landscape by Frances Hodgkins languishing in the British Embassy in Brussels. After some delicate negotiations with the Foreign Office, the Hodgkins was purchased for the Department at its original 1945 price of £270.00.

Frank's stellar rise continued and by 1962 he had been appointed to the ambassadorial post of New Zealand's Permanent Representative to the United Nations in New York. In the early 1960s, New York was the world's most exciting city, exploding with an exuberant creativity that was fuelled by a youthful population and the financial might of Wall Street. Lyn took to it like a duck to water, skilfully juggling her diplomatic duties with her artistic interests and the long hours she spent in her dark room. Thanks to her love of art and music, she soon made some close friends among New York's cultural elite, through whom she later met such legendary figures as Rothko and Chagall. Friendships also blossomed with their UN colleagues and, before long, she and Frank were leading a vigorous social life that ranged from diplomatic dinners at their brownstone on 73rd Street to late-night parties on the Lower East Side. Down the road in Washington, the mood was equally upbeat. The Kennedys were presiding at Camelot and Martin Luther King had dreamed a dream.

On 22 November 1963, Lyn was giving a ladies' lunch party. They had just sat down in the dining-room which Lyn, as usual, had hung with

New Zealand paintings. The guest of honour was the wife of a prominent Congressman who was close to the Kennedys, and the guest list had been carefully chosen with just the right blend of high-level diplomatic wives and interesting friends to make a congenial party. With a nod at her maid, who was to serve the hors d'oeuvre, she turned to the guest on her right. The conversation was humming and her party was going perfectly.

'You've got to speak to Paul.' Her maid was whispering urgently in her ear, 'He's on the telephone.' Lyn listened with irritation. Paul was the office driver and he had no right to interrupt her lunch party. She waved the maid away and turned back to her guests. The maid vanished only to reappear a moment later. 'You've got to talk to him,' she said. Lyn rose from the table with a practised smile and hurried from the room. 'What is it, Paul?' she asked. She would have to talk to Frank about this. 'The President has just been shot at Dallas,' he said.[15] Stunned, Lyn replaced the receiver and took her guests straight upstairs to the television. She turned it on and for the next hour they stood watching it in silence, unable to believe the tragedy that was unfolding.

After the assassination of John Kennedy, the dark shadow of the Vietnam War began to dominate US–New Zealand relations. In 1966, Lyndon Johnson and his wife, Lady Bird, made a whirlwind visit to New Zealand with the principal objective of enlisting support for the War. Despite the growing protest movement, they were greeted with wild enthusiasm and in 1968, Prime Minister Holyoake and his wife, Norma, were invited back to Washington. With a war on their hands, the Americans were only too anxious to woo their small Pacific ally and in contrast to the brief meetings granted to New Zealand Prime Ministers today, the Holyoakes were invited as official guests and lodged in splendour at Blair House, opposite the White House.

On the Holyoakes' first afternoon, Lyn found herself sitting on a sofa with Norma, in front of a bunch of journalists. A year earlier, Frank had reached the lofty pinnacle of Ambassador in Washington and, as the Ambassadress, Lyn was on duty with Norma. All morning the media had been in hot pursuit of L.B.J. and Holyoake. Now it was Norma's turn and for over an hour the Washington press corps had been trying desperately to elicit some newsworthy response from her. From the sidelines, Lyn could have produced a dozen suitable replies, but she was far too savvy to upstage the wife of her Prime Minister. As the interview ground to a sticky halt, one brave soul made a final attempt. 'What about sport?' he asked. Norma beamed. 'I was a champion hurdler at school,'[16] she said. There was a shocked silence. The notion that the almost spherical figure of New Zealand's 'First Mum' could ever have become airborne defied belief and the assembled journalists put away their notepads and departed.

That evening, L.B.J. hosted an official dinner for the Holyoakes at the White House. The party took place in the neo-classical elegance of the State Dining Room, where well over a hundred guests could be accommodated at round tables. Seated on the President's right, Norma seems to have managed rather better than she had with the press corps. But it was Lyn who won the day. Seated on the left of the most powerful man on earth, she brought all her diplomatic skills to bear and they got on famously. After dinner everyone moved to the Blue Room, where L.B.J. invited each of the ladies on his table to dance. Then later, as he and Lady Bird were bidding farewell to the Holyoakes, he turned to Lyn with a huge smile and gave her a bear-hug.

On his return to Wellington in 1973, Frank became Head of the Ministry* while Lyn, who had spent so much of her life in his slipstream, was now hotly in demand in her own right. Over the years her outstanding photographic portraits (one of which is in the Royal Collection at Windsor) and her role in establishing the art collection had not gone unnoticed. Moreover, she had a knack for picking winners and many of the works she had chosen for the Department had already trebled or quadrupled in value. The first body to snap her up was the Board of the National Museum and Art Gallery, the precursor to present-day Te Papa. This was followed, not surprisingly, by an invitation to chair the Gallery's Art Selection Committee. In due course, she also became Chair of the Gallery's Council and later she was asked by the Electricity Corporation to put together their magnificent Rutherford Collection.

Shortly after his retirement from the Ministry in 1980, Frank came to stay with us in Washington. There was some problem with his eyes, I was told, and he was coming to see a doctor. He arrived at our house, a small dapper figure with thick glasses, who moved cautiously from room to room. 'It's glaucoma,' he explained and I nodded uncomprehendingly. The following day I drove him to his appointment, dropping him off at a busy intersection where two great arteries of the city meet. He waved vaguely in my direction, and as I drove away I saw him standing uncertainly on the sidewalk peering

---

*   In 1970, the Department of External Affairs was renamed the Ministry of Foreign Affairs. From 1988–1993 it was known as the Ministry of External Relations and Trade and in 1993 it took its current name of Ministry of Foreign Affairs and Trade.

A serious photographer. Lyn Corner perched on a parapet of Lincoln Castle in order to get a perfect shot of the Cathedral, mid 1950s. (By kind permission of Lyn Corner)

up at the buildings. On his return, he said little. But it must have been one of the worst days of his life because the top American eye specialist, on whom he had pinned his hopes, had told him that he could do nothing to save his sight.

Two decades later, I found myself with an hour to kill in the little town of Wanganui. Driving up through the park, I stopped in front of the Sarjeant Gallery and slipped inside. The great domed hall was flooded with light and apart from a solitary staff member, I was alone – or so I thought. But as I turned to stroll past the pictures, my ears caught a faint sound like the twittering of birds. It was coming from one of the bays in which a short-term exhibition had been hung and as I headed towards it, I saw two little figures, small-boned and frail as sparrows, standing in front of a painting. Their heads were close together, his steel grey and hers still with traces of the silky sheen that had caught his eye so long ago.

To my untutored gaze, the canvas by Mrkusich that Lyn and Frank were admiring was devoid of features, but they were discussing it eagerly, Lyn with deft nods and gestures as she described the brushwork and Frank with all the gravitas of a discerning critic. Nothing had changed in the world of art and beauty which they had always shared – except that they only had one pair of eyes. Totally absorbed in each other, they moved into the second bay, Frank with outstretched arms and Lyn guiding his steps. Hovering in the doorway, I watched her shepherd him gently towards the next painting and then I crept away.

Today the Ministry has parted with most of its treasures. During the 1990s the Government introduced a crippling levy on art works, which forced the Ministry to cull the finest paintings from its collection. Among the beneficiaries were Te Papa and Government House, but New Zealand's Embassies and High Commissions are greatly the poorer and Lyn's vision of bringing the best of her country's art to the world has been lost for ever.

CHAPTER 5.

The Girl from Eketahuna

Alison was raised just outside Eketahuna, a sleepy little township that lies in the dusty hinterlands north of Wellington half way between Masterton and Woodville. From Eketahuna, Wellington seemed like the big smoke and when seventeen-year-old Alison left home to look for a job in the city her mother must have welcomed the news that she was living in a Baptist hostel. But Alison's new digs were not quite as sedate as they sounded; the Baptists had opened the first co-ed student hostel in New Zealand and it was there, a week later, that she met Jim Howell. Before long they were dating and on 14 May 1966, the shy, untravelled Alison found herself walking down the aisle on the arm of a good-looking young man, barely two months her senior, who was planning to show her the world.

Jim's plans were not just a pipe dream. Like Alison, he was paying his way through university with a part-time job, but as a 'student cadet' at the Department of External Affairs, he already had a foot on the diplomatic ladder and once he had completed his degree, he would be eligible for an overseas posting. Shortly after their marriage, Alison gave up her own studies to take a better paid job that would support both of them while Jim became a full-time student. At the time, this was nothing unusual. The man was always going to be the chief breadwinner – especially when they started a family – and his career was the one that mattered. In the meantime, neither he nor Alison had the faintest idea of where or when they might be posted. Despite its rapid expansion, the Department's appointment processes were still shrouded in mystery; there was no prior consultation and officers (and their wives) were expected to accept whatever they were offered.

In July 1967 the summons to the Assistant Secretary's office finally came. 'We're looking for somebody to go to Saigon,' he said, glancing up from his papers. Jim was flabbergasted. He had been married for barely a year and they were sending him to a war zone. 'Can I think about it?' he spluttered. The Assistant Secretary gave a curt nod. 'It's a two-year posting,' he said, 'with no home leave, but you'll get married allowances.'[1] His pale blue eyes rested momentarily on Jim's face before he turned back to his paperwork. The interview was over. Jim stumbled out of the room and rang Alison.

Over forty years later, Alison still struggles with her emotions when she talks about her father's reaction to the news that his only child was going to Saigon. Even in Eketahuna, everyone knew that the Vietnam War was ugly, and he broke down and cried. Alison's mother was more stoic, but she cared just as deeply, and over the next two years she typed up all of Alison's letters and filled two albums with every bit of coverage on Vietnam that she could find in the local newspapers.

When Alison and Jim stepped off the plane at Saigon's Tan Son Nhut Airbase on 1 December 1967, they were confronted by a vast array of military and civilian aircraft. The Americans were pouring thousands of additional troops into Vietnam, making Tan Son Nhut one of the busiest airports in the world. The noise was deafening. On the military runway, fighters were taking off and landing in a continuous stream and outside the main terminal the fleets of 707s that had been chartered to transport the troops were queuing up, six deep, to discharge their passengers. The Howells exchanged glances. Coming straight from Auckland, they had been pretty impressed by the airbase at Darwin, but that paled to nothing beside Tan Son Nhut.

As they drove away from the airport, Alison's first impressions were of the traffic. Great convoys of trucks and armoured vehicles – and even tanks were ploughing their way along the main highway, surrounded by a chaotic mass of cars, scooters and three-wheeled lambrettas. Above the din of the traffic came the constant roar of aircraft, and when they finally reached the old colonial hotel where they were to spend their first two weeks, she fled thankfully to their room. But the day had hardly begun and by the time she had visited the Embassy, which lay directly opposite the heavily guarded residence of the US Ambassador, and sat through lunch served by the Embassy servants, Alison's mind was reeling. As a mere wife, she was completely unbriefed – apart from a reminder about her 'representational duties'.* Worse still, she had discovered that except for the handful of New

---

*   For diplomatic wives 'representational duties' meant everything from cooking dinner parties to attending official functions.

Her first overseas trip. Alison Howell shortly after her arrival in Saigon, December 1967. (By kind permission of Jim and Alison Howell)

Zealanders employed at the Embassy, she was unable to communicate with anyone. No one in Wellington had ever thought of asking her if she spoke French.

That evening Alison got her first glimpse of their new home, a spacious villa, with a large garden located in an outlying suburb in what must once have been countryside. With its imposing circular balcony, the villa looked a lot grander than most of the houses in Wellington and in her first letter home Alison describes it as 'most attractive'.[2] What she fails to mention to her parents is that they were the only Europeans in the area and that the villa was flanked by a shanty town.

Once they moved in, Alison and Jim discovered some further drawbacks:

Our house is on the return circuit to Tan Son Nhut and there is a never-ending stream of returning choppers and fighters overhead. During the day … both runways are in use by aircraft on bombing and supply dropping missions with never a break. At night artillery and mortar fire on the city surrounds sounds like a rolling thunder that one only notices when it stops. Flares are dropped continually on the city boundaries and beyond. They fall so slowly and burn so brightly that the night sky is really attractive …[3]

The flares, of course, were not just for show. They played a crucial role in the defence of the city. Camouflaged by their trademark black pyjamas, the Communist-backed Viet Cong carried out most of their terrorist attacks at night and the US practice of dropping flares was an effective deterrent.

For the first couple of weeks, Alison was caught up in a whirl of farewells for their predecessors, who were still in residence at the villa. But once they had left and Toni and Margaret, who worked at the Embassy, and the 'army boys' who staffed the headquarters of New Zealand's small combat force in Vietnam, were back at their desks, her life came to a grinding halt. There were no other wives to befriend her and Jim was busy at the office. 'There was a lot of empty space in my life,' she recalls, 'and a lot of time when I was sitting playing patience or reading.'[4] Marooned down a narrow alleyway, in the middle of a teeming Vietnamese neighbourhood, she did not even dare to go out for a walk

On Christmas Day their Embassy colleagues, who numbered only five, came for dinner. Everyone chipped in. Toni made a special soup, while Alison produced the turkey – and trimmed the mould off the fruit cake that Margaret's mother had sent up from New Zealand. Also present was Birthe, the Danish wife of the newly appointed Head of Mission[*], Paul Edmonds[†], who had arrived only a few days earlier in a flurry of furs and designer clothing. It was Birthe's twenty-fifth birthday and the Howells had been instructed to provide 'plenty of champagne.'[5] Despite the bubbles, however, it was hard to feel Christmassy, especially as the main celebration for the local population was still over a month away.

Ever since her arrival in Saigon, Alison had been looking forward to Tet, the lunar New Year, when the entire population took a holiday and the streets erupted in fireworks. To add to the anticipation, the Viet Cong had announced a seven-day truce during which they would halt their attacks and it would be safe to drive outside the city. As the New Year approached, the excitement mounted. On the eve of Tet, Alison's neighbourhood resounded with exploding firecrackers and at the Embassy all the locally employed Vietnamese took off early. That night, shortly before midnight, she and Jim were woken by a roar of fireworks, which exploded into the night sky in a

---

[*] The term Head of Mission is used for anyone in charge of a diplomatic mission, usually either an Ambassador or High Commissioner. Paul Edmonds was Chargé d'Affaires with the rank of Minister, but was later promoted to Ambassador.

[†] Since his early days in Apia, Paul had lost none of his charm, but he had ditched his Samoan bride.

dazzling display of pyrotechnics that continued well into the small hours of the morning.

The next day was a holiday and taking advantage of the truce, Alison and Jim made their first (and only) trip to the celebrated beach at Vung Tau. It was a glorious day and as she lay on the golden sand beside a turquoise sea, Alison reflected idly on what she was going to wear to the pyjama party that evening. It was hosted by an Australian diplomat and it should have been a good party; there was plenty of booze and all the guests had made an effort to dress up – some even came as Viet Cong in black pyjamas. But the news that the truce had been called off had made everyone edgy. Rumours were flying and the old hands reckoned that something odd was going on. Tonight was the high point of the New Year celebrations, when the fireworks traditionally reached their zenith, yet the streets were silent as the grave, with scarcely a soul to be seen. The party broke up early and after their disturbed night and the long day at the beach, Alison and Jim drove home and crashed into bed.

The telephone beside their bed was ringing. Jim stretched out an arm and picked up the receiver. Alison could hear a woman's voice on the line. It was Margaret and she sounded worried. 'Yes, of course, we got home safely,' said Jim, glancing at his watch. They must have slept like logs because it was already nine o'clock. 'What's the problem?' As Margaret replied, Alison could tell from Jim's expression that it was something serious. 'There's been an attack on the American Embassy,' he told her, 'at about 3 a.m. this morning. Apparently a whole lot of other places have been hit as well and there are quite a few Viet Cong around.'[6]

They dressed quickly and drove into the office. On the way they passed the Philippine Ambassador's residence. Its iron gates had been blasted in by rockets and further down the road they saw the bodies of the perpetrators still lying where they had been mown down by machine guns. Once they reached the Embassy, Jim and his colleagues tried to piece together what was happening. The radio reports were still pretty confused, but the news that the Viet Cong had broken into the US Embassy and mounted attacks on all the major towns and cities in the country was already reverberating around the world.

By the time the Howells drove home for lunch, the sky was buzzing with helicopter gunships. Thousands of Viet Cong were holed up in the suburbs, where the Americans were bombarding them ruthlessly. For a while they sat out on their balcony, from where they had a grandstand view of the mop-up operation. To Alison, the whole situation seemed quite surreal, but Jim was observing everything keenly:

Early in the afternoon, they were using mostly the common Huey chopper with rocket pods and 30.cal and 50.cal machine guns … Later in the afternoon the rockets were being fired from almost overhead and the machine gunning in the area was indiscriminate … Our neighbourhood is simply packed with Vietnamese. But small squads of VC must have been around as the choppers were just blazing away continuously … God knows how many civilians* have been killed.[7]

When the Security Officer from the Australian Embassy phoned to say that they were moving their staff into secure houses, Jim and Alison decided to head for the Embassy, where the rest of the staff had taken cover. Bullets were whistling around the villa and, for the first time, Alison felt afraid.

The gunships were circling ever closer; there were snipers in the area and it wasn't safe out at our house. … Our street could have been blocked off. But before we left, I had to get supplies because we had to have something to eat. We kept our groceries up in a little room under the roof and to get to it you had to go out … along a little balcony up on the top … We had snipers overhead … and I had to crawl underneath the height of the balcony so that I wasn't visible …. There were stray bullets everywhere and I was really frightened … But I still did it.[8]

It was a huge relief to be at the Embassy, even if they were sleeping on a pile of cushions in Jim's office and washing under the garden tap. But it was hardly peaceful. There was constant sniper fire from the old French cemetery at the end of the road, which was crawling with US troops after Viet Cong had been spotted digging up the graves and extracting guns and ammunition from the coffins.

Food was another problem. Alison's 'groceries' consisted largely of a curious combination of New Zealand delicacies, such as toheroa soup, and assorted cocktail snacks imported from Singapore. Everyone else was in the same boat, but fortunately the 'army boys' had come up trumps, producing boxes of C-rations and taking it in turn to guard the Embassy. As the only wives, Birthe and Alison did the cooking together, an arrangement that strained their tenuous relationship to the utmost and culminated in a serious falling out over cocktail sausages. Alison thought they should be heated in water, while Birthe insisted that they should be fried.

Although Birthe was only a couple of years older than Alison, she was far more sophisticated. She was also well versed in all the little strategies

---

* Historians estimate that the number of civilian deaths in the Vietnam War may have exceeded 2.6 million.

employed by diplomatic wives for survival and social advancement. As a former secretary at the Danish Embassy in Jakarta, she had often watched the Embassy wives swanning off to committee meetings and coffee parties. Now that she had married Paul Edmonds, it was her turn and she had no intention of sharing one scrap of her insider knowledge with Alison. Instead, they spent most of their time sitting several yards apart on the terrace – in stony silence.

To help to pass the time, Alison wrote soothing letters to her parents: 'I am sitting out on the veranda at the Embassy, where we have been staying for the past week. It's very peaceful and pleasant here, apart from the overhead noise of aircraft.'[9] But back in Eketahuna, Alison's parents were getting a very different story. For fifteen days straight, the headlines of the *Dominion* had been dominated by dramatic reports of fierce fighting in Saigon, accompanied by gruesome images of dead bodies on the streets.

On 6 February, the front page of the *Dominion* showed a US soldier taking aim from behind a tombstone. This was followed the next day by a report on the running battle with the Viet Cong still holed up in the old French cemetery, which Alison's parents knew from their well-thumbed map of Saigon was within yards of the Embassy. In her letters, Alison plays down the press coverage: 'It's a pity, really, that such a sensation was made of the story.'[10] But quite how reassuring her parents would have found Jim's claim that the cemetery was 'too close for them [the Viet Cong] to use any mortars from there on the Embassy'[11] is open to question. The Department, meanwhile, had seen no need to elaborate on Holyoake's brief statement that 'all New Zealanders were safe and well'.[12] In the end, it took a stern telephone call from Alison's feisty grandmother, 'Nana Wainwright', to get any information on the fate of the staff at the Embassy.

Jim, of course, was in the thick of things. The Embassy had no communications equipment and as the most junior officer he had to deliver the despatches for transmission to the New Zealand Army headquarters. This involved him in a daily hair-raising run down Tran Quoc Toan, the main artery leading to the Viet Cong stronghold of Cholon, which had become little less than a shooting alley. 'He didn't even have a flak jacket,' Alison recalls, 'but I think I must have been a bit phlegmatic about it … I had to be in a way. There was no point in getting hysterical.'[13] Nevertheless, she must have been thankful when he returned.

When Jim announced that he was off to visit the New Zealand civilian surgical team in Qui Nhon, where there had been some heavy fighting,

Alison Howell boarding an open-sided 'Huey' under the eye of one of the US gunners, Saigon 1968. (By kind permission of Jim and Alison Howell)

Where the staff holed up during the Tet Offensive: the New Zealand Embassy in Saigon. (By kind permission of Jim and Alison Howell)

Alison accepted it stoically. He was due to fly up on a military plane, but it was only an overnight trip and he would be back the following evening. Two days later there was still no sign of him. 'When's Jim coming back?' asked Paul. Alison had no idea and had thought Paul knew. 'Well I think you'd better find out,' he said.[14] They were all sitting out on the terrace and he was trying to raise a laugh. Alison gritted her teeth. After a fortnight's incarceration with Birthe, Paul's flippancy was almost the last straw.

The next day, she discovered through the Red Cross that Jim's plane had been diverted and that he would not be home until the following morning. Unable to endure the thought of another night at the Embassy, she headed back alone to the villa and collapsed into bed. At 1.00 a.m. the Viet Cong launched their second major attack on Tan Son Nhut:

> The noise woke me up, and I was able to watch out the window …
> standing well back in the darkness. I could hear the thumps and bangs
> and see the smoke rise, and then see the glow of the fires. I listened
> to the news (American Forces radio has news items every hour for
> 24 hours) and got the gist of what was happening. Then I closed the
> windows, turned on the air conditioning to drown out the noise and
> slept till morning.[15]

Her phone was not working and when she awoke, she was astonished to find Birthe on the doorstep, despatched by Paul, who had been mortified to discover that the youngest member of the Embassy had just spent the night alone in an unguarded villa. By early afternoon, even Alison admits that she was getting 'just a bit worried' about Jim.[16] But he turned up eventually, tired and dishevelled, having flown most of the length of the country.

After that things quietened down. The Howells remained at home and by the end of February the last pockets of resistance had been wiped out by the Americans. Militarily the Tet Offensive was a resounding defeat for the Viet Cong, but it had a devastating impact on US public opinion. Stunned by the attack on their Embassy and horrified by the photographic coverage of the aftermath, Americans joined the anti-war movement in droves. When the South Vietnamese police chief was shown executing a Viet Cong prisoner on television, public outrage knew no bounds. LBJ's ratings plummeted, destroying his chances of re-election and triggering the eventual withdrawal of US forces from Vietnam.

For several months after Tet, normal diplomatic social life in Saigon ceased. A night-time curfew ruled out dinners and cocktails; food was in short supply and there were constant rumours of a new offensive. Trips to the beach were banned and for their weekend recreation the Howells used to drive around the bombed-out suburbs inspecting the ruins. By May, when a German diplomat was shot in Cholon, even that had become too risky. 'Life is very restricted', Jim told his in-laws, 'we don't even feel free to travel around Saigon ... As I'm writing American Phantoms are bombing somewhere across the way ... Thank God they're friendly.'[17]

After the evacuation of the Australian wives (under protest), Alison's immediate circle shrank still further and her greatest friends became the members of New Zealand's fourteen-strong surgical team. For them, the villa was a haven and on their frequent trips back and forth from their base in the provincial city of Qui Nhon, team members would turn up at any time of day or night, knowing that Alison would give them a warm welcome – and a good dinner. Such figures as the selfless surgeon Jack Enwright, who spent ten years in Vietnam, and Peter Eccles Smith, who was team leader during Tet (when they carried out 136 operations in four days to the constant sound of gunfire) were regular visitors. In return, Alison was often the recipient of generous contributions of food from the US Commissary, to which the team had access.

The despatch of a civilian surgical team in 1963 was the New Zealand government's first response to US pressure for support in Vietnam and prompted the establishment of an office, which was later upgraded to an Embassy.* Organising the team's pay and rations was one of Jim's chief responsibilities and Alison, who had always preferred nurturing to networking, was a natural in the role of 'camp mother'. Serving up New Zealand lamb (flown in from Singapore) and pavlova to the battle-weary doctors and nurses from Qui Nhon was far more her style than the lavish parties, with oysters and caviar, that Birthe was throwing.

As diplomatic social life revived, Birthe was finding keeping up with Paul Edmonds tougher than she had imagined. He was fifteen years her senior and, with his legendary network of contacts, people flocked to his parties, where he would work his way around the room with a bottle of champagne tucked under one arm, apparently drunker than anyone. Surrounded by beautiful Vietnamese women, he often continued partying late into the night. The following morning, however, he would sit down and dictate a brilliant despatch, in which he recalled everything of significance that had

---

* In August 1964 the sole staffer, Nathalie England, was lucky to escape serious injury when the Viet Cong detonated a bomb in the Caravelle Hotel, just above the suite occupied by the New Zealand offices.

been said to him the previous evening. Undoubtedly the quality of Paul's reporting owed much to his close rapport with the Vietnamese, but it is also rumoured that he gained some of his most useful information from frequenting 'the same girls as the generals'[18] – which cannot have been easy for Birthe.

Despite many weeks of preparation, the Holyoakes' visit to Vietnam got off to a bad start. Thanks to a grounded plane, they arrived nearly twenty-four hours late after Jim and the Second Secretary, John Clarke, had spent half the night on the Embassy phones trying to discover what had happened to them. As she made her way cautiously down the steps of the aircraft, Norma scanned the little group lined up on the tarmac to greet them. She knew Paul by sight and she supposed that the blonde in a tight white suit and high heels must be his new wife. His two officers were also there, but there was no sign of the girl from Eketahuna. Her face clouded. As a seasoned political wife, she had a healthy respect for the electorate and the good people of Eketahuna had been returning her husband to Parliament for the past twenty-five years. The parents were decent folk, too, and the least she could do was shake the girl's hand.

Birthe was extremely put out when Mrs Holyoake's first remark to her was 'I was expecting two wives.'[19] Alison, of course, had been left at home. Everyone (especially Birthe) had agreed that the wife of the Third Secretary was far too insignificant to be part of the official party. What followed was in the best fairytale traditions. A pumpkin was summoned and Cinderella was brought to the ball, in this case the State Guest House, where the Holyoakes were staying. Now dressed for a State reception, Norma and Keith swept downstairs like royalty and immediately picked Alison out from the rest of the party. Overcome with shyness, Alison was briefly introduced to them before everyone was driven in an armed motorcade to the Presidential Palace. Later, when the State reception was over, Norma drew Alison aside for a motherly chat.

In this nurturing role, Norma was at her best. She immediately put Alison at her ease and gave her the sort of advice that she should have had at the outset of her posting. But the crowning moment came right at the end of the evening, when Kiwi Keith gave Alison a smacking kiss on both cheeks before he and Norma retired to bed. Naturally her parents heard every detail, although at the bottom her letter, Alison added a scribbled PS 'all and sundry don't need to know about our comings & goings – or about the kisses.'[20]

Birthe Edmonds playing it cool during an official visit to the Philippines contingent at Tay Ninh, Vietnam 1968. Left to right: Ambassador Paul Edmonds, Philippines Commandant, Birthe Edmonds, Alison Howell.

(By kind permission of Jim and Alison Howell)

The Holyoakes' visit evened up the score between the two wives and perhaps taught Birthe something about New Zealand democracy. A few weeks later, both Howells were included in one of the numerous 'joy rides' that Birthe and Paul had been taking around the country. They travelled in a UH-1 Iroquois, universally known as a 'Huey', which also carried a couple of gunners to shoot down any stray rockets. It was Alison's first helicopter ride and a photo of the occasion shows a slim girl in white jeans stepping into an open-sided chopper with a confident smile. In another shot of the trip, she and Birthe are sitting side by side with the Philippine Commandant whom they were visiting. Clad in Gucci-style loafers and a mini-skirt, with a cigarette poised in her hand, Birthe looks the height of cool. But with a stylish new Saigon haircut and a becoming tan, Alison more than holds her own.

For Alison, the encounter with the Holyoakes was a major turning point. Shortly afterwards, acting on Norma's advice, she called on the largest volunteer agency in Saigon, the Catholic Relief Services, and put her name down. 'At least it will satisfy Mrs Holyoake',[21] she told her parents. Within a few days she had become part of a volunteer team working at the huge Go Vap orphanage in the suburbs of Saigon, where dozens of unwanted babies lay in pools of urine or sat rocking themselves in their cots. Many of the children were Amerasian, 'born as a result of the American war effort', as Alison puts it, who had been gathered up by the nuns with trucks and drivers borrowed from the US Air Force. Go Vap was full to bursting point and the overworked Vietnamese staff barely had time to feed the children, let alone give them the love that they so desperately needed. Alison was asked to help with the pre-schoolers, teaching them how to feed themselves and even how to play. At the sight of so many neglected 'tots', Alison's heart melted. 'Some real cuties', she writes, 'and I have to be careful not to become too sentimental over them.'[22]

Like the surgical team, Go Vap became an important part of Alison's life. On Christmas day she spent the morning there. 'Lucky we went', she notes, 'because there was scarcely any staff to feed the children.'[23] By February, she was able to report that the playgroup was 'really coming along' and that the children were starting to play 'instead of just sitting as they used to.'[24] Other things were also falling into place. As Jim developed his professional contacts, the opportunities for her to fulfil her 'representational duties' increased. She and Jim gave some dinner parties and she even tried to learn some French.

Her own circle was expanding too. Through her volunteer work, she was coming into contact with inspirational figures like Mother Mary Floride, a New Zealand nun who had been working in Vietnam for over forty years. She also met the heroic Sister Mary Laurence from Auckland, who in April 1975 was airlifted out of the US compound barely twenty-four hours before the North Vietnamese tanks rolled into Saigon. Similarly, the recent arrival of a youthful Red Cross team, comprising such remarkable individuals as Jerry Talbot, who became Secretary-General of the New Zealand Red Cross Society, and the Masterton nurse Moya McTamney, who was later awarded the Florence Nightingale Memorial Medal, brought further rewarding friendships.

During a week-long visit to the surgical team in Qui Nhon, Alison was introduced to the team's physician, the gifted paediatrician Margaret Neave, whose skill and commitment have left a lasting legacy to the local children. In a later interview, Margaret portrays the work of the team with chilling accuracy:

> Patients were brought in from the city and surrounding countryside … They travelled by anything from helicopters and trucks to hammocks which relatives carried for miles over terrible roads. Bombs, landmines, booby traps, sniper fire, collision with military vehicles meant that amputations and head and abdominal surgery were the surgeons' stock in trade.[25]

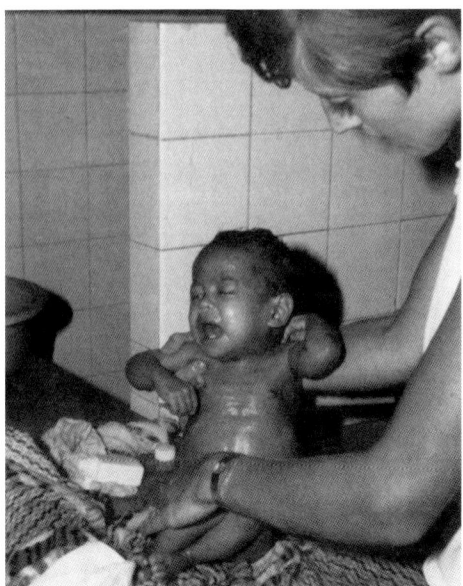

A legacy of the American war effort. Alison bathing one of the abandoned babies at Saigon's Go Vap Orphanage, 1969. (By kind permission of Jim and Alison Howell)

Throughout Alison's visit, the two operating theatres were working flat out. Emergency cases were sent straight to a 'waiting room', which she describes as 'a very sad place', with patients lying on stretchers on the floor with their relatives beside them. 'The Vietnamese accept the fact that they have to wait … often for hours and hours'.[26] But quite a number died before they could reach theatre.

The grim realities of the Binh Dinh provincial hospital, where the team was based, were a far cry from the glamorous high-society world in which Birthe was moving. But now that Alison had found her own role, the stark contrast between her life and Birthe's no longer bothered her. In a country torn apart by war, keeping open house for the surgical team and working with orphans seemed far more worthwhile than attending ladies' lunches and giving cocktail parties. Moreover, the Edmonds' marriage was in deep trouble. Birthe was finding Paul too hot to handle and, in early April, she departed on holiday and never returned.

In the meantime, visiting Go Vap had become 'the latest craze amongst the diplomatic wives'[27] and almost every week Alison found herself taking new recruits to the orphanage. By this time she had become a key member of the team, but typically she preferred to keep a low profile. When one pushy wife got her picture in the press, she told her parents indignantly, 'I have no intention of publicising any work I have been doing here. Charity work of some kind is just part of the wife's duties … it just so happens that the need here is maybe greater.'[28]

In September, the desperate neediness of some of the orphans was brutally brought home to her when she joined a tour of inspection of a country annexe of Go Vap. Hidden in a tiny room adjoining the pig sties, she and her companions came upon five crippled boys lying on two beds. They were polio victims; several were blind and a couple were mentally handicapped. The staff had tried to conceal their existence. 'The boys were delighted to have visitors', Alison told her parents, 'but we were all pretty upset.'[29] In the final days before the fall of Saigon, some of the Go Vap orphans suffered an even more tragic fate. On 4 April 1975 the first mission of 'Operation Babylift', which was evacuating hundreds of Vietnamese orphans to the US, crashed shortly after take-off, scattering the paddy fields around Tan Son Nhut with dozens of tiny corpses. By then, however, Alison and Jim were long gone.

In early November 1969, the Howells caught the 'Freedom Bird' home. For the GIs, a tour of duty lasted thirteen months. Jim and Alison had done twenty-three and, although they had local leave, for both of them it had been a baptism of fire. 'The best part of Vietnam was getting away,' said Jim, 'and the sense of ultimate relief in getting out, in a way that I've never felt in any other post … Seeing those planes leave and thinking, God, one day I'll be on one of those.'[30]

CHAPTER 6.
....

A Passage to India

(letters home from a first posting)

Oberoi Hotel
New Delhi
12 September 1968

Dear Mama,

We went to see our flat yesterday. Never, never in my life have I been so depressed … It is sheer hell … Life there for three years with children would be almost impossible.

I don't know what we can do about it. We are trying to change the flat if administration will let us. The flat has no water at the moment and is frequently without it. It has a lousy Indian landlord … who never fixes anything.

I'm so glad I bought everything I did in Wellington. I assure you that nothing was bought in vain and I only wish I could have bought more. I thought people were being unnecessarily fussy. But they certainly weren't.

The local soap powder doesn't lather or clean nor does the local soap. You might think this is odd – but really it doesn't work. I have spent today day-dreaming about bars of sunlight soap and bottles of Ianola, Bliss. Things are unprocurable – just as stated in the post report … We will just have to do without.

All I really want at the moment is an electric jug which works on an Indian wall socket, a packet of sunlight soap … and lots of baby food.

Lots of love from us all
M.*

***

---

*   Moina Simcock, who had just arrived in Delhi with her husband, Adrian, and her eighteen-month-old son, Nicholas.

Oberoi Hotel
New Delhi
19 September 1968

Dear Mama,

*India is an impossible place. Nothing gets done. Our flat is quite hideous –
no water for most of the day, no electricity for days on end. It is so dark and
uninspired, really it is. The kitchen is unsanitary & the whole place more
than indescribably awful. I hope we don't have to live in it, but the High
Commissioner won't budge.*

*I wonder if you could do some things for me. We really can't swim
satisfactorily here, because if we put our heads under the water we are
likely to lose our hearing or at the least grow fungus in our ears. So could
you please send us some ear plugs for swimming, they are rather tiny so if
you put one pair in a letter in some discreet manner & send it through the
bag & then another pair in another letter that would be quite wonderful.*

*We have been to three parties already! They were most enjoyable, but I
don't like some of the extensive socialising which goes on here … I am
already being bulldozed by the High Commissioner's wife (& heavily
bulldozed by a giant earth-moving machine) into a number of social
activities which are under the guise of charity.*

Lots of love from all of us
M.

***

Oberoi Hotel
New Delhi
26 September 1968

(In bed with Nicholas at 4 am)

Dear Mama

*Well we have a fairly long tale of woe. I have had bacillary dysentery
… Evidently I have had it since the day after our arrival in India. It is
quite hideous & quite unlike anything you can imagine. Anyway now
I'm on an intensive weekly course of drugs – 3 different types. One is
Chloramphenicol & the packet contains this awful warning:*

'Serious & even fatal blood dysorasias are known to occur after
the administration of Chloramphenicol … Bearing this in mind,
Chloramphenicol should not be used when other less potentially
dangerous agents will be effective.'

*I'm telling you that after passing blood every few minutes for 24 hours
I'm thrilled to have Chloranphenicol. In fact I'm feeling quite normal now
(almost). But I have to look forward to a diet of boiled eggs & boiled rice &
weak tea only for the next three days.*

*Nicholas gets terribly upset if we are not both around him all the time. If
either of us is not there he gets upset … He now distinguishes between us &
has become very clinging to both of us. I have to go everywhere with him or
else he is extremely upset and 'Mummy, Mummy' fills the hotel. The maids
etc. say to me 'He doesn't like Indian people' … He does like Indian people a
lot provided we are there, preferably holding onto him, and he will show off
with even greater skill than when he was younger. That's saying something.
Provided we never leave him he is now quite happy, but if we have to go out
it upsets him for the next 24 hours.*

*We have had a hairy time trying to get some accommodation fixed up. All
most upsetting. The office at first didn't appear to be at all helpful about our
flat … However we think we have found a way out of the lease. Evidently
the whole thing was illegal … We met a chap at a cocktail party who said
'Before your office force you to live there, just check the registration of the
lease.' Well, when we found the whole thing was illegal, the office were
much more helpful. Really, they don't want us to live there. They just didn't
want to ruin our country's reputation by breaking a lease.*

Adrian is off to Nepal next week with the High Commissioner, who is
going to present his credentials to the King of Nepal. He is borrowing a
tail coat from an Irish friend of the First Secretary's, who evidently is of a
similar build. It should be extraordinarily interesting. In the meantime I
shall be in a hotel with Nicholas crying for his Daddy.*

*Lots of love
M.*

***

---

* As Third Secretary, Adrian Simcock was the most junior diplomat at the New Zealand
   High Commission in Delhi.

Oberoi Hotel
New Delhi
3 October 1968

Dear Mama,

Our housing problems still remain unsolved – nothing whatever has been done yet. Here I sit in the hotel with Nicholas while Adrian prances round in a morning suit ten sizes too big in Kathmandu. Life is ludicrous …

The flats here are pretty hideous. All the good ones are quickly snapped up & the ones available to let are ghastly … I can't find a thing, with Nicholas, no Adrian, no car & unreliable land agents, who are complete rogues & who leave one stranded in a taxi with the bill to pay. I have never in my life met so many rogues, scoundrels, liars and confidence tricksters as I have met in the last two weeks … Enough to last me for a life time, or several lifetimes …

This morning I bought an electric kettle so that I can heat Nicholas up some food in the hotel. I have just plugged it in. The plug is extremely hot & the kettle is leaking out of all three feet … Really this place is amazing.

I hope you are all well & enjoying yourselves.

Lots of love
Moina

***

Oberoi Hotel
New Delhi
October 1968

Dear Mama

I think that the ear plugs (2nd & 3rd pairs) had better come some other way. The first pair arrived all in a beautifully sealed envelope supplied by the NZ Post Office stating that unfortunately the envelope had been 'damaged in the post'. Very kind of them! If you could put the next pair in a thick envelope it might be better.

Adrian is still in Nepal and is to be there for a whole week more. Never have I known the time to drag so. Every day seems to have a thousand hours in it. When Nicholas cries for Daddy, I have the inevitable diarrhoea;

& we sit in a hotel knowing almost no-one* & having nowhere to go, & not knowing where to go anyway.

What is so much worse, though, is the fact that I can do nothing constructive about getting a flat ready for us. I'm pretty furious with some people in the office. They are a lot of muddlers … Today I have been told that Wellington won't break the lease, so I can't look around for a new flat. They probably don't know how impossible it all is.

If I were given the opportunity I would catch the first plane home …

Lots of love to all the family
M.

***

Oberoi Hotel
New Delhi
16 October 1968

Dear Mama,

Thank you for your sympathetic letter … Also thank you for the ear plugs. These ones arrived quite safely.

We have been here over a month now and still nothing is settled about our flat & we are paying 66% of A.'s salary in food & lodging. The Canadian Foreign Service makes their officers contribute 25%, but our administration's idea is to get officers out of a hotel in a big hurry … We are also in the difficult position of having to support four servants† because the flat has to be watched & kept clean as it has government furniture in it. In India a house would quickly be emptied if things weren't checked up on.

Now that A. is back from Nepal, Nicholas has settled down quite well. The waiters & housemaids adore him and he is also a great hit with our cook (an old rogue!). Every morning Babu says to him 'Good Morning Sahib' and bows … He accepts servants as a fact of life & rather likes them.

---

*   Moina's loneliness was exacerbated by the absence of all the other wives at the High Commission. The First Secretary's wife had taken her children to the High Commission's summer house at Kasauli; the Second Secretary's wife was in hospital having a baby and the High Commissioner's wife had accompanied her husband to Nepal.

†   Moina's large household was quite standard in India and consisted of a cook named Babu Khan, an 'ayah' (nanny) named Grace, a 'sweeper' (cleaner) named Dipak and a 'dhobi' (laundryman) named Hira Lal.

Yesterday he spilt some dinner on the floor. Very sweetly, he announced 'Babu, clean it.'

We all send lots of love to you & all the family
A.M.N.

***

Oberoi Hotel
New Delhi
31 October 1968

Dear Mama,

Here's what I would like for my birthday HAIRSPRAY. Please send it ordinary parcel post by sea. As it will be the cool season it will arrive in good condition … I would love a bottle of spray-on deodorant too – not roll-on or stick as these don't travel so well … Adrian would like a little jar of Marmite. It doesn't matter if it doesn't arrive till March as it is still the cool season & I wouldn't think it would matter to Marmite anyway. (Adrian has just said not Marmite, but Vegemite.)

Today I saw the National Film Unit production 'Amazing New Zealand' & I felt so homesick. It's much worse to see these things. I feel fine as long as I'm not reminded of home …

Lots of love
M.

***

Oberoi Hotel
New Delhi
13 November 1968

Dear Mama,

It's all hopeless and we have a landlord who is a great ugly liar …

The day we were to move into our redecorated and re-renovated flat, the landlord said he wanted to break the lease. We (us personally & the office) had spent quite a bit of money trying to get the place habitable … The office had installed air-conditioners & a stainless steel sink and had painted the

A PASSAGE TO INDIA · **87**

kitchen cupboards. I had spent many hours (and quite a lot of our money) on curtains … Then the landlord rented the whole building behind our backs so he wanted to get out of the lease … Now he is claiming rent until 1971 from the office. Of course he won't get it. The office aren't even talking to him as the whole lease was illegal anyway.

Our lift van is due to arrive any day. Where it will be put, I do not know.

Lots of love
M.

***

14 Jaipur Estate
Nizamuddin East
New Delhi
31 December 1968

Dear Mama, Dad, Diana, Warwick & John,

We are now vaguely settling into our house in Nizamuddin. At the moment the place is full of plumbers, painters and tailors and everything is quite chaotic … I have just hired a new cook* who sports a jaunty red turban, makes beautiful mince and apple pies, lovely curries, superb bread, & real NZ style roast dinners … Perhaps he will stay.

On Christmas Day we went to church at the Episcopalian Church in Parliament Street. It was odd to hear the familiar Anglican service in such remote surroundings. It didn't seem quite real. After church we returned home to be garlanded with marigold by our servants …

The High Commissioner's Christmas lunch was a real New Zealand affair – most of the New Zealanders in Delhi were there – 28 of us, including children & we sat down to a typical family Christmas dinner with crackers & hats, roast turkey, baked potatoes, peas, plum pudding & children everywhere. Afterwards we had presents from the tree. Again, children & wrappings everywhere – we could have been in New Zealand.

Lots of love to everyone at the Lake†
M.

***

---

*   Moina's suspicions that Babu Khan was a 'rogue' proved well founded and she replaced him with a Sikh named Ram Baux Singh.

†   Lake Tarawera, in the North Island of New Zealand, where Moina's extended family always spent their summer holidays.

14 Jaipur Estate
Nizamuddin East
New Delhi
14 January 1969

Dear Mama,

Life here is rather complicated. The ayah has an infectious parasite living in her intestines. My dhobi has a TB cough. My cook is flogging my groceries and my sweeper has nowhere to live and is asking for a rise. However, these domestic details are nothing when compared with our latest drama – our lovely, new, beautifully undriven Mercedes* was severely damaged in Bombay. It was damaged in the loading & unloading of the ship. So our car is in Bombay with the roof all crumpled in, the back window now non-existent and the sides requiring extensive panel-beating … We have cabled Germany saying that we won't accept delivery, but I think we will have to or have nothing.†

Lots of love
M.

***

14 Jaipur Estate
Nizamuddin East
New Delhi
16 February 1969

Dear Mama

We are rather busy at the moment and I've been rather wicked & telling lies in order to get out of cocktail parties … I felt I had just done so much I couldn't go out again so I didn't go to a dine & dance, but gave some lame apology & stayed at home and cooked a cheese soufflé. Sometimes I feel if I go to another cocktail party & have to get dressed up & be polite again I shall go cranky … I just long for an hour alone with a book.

Lots of love
M.

***

---

*   During the 1960s and '70s, many New Zealanders living overseas bought new cars in order to take advantage of the exemption on the very high import tax on motor vehicles in New Zealand.

†   This proved true and they drove the patched-up Mercedes for the rest of their posting.

14 Jaipur Estate
Nizamuddin East
New Delhi
25 February 1969

Dear Mama,

Today I went to the doctor, and am thrilled to relate that I am 4 weeks pregnant. Don't tell anyone please as it is terribly early … You can hardly imagine how I found out … I hadn't had a period since I left NZ. I'd been fairly upset living in the hotel – in fact very upset – and evidently my system was in sympathy with my cause. So I rushed off to a gynaecologist …

On my way home from the doctor a gang of about 40 youths forced me to almost stop the car, leered, jeered & and made very rude faces, gestures & hideously lecherous noises & then threw a bucket of water all over me. I kept the car moving slightly & drove steadily on. I was FURIOUS & nearly went straight to the High Commission to complain, but decided that it was a bit theatrical … So I drove home, saw the funny side of it and was glad in retrospect that it was only water & not paint.

Lots of love to you all
M.

***

14 Jaipur Estate
Nizamuddin East
Bag Day*
New Delhi
8 May 1969

Dear Mama,

I tried to write to you last night, but it proved impossible as we were again without electricity and spent the evening taking turns in a cold bath by candle light …

After I last wrote to you Nicholas got an Indian type bug and ran temperatures of 104°F for several days & lost a lot of weight. When I saw the slides which I took at the end of the winter of a chubby little boy, I could hardly believe the damage the summer has done already … He spent quite

---

*   The day on which mail was sent by diplomatic bag to New Zealand, usually weekly.

a bit of the time last month unable to eat and vomiting from the heat.* To get A. to eat also requires a positive effort. I've now been reduced to taking him mangoes and ice-cream while he lies in a cold bath.

Lots of love
M.

Sorry about splodges – perspiration not tears.

***

By mid-May, Moina and Nicholas had retreated to the High Commission's rented house in the hill station at Kasauli, where the wives and children used to spend the worst of the summer months. At weekends, the husbands would make the seven-hour drive from Delhi to join them. After the blistering heat of the plains, the rambling stone house, with its enormous, cool rooms and sweeping views of the Himalayas, proved a lifesaver and their health improved rapidly. Towards the end of May, the Simcocks treated themselves to a few days in the nineteenth-century glory of Clarke's Hotel in Simla, which was only a couple of hours' drive from Kasauli. Moina was enchanted:

Clarke's Hotel
The Mall
Simla
31 May 1969

Dear Mama,

We are having a lovely time here. We have a suite with a separate bathroom, separate dressing room, lounge with fire & smoking room with a bay window, & of course a bedroom … The climate is glorious and the walks in the pine forest are delightful. The shopping is good fun too. Lots of oddities and relics of the British Raj in all its splendour abound. There is a picturesque railway which runs up here and looks just as if it has come out of a fairy story.

Much of her letter, however, is devoted to the unfolding saga of her underwear:

---

*   During the summer months (April–October), temperatures in Delhi remain above 40ºC night and day and at times reach as high as 50ºC.

Dear Mama, I'm desperate for breeks. You will recall that I bought 2 dozen pairs of breeks in Wellington before I left, but they were all cotton knit & they cling and grab the cotton material of unlined dresses. To say one needs cotton breeks in a tropical climate is a complete fallacy. I'll have to save up my 24 pairs & wear them in NZ, where I wear petticoats. The very best sort of breeks are Dacron or nylon, generously proportioned and of conventional design obtainable anywhere in Woolworths. Bikini breeks or any cute shape are useless ... You with your great nylon bags would be ideally equipped. Could you please send me either some maternity breeks or OS nylon ... I'm so sorry to ask for these, particularly when I already have 2 dozen cotton ones ...

Lots of love to you all
M.

***

Kasauli Hill Station
Himachal Pradesh
9 June 1969

Dear Mama,

I have a bra problem ... Could you possibly send me one 34B and one 36B nursing bra ... Although the situation here is improving rapidly, no nursing bras are made ... The Indian erotic ideal may be to have breasts like mangoes, but as far as I can see the bras wouldn't hold anything other than green limes.

Lots of love
M.

***

14 Jaipur Estate
Nizamuddin East
New Delhi
4 July 1969

Dear Mama,

Please send me several cards of NZ boil-proof elastic. I nearly lost my breeks in town yesterday. Most embarrassing. I had bought some Indian elastic HORSE KNICKER ELASTIC BEWAR OF IMITATION and put it in water to shrink before putting it into my breeks. It went bright blue & then all wrinkly.

Lots of love
M.

⁣⁣*

14 Jaipur Estate
Nizamuddin East
New Delhi
15 July 1969

Dear Mama,

Thank you for the 4 pairs of breeks ... The white Dacron ones fit perfectly, and the banded breeks do now. They hung so low on me that you could see them hanging under my dress, but I have shortened them 5 inches and they are marvellous. I keep feeling that you must wonder why on earth I can't get things here. I assure you I do try the local product & am not one of those fussy people who think everything Indian is bad.

Poor wee Nicholas is very sick again, and has been running high temperatures and vomiting everything ... Every day he gets thinner & looks more black around the eyes ... I tried to give him penicillin myself when his temperature was 104°F on Sunday and I felt a bit frightened, but he only vomited it up.

Later:

I'm feeling much saner after a rest in the air-conditioned room.* Nicholas hasn't returned the ice-cream he's just eaten and his temp is only 101°F.

---

*   Only the bedrooms in their house were air-conditioned.

P.S. Unfortunately wrong about that ice cream.
P.P.S. Dacron briefs are divine.

From a more cheerful, loving and extremely grateful
M.

***

14 Jaipur Estate
Nizamuddin East
New Delhi
1 October 1969

Dear Mama,

Thank you very much for ringing. I'm sure the reason we couldn't talk was due to some stupid operator not plugging in the right connection. I heard Dad quite clearly as tho' he was just down the road and I could hear the poor operator in London trying to get Delhi to plug me in. Finally I said to London 'I can hear everyone quite clearly.' London replied 'Yes, but the Delhi operator can't.'

A. and I are feeling rather homesick. We have made friends & know our way around here, but we miss N.Z. and the lovely life we had there. I think the place we long for most is the Lake.* It would be wonderful to take Nicholas there. I'd love him to play by the water at the beach and be nice and cool and not all covered with prickly heat … Adrian and I had a holiday today (Gandhi's birthday) & felt more homesick than ever … It isn't that Delhi is so horrible, it is just that N.Z. is so many thousands of times better.

Love
M.

On 11 Oct 1969, the Simcocks' second son, Christopher, was born at the Holy Family Hospital in Delhi. Although Moina had been dreading it, and arrived armed with dozens of syringes sent by 'Mama' and gallons of disinfectant, the birth went without a hitch.

---

*   Moina's longing for Lake Tarawera is a recurring theme of the letters.

Despite her fears, the birth in Delhi went without a hitch. Moina Simcock at the christening of her second son, Christopher, 1969.

(By kind permission of Adrian Simcock)

14 Jaipur Estate
Nizamuddin East
New Delhi
25 November 1969

Dear Mama,

Your wonderful, wonderful parcels have arrived! I'm thrilled with all the contents especially with the mosquito net, baby chair and sox for Nicholas. It is just marvellous not to have Christopher being bitten & Nicholas having warm feet. As for the baby chair – it is the answer to a Mother's prayer … It is such a relief that they have arrived safely.

Lots of love
M.

***

14 Jaipur Estate
Nizamuddin East
New Delhi
4 February 1970

Dear Mama,

This new cook of mine is marvellous.* He is reliable & nice. I just can't believe it & keep wondering if he will leave us for higher places or if he has an unrevealed illness or drinks or steals or something. So far, however, he seems to be exactly the man for me and if he is still here when you arrive, it will be wonderful. We will have no cooking or dishes to do ever!

Lots of love,
M.

In February 1970 Moina's parents arrived for a lengthy stay, during which they all took a holiday in England. After her mother's visit, Moina sounds far more settled. Her household was running like clockwork and, with a full-time nanny and a cook, she was spending most of her mornings playing tennis and bridge. 'Life is pretty cushy for a Memsahib', she tells her mother breezily, and even the diplomatic round had its compensations.

14 Jaipur Estate
Nizamuddin East
New Delhi
19 August 1970

Dear Mama,

Life goes on here in much the same way … We go out most nights in a week and I have had 3 large buffet dinners in the past 3 weeks with another one this Friday night … I have worn my new white lace suit on average 4 times a week … Paddy Dunlop† told me that I had made a great impact on the Norwegian Ambassador … Most gratifying.

Love
M.

***

---

*   Moina was now on to her third cook, Joseph.
†   Wife of the Counsellor at the High Commission.

14 Jaipur Estate
Nizamuddin East
New Delhi
Boxing Day 1970

Dear Mama,

We have had a very Christmassy Christmas with parties and presents galore … The High Commissioner was to have his usual Christmas lunch, but he rather lost his enthusiasm, so all those New Zealanders who were not catered for in any other way came here for Xmas dinner … It was a New Zealand do-it-yourself dinner. We are all afflicted with Christian servants, hence the co-operative effort. Also it was a nice change & all rather un-Delhi-like. I felt like an N.Z. housewife – but at least Dipak washed the dishes. (Thank heaven for 1 Hindu.)

We had every Christmas detail – a superb tree which we put up 2 weeks before Christmas with masses of red, green & white candles, Xmas bells (lovely brass ones) lacquered decorations and even mistletoe. I made your recipe for mince tarts, your wedding cake recipe for the cake & your stuffing recipe for the turkey. The plum pudding burned furiously, the crackers banged stupendously (in a rather lethal gunpowdery way) and the itinerant bands played loudly and untunefully. It was a fantastically successful day and the dinner finally finished at 5 pm.

Lots of love
M.

But within a matter of days Moina's well-ordered household had been turned on its head.

14 Jaipur Estate
Nizamuddin East
New Delhi
4 January 1971

Dear Mama,

This has been a hectic and impossible week. I could write a book about JOSEPH.

Lots & lots of love
M.

***

Garlanded with marigolds by their domestic staff, Adrian and Moina Simcock and eldest son, Nicholas, celebrate Christmas in Delhi, 1970.

(By kind permission of Adrian Simcock)

14 Jaipur Estate
Nizamuddin East
New Delhi
29 January 1971

Dear Mama

I have been trying to write for the last three weeks, but I have had virtually no staff. Joseph left for Madras (apparently his house is falling down), Dipak has had a flu' type virus all week and is now away and Grace has dropped her teeth and is off in the afternoons to have them reassembled ...

Love
M.

***

14 Jaipur Estate
Nizamuddin East
New Delhi
12 February 1971

Dear Mama,

Joseph is still in Madras and we have no news of him at all and Dipak is in the village at his brother's wedding. I'm frantically dusting – the dust is thick after 1 day of rain since last September – and cooking.

Love
M.

***

14 Jaipur Estate
Nizamuddin East
New Delhi
22 February 1971

Dear Mama,

Joseph has gone …

As for Dipak, he announced that he wanted to go to his brother's wedding … Actually we don't think he has a brother, let alone a wedding, but he has a young wife in the village … but she won't come to Delhi to live with him as her mother-in-law says she has to help her to look after the buffalo.

Well it's either the wife or me & the wife can have him.

Lots of love
M.

***

14 Jaipur Estate
Nizamuddin East
New Delhi
1 April 1971

Dear Mama,

Life continues its crazy course. I've replaced Dipak fairly satisfactorily and I have a new cook on trial, who incidentally is a Buddist. I've now had the lot:

Babu Khan – Muslim (U.P.)
Ram Baux Singh – Hindu (Rajput Singh)
Joseph – Christian (Madrasi)
Puranjoy Barua – Buddist (Bengali from E. Pakistan)

In the short time I've had Barua, I've had to entertain frantically to make up for the months when I was servantless. I've had a garden party – buffet and barbecue for 30, formal dinner for 8, formal dinner for 4, ladies' coffee party for 12, child's party for 14, Sunday lunch for 8 & champagne etc. for 26 last Sunday to farewell the H.C.

I'm just off to the airport again and with Delhi belly. I'm trying to plan my day according to the availability of loos.

Yours in haste!
M.

By the time she wrote her next letter, Moina had discovered that she was pregnant again. But her chief concern was the impending political crisis.

Oberoi Hotel
New Delhi
27 April 1971
(At the hairdresser)

Dear Mama,

*We have been very worried about the possibility of war with Pakistan …
War is the last thing India wants & Mrs G[Gandhi] has been doing her best to avoid it. However Pakistan is being deliberately provocative. Bhutto erroneously believes a war with India would weld Pakistan together. Of course, it would be impossible for anything to unite East & West again. East would have to have a considerable degree of autonomy, if not complete nation status …*

We had planned to drive to Kashmir on 6 May for a 10-day holiday, but now we are in a quandary … The border situation is very tense and if the Pakistanis attack, they will attack Kashmir …

Love
M.

Moina was clearly well-informed on the crisis, which had been brewing since the general election in Pakistan in December. On 25 March, matters had been brought to a head by a brutal crackdown by West Pakistan on the insurgency in East Pakistan (present-day Bangladesh). Thousands of civilians were massacred and eight million refugees fled to India. This put India and Pakistan at loggerheads, with India supporting the Bangladeshi independence movement, and with the Pakistan Air Force making increasingly bold incursions into Indian territory.

Kasauli Hill Station
Himachal Pradesh
24 June 1971

Dear Mama,

Adrian went to Calcutta and visited the refugee camps a couple of weeks ago. He was absolutely appalled at the situation and the condition of the refugees. He said that there is no wonder that they are dying of cholera.

We are most definitely anxious about the Indo-Pak situation, but thank goodness we got our Kashmir trip, and were not put off by a number of our learned colleagues.

We are now in Kasauli for our last week. The monsoon has cleared the air of its heavy dust pall and we can see rows of snow-capped Himalayan peaks. Our neighbour claims that we are looking at Tibet … I rather dread the return to Delhi to the heat, the inevitable monsoon illnesses & the unending cocktail parties.

Lots of love
M.

This was the Simcocks' last summer in Delhi. They were hoping to be home by Christmas, but to add to Moina's worries the Ministry of Foreign Affairs still had not notified them of their departure date. Moreover, at five months pregnant, she was not looking forward to the move.

Kasauli Hill Station
Himachal Pradesh
26 June 1971

Dear Mama,

This life is certainly not full of joy when it comes to moving around with young children. On the one hand I'm longing to see you, and for the children to see you and enjoy life in N.Z. I also couldn't bear another Christmas in Delhi – all that bakhshish and brass bands and marigolds. Yet the whole upheaval appals me – and that horrid, horrid feeling of homelessness and disorganisation … Sometimes what I crave for more than anything else in the world is just a nice settled life in N.Z.

Love
M.

***

14 Jaipur Estate
Nizamuddin East
New Delhi
2 August 1971

Dear Mama,

We are all rather preoccupied with Bangladesh and the Indo-Pak situation. It is hard to think about anything else. I haven't given the new baby a thought. We are genuinely worried about the prospect of war … September seems to be a likely time – or maybe early October … I could be in the hospital with 'Jonathan' with Pak planes overhead – I only hope that the Indian MIGs are as good as the Pak Mirages.

Later:

A. came back from the office the other day with news of plans for evacuation in case of war. 'Well,' said A. 'We will just have to decide what is the last date we can evacuate you, or whether you will just have to stay here.'

Lots of love
M.

***

14 Jaipur Estate
Nizamuddin East
New Delhi
8 September 1971

Dear Mama,

I haven't written for a while as A. has been rather ill, and I've been terribly busy looking after him and doing all the jobs he would have done had he been well … I find I can't sleep at all & keep waking up in the night wondering what I should do next. We don't know whether he has (a) chronic amoebic dysentery plus infectious hepatitis or (b) amoebic hepatitis … Now he is on the mend and the doctor says he should be back at work by October – just in time for the new baby!

Love
M.

On 9 October 1971, Moina gave birth to her third son, Jonathan. With three children under five, she was feeling increasingly vulnerable and in her final letter from India, she spells out her predicament with her usual frankness.

14 Jaipur Estate
Nizamuddin East
New Delhi
8 November 1971

Dear Mama,

Things are very serious … The Army and Air Force have been on the alert 24 hours a day for the past six weeks and the general consensus of opinion is that war is definitely going to occur … For Pakistan to embark on a war is complete suicide … So one can expect any crazy course of action from a desperate people … Now the problem is WHEN.

Once the war starts, it may be very difficult to leave Delhi, so we would have to leave BEFORE war breaks out. And that is a very difficult decision to make – to leave Adrian here … Jonathan is still waking every 3–4 hours all through the night and I don't know how I would have the strength to manage those three boys alone … So we just keep hoping. The prospect of war is so horrible we don't want to believe it will happen.

Lots of love
M.

At 5.35 p.m. on 3 December 1971, the Pakistan Air Force bombed nine Indian airfields along the western border. Delhi was on high alert and within seconds the whole city was resounding with the wail of air-raid sirens. When the attack happened, Moina was sitting under a hair dryer at the Oberoi Hotel and never heard a thing, but by the time she emerged India had retaliated and the two nations were at war.

The next few days were a nightmare. An air attack was expected at any moment and the sirens went off constantly. At night there was a blackout. Nobody went out. Instead they huddled at home, behind closely drawn curtains, straining for the sound of aircraft. But the Simcocks' greatest concern was how they were going to leave. All the international airlines had cancelled their flights and the domestic carriers were booked solid for weeks.

On 11 December, Adrian and Moina, with their three small sons and fourteen pieces of baggage, finally left Delhi. Through the good offices of an Indian friend, they had miraculously acquired seats on a domestic flight to Bombay, where a handful of international airlines were still operating. But their troubles were far from over. In Bombay, tensions were running even higher than in Delhi. After a night fraught with air-raid warnings, they were collared at the entrance to the International Terminal by the captain of their Swissair flight to Singapore, who was keen to get his plane off the tarmac as quickly as possible. They were bundled aboard, only to be off-loaded in Bangkok because their flight had been diverted to evacuate the foreign community from Dhaka. Surrounded by their baggage, they camped in the concourse until late in the evening, when they were at last able to continue their journey. By 16 December the war was over, resulting in a resounding defeat for Pakistan and the creation of Bangladesh.

Twenty-five years later, the Simcocks made a second passage to India. But this time Adrian was going as High Commissioner and the story was very different.

CHAPTER 7

The Iron Lady

Ambassadresses, like duchesses, have always enjoyed a mixed press. All too often they are depicted as dictatorial figures, ruling over their embassies with a rod of iron and pressing junior wives into an endless round of duties. In some more traditional diplomatic services, such women still exist, but a careful survey of New Zealand's senior wives has produced only one really authoritarian ambassadress, whose fame rests on her ill-fated attempt to produce a handbook for diplomatic wives.

Today the handbook lies gathering dust, but its contents are far from forgotten. 'I believe,' one wife told me recently, her eyes flashing, 'that it said we had to curtsey to the Ambassador – and then walk backwards out of the room.' I listened politely. The handbook says nothing of the sort, but it does contain a few unpalatable home truths, such as her comment that 'New Zealanders are all too inclined to be un-punctual and equally insensitive about knowing when to leave.'[1]

Apart from such blunt observations – and some assumptions on the willingness of wives to serve as unpaid adjuncts to their husbands – the handbook is full of helpful advice on everything from writing a thank-you letter to where one sits in the car. It was not dreamed up in isolation, but drew heavily on existing manuals prepared by the Australian, Canadian and British diplomatic services (which purportedly include an instruction to British wives to be 'kind to the Colonials'). For someone who was as ignorant of diplomatic life as I was, some clear guidelines of this sort would have been a godsend and would have saved me from some memorable blunders.

The real trouble with the handbook was not its contents, but its timing. The first draft appeared in 1974, when New Zealand feminists had made common cause with the Vietnam protest movement and the agitation for women's rights was at its height. To the young women of the '70s, the notion that a wife's social position depended entirely on the rank of her husband and that she had a 'duty' to engage in representational activities was like a red rag to a bull. 'They were a stroppy lot,' said one older wife sadly. The handbook never stood a chance and was promptly consigned to the archives. As a result, New Zealand's diplomatic wives, unlike their closest counterparts, are still sent out into the world as players in a complex political game without the benefit of a rule book.

Ironically, few of the young firebrands who dismissed the handbook so scornfully would have had any idea that the stately woman who wrote it not only had an MA in French and a fencing blue, but was also a crack shot with a rifle and a fully qualified truck driver. Furthermore, when she was their age, far from playing a submissive female role, she was engaged in one of New Zealand's most secret wartime operations.

Marguerite Scott was a remarkable woman and she came of remarkable stock. Her brother became an Air Vice-Marshal in the RAF, with a string of wartime decorations and a knighthood, and she was in the same mould. Doubtless had she been a man, she too would have ended up at the top. Both of them knew how to keep a secret. In her brother's case, this involved flying the H-Bomb to Christmas Island for tests without informing the US airbases at which he was refuelling of his payload. In Marguerite's case, it meant telling no one of her wartime service until forty years later, when one of her colleagues gave an interview to the press.

Marguerite joined the newly formed Women's Royal New Zealand Naval Service in late 1942 after an interview with the redoubtable Ruth Herrick, Commissioner of the New Zealand Girl Guides and schoolmate of Katherine Mansfield, who had recently been appointed Director:

> 'Ah', said the Commandant, who had made a smooth transition from the crisp navy serge of a Girl Guide officer to the tailored navy serge and tricorne of a Wren officer, 'the Wrens are looking for girls like you. The navy has technical, extremely hush-hush work for University graduates, to be carefully vetted and trained … [But] as the work has the highest secrecy rating, I cannot give you any idea of the duties, because I myself shall never know what they are.'[2]

The job for which Marguerite was recruited was at the forefront of contemporary technology and involved the filming of radio signals from enemy vessels in order to establish their identity. Known as radio finger printing, the system was already in use at Britain's top-secret Bletchley Park and in May 1941 it was responsible for identifying the course of the German battleship, *Bismarck*, which was then sunk by the Royal Navy. In New Zealand, it was used to keep track of Japanese naval strength in the Pacific and to monitor the movements of Japanese submarines stationed in Papua New Guinea.

The operation was based in an isolated farmhouse in Blenheim, not far from the Waihopai Valley, where some of New Zealand's most sophisticated monitoring equipment is located today. The all-female 'crew' consisted of four classifiers of which Marguerite was one, whose task was to identify the unique characteristics of the individual radio transmitters, and four telegraphists fluent in the Japanese Katakana code. As the sole heavy duty licence holder, Marguerite also drove the truck which was their only means of transport.

Apart from a female petty officer (who was not allowed into the operations room), the eight women lived in complete isolation, enclosed by an eight-foot barbed wire fence, which was patrolled by a detachment of elderly Home Guards. The women worked in shifts and were on a war footing twenty-four hours a day. Bound to secrecy, with no encouragement or feedback from their superiors, they were tied to a relentless routine that could well have led to tensions. But imbued with a wartime sense of mission they became the best of friends, sharing cooking and cleaning duties and developing a flourishing vegetable garden.

Life was not unrelieved toil. From time to time the local farming families invited them to Sunday lunch, and by taking it in turns they could attend parties and concerts in Blenheim. There were also some professional high points, such as the 'brief crystal-clear transmission' from a Japanese submarine in Cloudy Bay which was 'just over the back fence'[3] from their base. When the transmission came through, the girls were so excited that all eight of them stayed up for the whole night.

At the heart of the operation was a hair-raising piece of equipment plastered with 'High Voltage' and 'Danger' stickers, which Marguerite describes as 'an obscure, precious and expensive Pandora's box of experimental gear.'[4] To add to the fun, an adventurous naval officer named Merlin Minshall (who was reputedly one of Ian Fleming's models for James Bond) was sent out by British Naval Intelligence to install it. With the help of a bow and arrow, he and Marguerite managed to suspend the crucial aerial line from the biggest tree in the paddock, where it survived the repeated

Members of the all-female crew of top-secret 'Raupara Station' in Blenheim, c. 1943. Marguerite Boxer (later Scott), 2nd from right. (Break In, *Dec 1996: Frank Barlow* 'Awarua Radio (ZLB) the RNW connection')

flypasts of inquisitive pilots from nearby Woodbourne Air Base.

As the Americans gained the upper hand in the Pacific, the Japanese moved north and their radio signals became increasingly difficult to monitor. By mid-1944, 'Rapaura Station' had outlived its usefulness and Marguerite was moved back to Wellington, where she spent the rest of the war training male ratings in gunnery.

Early in 1946, Marguerite met a young naval officer named John Scott, who had recently joined the Department of External Affairs. They married a few months later and were almost immediately posted to Canberra. From the outset, Marguerite took her role seriously. Like many whose formative years had been spent in the forces, she saw life in terms of service. For her, the prime duty of a diplomatic wife was to support her husband at his post. In a later interview, however, she admits that some of her early efforts at diplomacy were 'a big mistake' and that her attempts to call on the senior ambassadresses in Canberra were 'way out of place'.[5] She had been ill advised by someone who knew nothing about protocol. The humiliation rankled with her for the rest of her life and may well have fuelled her determination to instil the do's and don'ts of diplomatic etiquette into others.

Clever and competent ('my head was screwed on fairly tightly'),[6] Marguerite soon learnt the ropes. Postings to New York and London followed, with promotions for John to match. Slotted between diplomatic duties and packing cases, three little girls were born. By the time John's first ambassadorial appointment, to Japan, came through in 1965, Marguerite was at the height of her powers. With three diplomatic postings under her belt, she knew exactly how the diplomatic world operated and at a time when the Department's regulations for overseas staff still stipulated that wives had to make 'a full contribution to representational activities', she expected her junior colleagues to pull their weight.[7]

For official functions at the Residence, wives were required to arrive at least ten minutes early and to remain until the last guest had departed – and woe betide them if they were caught talking with each other rather than to the guests. Late arrivals and early departures had to be for a valid reason, which should be explained to the Ambassador beforehand. Excuses about children were unacceptable and parents were told to make whatever arrangements they could for babysitting. There was also homework to be done: 'You will naturally be a greater help to your host and hostess if you are clued up'[8] and for larger parties the guest list was to be studied beforehand. The wives obeyed meekly. Most of them were terrified of Marguerite and feared that their husbands' careers would suffer if they earned her displeasure.

Having licked her troops into shape, Marguerite channelled her energies into serving the interests of her country. Well versed in the art of networking, it did not take her long to discover that her most direct path to those in positions of influence was through the International Ladies Benevolent Society, to which the cream of Japanese society belonged. As an ambassador's wife, she had an immediate entrée and within a very short time she became its President, with responsibility for organising a wide range of charitable activities, including one of the most prestigious social events in the year, the Cherry Blossom Charity Ball.

The Cherry Blossom Charity Ball was one of Marguerite's great triumphs. Two photographs commemorating the occasion show her sitting next to the Emperor's brother, Prince Takamatsu, at dinner. Dressed in a full-length gown and long white gloves, she is listening attentively to the Prince with her large, intelligent eyes fixed firmly on his face and an expression of mild amusement. Even if her thoughts were straying to the months she had spent tracking Japanese submarines, and the long hours she had spent teaching gun crews how to shoot down the Kamikaze, she was far too professional to show it.

For a woman who ran her household like a command post, it must have been particularly galling for Marguerite that the notorious Nishikawa

The Cherry Blossom Ball in Tokyo. Marguerite Scott talking to the Emperor's brother, Prince Takamatsu, at dinner, c. 1967. (By kind permission of Veronica Scott)

incident happened on her watch, making her the only ambassadress in New Zealand's diplomatic history nearly to have lost her Residence. To be fair, the incident occurred when she and John were on leave, but in the collective memory of the Ministry it is still indelibly linked to her tenure.

The Embassy chauffeur, Nishikawa, was a pearl among drivers who, in the wild mêlée of diplomatic vehicles at official functions and National Days, always managed to secure the best parking place for the New Zealand Ambassador's car. How he did this, in the face of far greater powers, nobody dared to enquire, but it was rumoured that he enjoyed some special underworld status to which all the other drivers deferred. Among his many interests, Nishikawa kept an eye on real estate and during the Scotts' absence on mid-tour leave he decided to sell the Residence.

Apart from the butler and the maid, the Residence was empty and Nishikawa had no trouble in persuading the butler to pose as the New Zealand Ambassador, while he showed a potential buyer around the property. Quite how the Japanese butler managed to pass himself off as a Kiwi remains a mystery, but the buyer agreed to a deal immediately. Unfortunately for Nishikawa, however, before handing over the money, he decided to call in at the Embassy where John's deputy, Roger Peren, was astonished to learn that someone had bought the Residence. A painful exchange followed and the

Every inch the Ambassadress. Marguerite Scott boarding the plane to Seoul, Tokyo 1968. Left to right: Norma Holyoake, Keith Holyoake, Marguerite Scott, John Scott and Secretary of External Affairs, George Laking. (By kind permission of Veronica Scott)

buyer departed in confusion. Both the butler and the maid were pardoned, but Nishikawa vanished without trace and many years later the Scotts learned that he had died in jail.[9]

After Tokyo, Marguerite went on to become Ambassadress in New York, where she continued to maintain her impeccable standards. By this time, feminist authors like Betty Frieden and Germaine Greer were top of the best-seller lists and women worldwide were clamouring for greater freedom. But living in a cloistered world of silver trays and calling cards, Marguerite seems to have been quite oblivious to the enormous social changes that were going on around her. Shortly after her return home in 1974, she sat down and wrote the handbook. After nearly a decade as a high-ranking Ambassadress, she had no idea of the turmoil that was raging in the hearts of the younger wives and their indignant reactions to her carefully prepared manual on etiquette and protocol must have come as a rude awakening.

But as a woman who would have thrived on an independent career herself, Marguerite was not immune to the arguments of the Women's Liberation Movement. During the five years she spent in Wellington she underwent an extraordinary conversion, embracing her new-found feminism with all the zeal of a born-again believer. When John became Ambassador in Paris, she took advantage of a New Zealand Heads of Mission meeting to have a discussion on women's rights with her fellow ambassadresses. The outcome was a hard-hitting paper to the Foreign Service Association* (which wives were not permitted to join), in which she argues cogently for the right of diplomatic wives to work and voices their 'long-standing dissatisfaction' at being 'packaged and posted overseas regardless of personal commitments.'[10]

In Marguerite the younger women had gained a formidable ally, although how much the paper reflects the views of her peers is open to question. It is clearly her own work and also contains a page-long diatribe against the 'very considerable responsibilities and commitments' of senior diplomatic wives. She concludes on a sour note: 'Thus it seems abundantly clear that the government gets two for the price of one, which could be regarded as rather a shoddy arrangement for all concerned.' Marguerite's disenchantment with the diplomatic role, which she had formerly embraced so eagerly, reveals her bitter regrets. Feminism had certainly captured her, but another crucial reason for her change of heart would have been the realisation that her many years of unquestioning service had taken a heavy toll on her most vulnerable child, Veronica.

Veronica's Story

I went to New York when I was six months old and I came back when I was about four and a half or five ... Then we had two years in Wellington, where I went to my first school ... We went to London in 1958 until 1962, when I was aged eight to eleven ... There we lived in two different houses and we [elder sister Hillary and Veronica] went to a little dame school in North London ...

We came back on the maiden voyage of the Canberra ... I remember that I was only eleven because I was just not old enough to be allowed to swim in the adults' swimming pool ... We also went to England and returned from America by boat ... On our way home in 1955, when my younger sister was still a babe in arms, we travelled by train across the Rockies to Vancouver where we jumped on the boat to New Zealand. I remember sitting on that wonderful train with a glass roof, admiring the views as they went racing past ...

---

*   The Ministry's staff association.

I always seemed to be arriving in new schools mid-term, never on the first day with the other new children. I guess this reflected my father's posting dates and the different school years in northern and southern hemispheres.

Early in 1965, my parents were posted to Japan and I went with them aged fourteen … In Tokyo, there were only two available schools for foreign children. One was the American School, which was an hour and a half's travelling each way, and the other was the International School of the Sacred Heart, which was not far away. So that's where I went, which I have mixed feelings about … There were a lot of tight-lipped, disapproving Asian nuns. I only had to look at them and I was in trouble.

The 'real' Catholics went to a group called the Angels' Solidarity Class in which the Catholic girls were encouraged to report on any subversive conversations … At fourteen, I was busy questioning things … Do you really think there is a God? So I was labelled as an advocate of the Devil and I was named and shamed in front of the whole school …

After a year there, my parents send me back to a 'proper' New Zealand school … So I said farewell to my friends (again) and I returned to Nelson Girls' College, where my mother had been dux and head prefect and indeed my grandmother before her. I went into the Lower Sixth as a boarder … It was quite a culture shock. I arrived late in the term and didn't have a uniform. Everyone else was in uniform and I was wearing a wildly coloured Japanese silk shirt and make-up … I used to make my eyes up like Twiggy, with black lashes underneath, pretty precocious, I suppose, for a fifteen-year-old … A lot of the girls were the daughters of farmers and I felt that a lot of them looked at me askance and thought 'who the hell does she think she is?' … I just always felt quite different.

The school holidays were always a problem – we needed to be farmed out to friends of my parents, family members, or anyone who would take us! At the time the Ministry only funded one trip a year home to parents, wherever they were. My elder sister, Hillary, was at school in Wellington, privately boarding. Effectively that year in Tokyo 1965, when I was fourteen, was the last time that we three children lived together with our parents as a family …

My little sister, Debbie, was still in Japan … I think she missed me afterwards because she was in the Residence, next to the Embassy, and had no other children of her own age to play with. She became good chums with Yuki-san, the older housemaid … She also retreated into herself and read and read – a hundred books.

During the school holidays, Hillary and I would go to friends of my parents' ... In fact many of Marguerite's letters around that time are requests to friends to have me or Hillary for the holidays. At Christmas I would go out to Japan for six weeks. But my main recollection is of being farmed out to semi-strangers, who may have been friends of my parents, but whom I barely knew.

Getting home was pretty exciting and glamorous compared with boarding school ... Being around Christmas time, there would be cocktail parties galore. Everything was big and on a glorious scale. Also it was nice to be back with my parents, even if they were always busy and always going out to one thing or another. But it was very short. Six weeks is a short period of time ... Once I think in my three Nelson College years, Marguerite managed to wangle a visit back to New Zealand on her own. But she had to attach that to some other task ... to do with furnishing the new Embassy.

I stayed on for three years at Nelson College because I failed my exams ... Part of my trouble was poor concentration, but more importantly a lack of consistency meant I could never get a grip on the curriculum. Every time I moved schools, especially between countries, it was a different curriculum and even the same subjects were being treated in a different way ... The Latin pronunciation in Nelson didn't sound anything like the Latin in Tokyo ...

I'd started playing the guitar around then and listening, star-struck, to Joan Baez and Bob Dylan and just wanted to be like them ... We had a fantastic music teacher. I played clarinet in the orchestra and sang in the choir.

When I failed UE, I had to repeat the Lower Sixth year ... but this time I was accredited. Expecting to move on to university, I discovered that Mum and Dad had decided that another year in the Upper Sixth would do me the world of good ... I think the fact that they were still in Japan, without any indication of where to next had quite a lot to do with it ... But that extra year in the Sixth Form unsettled me. All my friends had moved on and somehow I lost heart and I lost momentum ...

I began to go off the rails in various ways. I used to pad off down to the Chez Eelco coffee bar – a revolutionary concept in 1968, and play my guitar on Sunday evenings at the folk club ... I had consented to go back for a third year in the Sixth Form on condition that I could board privately ... I was living with a young family near the school, but they weren't responsible for me and for that last year at school, I felt very lonely.

In 1969 I went to New York for a year with Mum and Dad when they went to the UN directly from Japan ... I can't remember if Debbie was there. As

The swinging sixties. Veronica Scott flanked by her father and her French boyfriend, New York 1969.

(By kind permission of Veronica Scott)

a family we weren't very bonded. We were just making these fairly arbitrary decisions according to convenience – or geography …

I went to Hunter College which was the first time I had had some academic success … It wasn't wildly radical like Berkeley … but the great thing was that I got really good marks … I don't remember making a lot of close friends, but I often went down to Greenwich Village to listen to folk singers. I used to walk all over New York exploring … I also went to the Alliance Française to smarten up my French.

I wasn't really included in diplomatic life … I remember being much more involved in Japan with lots of drinks parties in the early evenings and canapés being handed round, and learning how to make small talk with guests.

In New York I had a programme of my own … I went out with my French tutor at the Alliance – the first big/little love affair of my life … He was going back to university in Paris and I wanted to go back with him, but at the end of that year Mum and Dad insisted that I go back to university in New Zealand … They said that if the relationship was worth anything, it would survive … I guess I was very young, eighteen going on nineteen …

*I have a picture of myself in a purple, velvet dress and him with long hair.
Typical sixties.*

*I always wanted to please my parents, even though of the three girls I was
the most rebellious and wilful. I spent many years trying to gain their
approval, but doing all the wrong things … I think the time I missed my
parents most was from fifteen to seventeen because that's when you make
big decisions that affect the rest of your life …*

*By the time I returned to Victoria University in early 1970, I was quite
spoilt by the good life … but I was still completely clueless about what I
wanted to do. I've always felt the ground was shifting underneath me … I
also feel there's quite a big legacy from my early childhood … I'm not very
good at making long-term friends because in my early childhood friends
were something that came and went, and no sooner had you made a good
friend than it was time to move to another school or another country …
and that would be the end of that …*

*I think I grew up expecting my life to be somehow as glamorous as my
parents' and that has been the biggest challenge for me – recognising
that life isn't to do with cocktail parties and being chauffeur-driven and
presenting a perfect exterior … Sometimes the life I've made for myself
seems dull and disappointing by comparison …*

*Home, what is home? Is it where the diplomat's family retires to? Is it one's
place of birth? … I honestly don't know where I belong. Nothing has ever
really lived up to those early expectations.*

*I gave up university, went to Auckland and met up with a group of people
who were into music. We went off and lived in Coromandel, in Colville,
from 1971 to 1974 … Richard and I lived in a tent … There were some
amazing Swiss Family Robinson tree houses built by the original people,
cooking outdoors and so on. All that stuff, but we didn't go to that extent.
We found an old house on the edge of town with a huge garden and an
apple orchard … There were no rules. We were trying life out according to
whatever we felt like.*

*In 1974, when Mum and Dad were [returning from] New York, I went
bounding up to them at Auckland Airport as they arrived, in my long,
blue muslin dress with a big bump in the front and went 'Guess what, I'm
pregnant' full of excitement and the joy of motherhood. And Mum and
Dad just went 'What, Oh no, God!'*

In the circles in which the Scotts moved, attitudes to unmarried mothers
had changed very little since the days of the Pember Reeves. Fortunately

they were returning to Wellington, where Marguerite stood staunchly by her daughter. Veronica gave birth to a son, who remains her greatest joy. Since then she has lived 'several different lives', including twenty-five years overseas, working as a sub-editor for a UK national newspaper and later as a software test analyst. But like many diplomatic children, she has never known where she belonged and on finally returning to New Zealand she admits that 'I don't exactly feel I belong here either.'[11]

Marguerite, meanwhile, continued to campaign vigorously on behalf of the diplomatic wives. But her belated espousal of feminism is largely unknown and in the annals of the Ministry of Foreign Affairs this forceful and able woman is only remembered as a stickler for protocol and as the author of the infamous handbook.

CHAPTER 8

Chilling Out with Pierre

At Pierre Trudeau's autumn garden party for the Diplomatic Corps, Jane was the only person wearing a fur hat. By New Zealand standards, the weather was already distinctly wintry, but Pierre took her to task: 'Well, Miss Eyre, you shouldn't be wearing that till the snow comes,'[1] he said, indicating the rolling green lawns that swept down to the lake. The party was being held at his country 'cottage' at Harrington Lake, a charming Colonial-style house set in a beautiful park about thirty-five kilometres from Ottawa. Everyone tittered politely. Pierre was famous for his chat-up lines and at twenty Jane was one of the youngest and most attractive women present. He had been Prime Minister of Canada for barely six months, but already his charm and panache had gained him the title of Canada's most eligible bachelor – and thousands of female admirers.

It was October 1968 and Jane had recently arrived in Canada where her father, Dean Eyre, was the New Zealand High Commissioner. He was not a career diplomat, but a retired politician who had been personally appointed by Holyoake. To those who had spent long years learning their trade, the government's practice of rewarding political cronies with top-level posts was little short of an insult, especially as such appointments were often used to dispose of those who were past their sell-by date. Eyre's case, however, was slightly different. As a six-term member for Auckland's North Shore he was a National Party stalwart, who had held almost every portfolio except finance and foreign affairs. But, in November 1966, he had become a political liability when as retiring Minister of Defence he was widely reported as saying that the best solution to the Vietnam War was to drop 'a basinful of bombs'[2] on the enemy. It was an ignominious end to his political career and although he sued the newspapers – and won – he never lived it down. The coveted position of High Commissioner in London went to the future Governor General, Denis Blundell, and Eyre was given Canada as a consolation prize.

After her father's long years in Cabinet, Jane was quite used to mixing with high-ranking political figures. At the age of eight, she had sat on Prime Minister Sidney Holland's knee while he did card tricks for her. But Pierre Elliott Trudeau was in a very different league, and as Canada's answer to John F. Kennedy, he had created a nationwide frenzy of 'Trudeaumania'. After their brief exchange Pierre gave her an appraising glance and moved on to work the party. The guests were outside on the terrace and when the first snow flurries fell, everyone was taken by surprise. 'It seems you know our weather better than we do,' said Pierre, who had reappeared at Jane's side. Within a few minutes, he had invited her out to dinner.

During his fifteen years as Prime Minister, Pierre had a stable of attractive women, ranging from celebrities like Barbra Streisand and Margot Kidder to junior female officers in the Canadian Foreign Ministry. He also had a weakness for diplomatic daughters such as Jennifer Rae, daughter of the distinguished Canadian diplomat Saul Rae, with whom he had a well-publicised romance. But although he used to turn up at the New Zealand Residence in a white Mercedes convertible to take Jane out, their friendship never made the headlines. Even the staff at the High Commission knew nothing about it until nearly a year later. He lived at a hectic pace, often ringing up at short notice to invite her to the 'cottage', where they would swim across the lake. 'He was a very serious athlete,' Jane told me, 'and I never skied with him because he was far too good.' But he did teach her how to handle a canoe, Indian style, with a single paddle.

Initially Jane found Pierre difficult to get to know. He was 'very private' and 'very cool'. He was also nearly thirty years her senior. But he had always had a special rapport with youth, which culminated in 1971 with his marriage to Margaret Sinclair, who was a year younger than Jane. Like Jane, Margaret was the daughter of a Cabinet Minister, with whom Pierre felt very much at ease. He and Eyre also hit it off. As fellow politicians, they spoke the same language and the regular appearance of the normally elusive Prime Minister at New Zealand High Commission parties used to arouse considerable envy among the rest of the Diplomatic Corps. Eyre had always got on well with foreign dignitaries and, even after his unfortunate remarks on Vietnam, figures such as the Prime Minister of Singapore, Lee Kuan Yew, refused to condemn him: 'Made a gaffe, eh?' said Lee, when Eyre's comments were reported to him, 'I like him, hearty, blunt, earnest.'[3]

Although Jane is at pains to stress that she was simply one of Pierre's many girlfriends, if fate had not intervened in the form of a disastrous motor accident, their relationship might have developed into something more serious. Even so, 'half the Cabinet' came to visit her while she was recovering from her injuries, which suggests that she was very much the girl of the moment. Having broken both legs, however, she was no longer able to participate in any winter sports and after a lengthy convalescence she left for London. By this time Pierre was courting his future wife, but he and Jane remained good friends and they stayed in touch.

Four years later in 1973, when Margaret Trudeau was enjoying the same rock star status as her husband, Pierre and Jane met up in London. 'Who's that lady?' ran a hopeful headline, 'PM & "old friend" hit quiet spots'. Much to the disappointment of the press, their outing was a decorous theatre party, which concluded with nothing more scandalous than a quick drink at one of London's most exclusive nightspots. Ironically this was the only time that Jane and Pierre ever went to a nightclub together, but the gossip columnists were unimpressed: 'If anything should put the nail in the coffin of Trudeau the trendy swinger, this is it.'[4]

By 1977 the Trudeau marriage was on the rocks and the love story, which had started so romantically on a beach in Tahiti, had lapsed into a tawdry tale of marital wrangling and misbehaviour. While Margaret sought solace with the Rolling Stones, Pierre preferred to stick to his old friends and whenever Jane came to visit her parents in Ottawa, he would give her a call. 'Come for dinner and a swim,' he said. It was mid winter, but at his request a large indoor pool, which reputedly cost four times as much as the one at the White House, had been installed at his official Residence.

At the Prime Minister's imposing mansion at 24 Sussex Drive the swimming pool and the sauna are in an adjoining structure, which is connected to the house by a tunnel. Except for the security detail provided by the Royal Canadian Mounted Police, Jane and Pierre were alone and after a long swim and a bake in the sauna they decided to top off the evening with a traditional roll in the snow. Having known Pierre for nearly a decade, Jane no longer found him so intimidating and they were both shrieking with laughter as they plunged, scantily clad, into the icy garden. But when the door slammed shut behind them, Pierre stopped laughing. They were trapped outside and at -20ºC their survival time could be as little as fifteen minutes.

Jane Eyre at the time she met Pierre Trudeau, Ottawa 1968. (By kind permission of Jane Coke-Steel)

'Pierre was pretty het up,' said Jane, 'and there was no way we could get round to the front of the house because of the banks of snow.' As he began hammering on the basement windows, she remembers giggling hysterically. She had no idea of the danger they were in. But Pierre realised at once. He also knew that the security guards only patrolled the house periodically and that there was very little chance of them hearing anything from their upstairs office. The minutes crawled by and both of them had started shivering violently, when at the far end of a darkened passage Pierre saw the beam of a torch. One of the guards was making a routine check of the basement and after some renewed hammering he finally attracted her attention. It had been a close call and the next morning Pierre sent Jane a message to say that he had arranged for a handle to be put on the outside door of the sauna.

Not long afterwards Jane met her future husband in England. A year later a full-scale wedding took place in Ottawa, where Eyre was enjoying a second term as High Commissioner. Naturally the local press made much of Jane's name and, picking up on the fact that her new home would be comparatively close to Charlotte Brontë's birthplace, the *Globe and Mail* ran the headline

Pierre Trudeau arriving at the New Zealand Residence in Ottawa to toast Jane Eyre at her wedding. (By kind permission of Jane Coke-Steel)

'Jane Eyre back to Brontë country'[5] above its report of the wedding. But the lead story was Pierre, who arrived hot off the campaign trail – with a rose in his buttonhole – to make a toast to the bride.

As a veteran politician, Eyre must have relished this mark of high favour – although it is doubtful that Jane's friendship with Pierre brought any tangible benefits to New Zealand. What is certain, however, is that if the Prime Minister of Canada and the daughter of the New Zealand High Commissioner had been found frozen to death in the garden no one would ever have forgotten it.

CHAPTER 9

A Portrait of the Artist

From her very first posting in 1957, Piera fell in love with Paris:

> *It was a revelation. I'd never seen Cubist paintings in those lovely beige and gentle colours before ... Whenever I could get away from my young family, I used to go and look at these things and wonder about them ... And then there was that marvellous plenitude of museums and galleries that you could go to at any time ... It was a feast ... A life beyond one's wildest dreams and I embraced it with love and enthusiasm.*[1]

Piera's love for France dates back to her early childhood when, unlike most little girls in New Zealand, she had a French governess. In true Gallic fashion, the governess never spoke a word of English, so Piera learned to speak French long before she could write it. She and the governess became great friends and by the time Piera was handed over to the nuns at the age of twelve, she had acquired an impeccable French accent and a devotion to all things French.

At school not everything went quite so smoothly because Piera could not stop drawing and she covered every piece of paper in sight with sketches: 'Ever since I was a tiny girl, I've loved to draw ... I never took lessons ... I've always just "had it". In the end, she was sent to the Reverend Mother for scribbling on the back of her maths book. Today Piera's gifts would have taken her straight to art school, but in the 1940s few women gave any thought to a career. Instead she took a degree in languages and got married to a fellow student named John McArthur, who spoke even better French than she did and was destined for a diplomatic career.

During the early years of her marriage, Piera devoted herself to motherhood which, like everything else in her life, she did on a grand scale. With a family of six she had little time to develop her artistic interests, but she had always adored children and she revelled in her maternal role: 'We had such fun as a family ... People used to envy us.' Bounding with energy, she coped effortlessly with her numerous offspring. Even travelling the world with them held no fears for her: 'I felt so proud walking out at the airport to catch a plane with all these little kids with their shoulder bags ... and a little written note in case they got lost.'

John, meanwhile, was moving up the diplomatic ladder and after Paris and a period at home, postings to New York and Rome followed. With her husband's increasing seniority, Piera's representational responsibilities multiplied, but once again she took it all in her stride. She was a superb hostess and in a household where they rarely sat down with fewer than eight to meals, a lunch or a dinner for twelve was neither here nor there. As far as she was concerned, entertaining was all part of the job: 'It had to be done, so I did it gladly.'

John's first post as head of mission came in 1973, when the New Zealand government decided to open embassies in Chile and Peru, with an ambassador resident in Santiago. Despite the lure of a lucrative milk powder deal, the government could hardly have chosen a worse moment for its first venture in Latin America. Stirred up by the economic reforms of its President, Salvador Allende, Chile was in a state of turmoil. The right-wing opposition was up in arms and yet further unrest was being fuelled by the US government, which was deeply suspicious of Allende's Communist affiliations. By October 1972 waves of strikes were paralysing the country, inflation was soaring and rumours of a *coup d'état* were rife. The position of New Zealand's first Ambassador to Chile and Peru was clearly not an assignment for the faint-hearted, but the McArthurs were undaunted and when John was offered the job they saw it as an adventure.

For the Counsellor Don Hunn, and his wife Janine, to whom the task of setting up the Embassy had been allotted, living in a hotel room (which also served as the office) was all too familiar. They had already spent weeks in a hotel in Suva when they had opened the High Commission in Fiji. The greatest problem in Fiji had been the shortage of housing and they were braced for similar difficulties in Chile. But in Santiago, thousands of wealthy Chilean *momios* were fleeing the country, and for a fistful of US dollars Don was able to acquire two enormous houses to accommodate the staff, plus a charming European-style building for the office.

By the time John presented his credentials to Allende in March 1973, Chile was lapsing into chaos. Thousands of women marched through the streets, banging their empty saucepans in protest at the food shortages, and Piera remembers seeing truckloads of workers waving pitchforks heading off to take over the *estancias*. Shortly before the *coup* took place, the situation became so volatile that Don and the Embassy driver dug a hole in the office garden to hide petrol so that the staff would be able to get to the airport.

After so many months of tension, when the *coup* came it was almost a relief. It began early on 11 September and Piera remembers John 'skidding round the corner from the bathroom, still shaving, shouting "It's happening. It's happening". From her bedroom, Piera could hear the planes passing overhead on their way to bomb the Presidential Palace. The noise of the bombardment was deafening as the planes wheeled round and flew back towards the hills to bomb Allende's official Residence. Within a couple of hours General Pinochet and his troops had gained control of the country, but Allende and his supporters held out at the Palace until well into the afternoon. His stirring last speech on live radio and his subsequent suicide have become the stuff of legends. Many still believe that he was assassinated.

After the *coup*, the city was engulfed in a different sort of madness. A curfew was imposed and thousands of Allende's supporters were rounded up and taken to the National Stadium where they were shot. Two New Zealand hippies were caught up in the chaos and Don, who had broken his ankle a week earlier, went limping down to the stadium to look for them. There were some tense moments when the military took away his passport, but he got the two men out and took them home. They hadn't had a bath for weeks and when Janine cut their hair, she found it crawling with lice.

Over the weeks that followed, Santiago was overrun with people trying to evade capture. The most prominent were being hotly pursued and anyone who could claim political asylum was looking for an embassy where they would be safe from arrest. In downtown Santiago, over two hundred *asilado* had taken refuge in the vast Renaissance-style palace that housed the Argentine Embassy. 'You'd go past,' Piera told me, 'and see all their bedding airing out of the windows.' Just down the road from the McArthur's mock Tudor mansion, the German Ambassador was sheltering forty refugees and it was only a question of time before someone approached New Zealand:

One Sunday morning John got a call from the guard at the Embassy to say that someone had broken in. He went off in the car to see what had happened … He rang me at home saying 'I'm coming home and I'm bringing someone with me. I want you to stand at the gate and make sure the coast is clear.' ... Eventually his car came down through the gates into the courtyard, then across the cobbles and into the garage. Out got a hefty figure that looked rather like a Belgian charwoman with a wig and a hat and an astrakhan coat. He bowed to me graciously and said in very good English, 'Madame, I ask your forgiveness for arriving in such a manner.'

Once he removed his disguise, Piera recognised the man immediately. It was the leader of the Trades Union Movement, Figueroa, who was one of the ten most wanted men in the country. His photograph had been on the front pages of the newspapers for weeks and with the military close on his heels, he had been moving every night. Piera showed him to a bedroom on a side of the house that was invisible from the street and for the next ten days he lived with them, much to the curiosity of the household staff: 'We told them that we had a visitor and that they were to be very courteous and mind their own business.' But, as far as asylum seekers went, Figueroa was quite a catch and before long Piera and John were able to hand him on (with a bag of flour and a bag of sugar to help with the housekeeping) to the Swedish Ambassador, who was collecting political figures enthusiastically. By this time Figueroa's girlfriend had moved in too and Piera confesses that she and John 'were quite glad to get rid of them.'

Piera's second *asilado* climbed through a window one warm summer afternoon, when she was drying her hair:

I was alone in the house, but I kept very calm and asked him what he wanted. He said he wanted to 'take refuge' ... so I suggested to him that it might be more sensible to go down the road to the Germans. I made him a cup of tea and gave him some ginger biscuits, which he'd never tasted before ... and then he left, having made sure that there were no police around ... He was terrified.

As befits a woman of her diplomatic experience, Piera is cautious in her political comments: 'I don't feel sad or happy about Allende. As far as I am concerned, he was a figure in history who played his role.' But the most junior of the three wives in the Embassy had no such reticence. At a diplomatic reception she was overheard denouncing the *coup*, and a few days later she had the distinction of being the only New Zealand diplomatic wife ever to have been declared *persona non grata* in her own right. Of course she had to leave. But by all accounts diplomatic life was not to her taste and after her departure (so I am told), her husband settled down very happily with a Chilean.

Far removed from the horrors of the stadium, the coffee parties and cultural groups of the diplomatic wives continued, and it was in the unlikely environment of one of these gatherings that Piera discovered her artistic vocation:

> There was a Canadian wife who ran a painting class ... It was a funny little group of women of various capabilities. One stopped for morning tea, brought in by the maître d'hôtel in his white jacket. They were all diplomatic wives or ladies devoted to worthy causes like Las Damas Diplomaticas ... and now and again a plaintive voice used to bleat 'Oh, I've forgotten how to make green' and dreadful things like that.

But these first painting classes were life-changing for Piera. All her youthful passion for art flooded back and once she began painting, she realised that she was never going to stop. Before long she had joined a serious studio run by a Chilean painter called Raoul Bustamente, where she could work from live models: 'For a couple of hours, I would be totally engrossed in drawing. Then I'd drive home to find John reading his paper, rather gruffly, with no comment in the study. He didn't even say "Where the hell have you been?".'

Of course John knew exactly where she had been. Art had become her all-consuming passion and she could think of nothing else. But any fears that he may have had that his wife would vanish permanently behind an easel proved unfounded. Piera had far too much zest for living for that. Nevertheless, her world view had altered radically: 'I became totally aware of seeing things and of looking at things.' She also became imbued with the spirit of the times, and both the magical realism of Gabriel Garcia Marquez and the surreal canvasses of Roberto Matta have left their mark on her style. One autumn afternoon in 1975, John telephoned Piera from the office. 'I'm coming home', he said, 'and I've got something to tell you.' His tone betrayed nothing and Piera wondered if someone had died. But as soon as she saw his face, she knew that the news was good. 'We're going back to Paris,' he said, pouring her a glass of champagne and Piera's heart leapt for joy.

Few people would dispute that the Residence in Paris is New Zealand's most beautiful diplomatic property. From the street the sober limestone façade, with its classical windows and cornices, gives little hint of the splendour that lies within. But once inside the mood changes and a sweeping marble staircase leads up to a suite of reception rooms that includes a magnificent *grand salon* with mirrored walls and a soaring thirty-foot ceiling. The scale of the *grand salon* is breathtaking, but it is by no means the Residence's only asset. Next door to it is a library, with tall oak bookcases and a fireplace, and on the other side of the hall is an elegantly furnished *petit salon*, which leads into a graceful dining room. Beyond this, at the far end of the hall, an *escalier d'honneur* curves up to the first floor, where a more intimate series of rooms forms a charming private apartment. Higher still, on the second and third floors, at least half a dozen further bedrooms can be found, with box rooms and attics galore.

'How many rooms has it got?' growled Muldoon, when he came to Paris as Prime Minister. 'A hundred, Sir', replied the French architect, who was trying to impress him. A mere forty would be closer to the mark. Nevertheless it is not a house that any male New Zealand diplomat would have dared to purchase. Fortunately, however, the task of buying the Legation* in Paris fell to a woman and she could see at a glance that this was the sort of house to which every hostess aspires. Furthermore, she had a hoard of French francs which she had every intention of spending.

When Jean McKenzie was appointed as New Zealand's Chargé d'Affaires to Paris in 1949, she no longer possessed the blonde good looks that had so endeared her to her elderly male bosses. But she still had an aura of glamour and, having worked in the Prime Minister's Department (and later in the Department External Affairs) for over twenty years, she was uniquely well placed to twist the arms of those who held the purse strings. The course of history also played into her hand. In 1949, the world was still picking up the pieces from World War II and when it emerged that New Zealand had been supplying the French territories in the Pacific on credit throughout the war, McIntosh realised that a considerable sum of money must be owing to New Zealand.

Given the parlous state of the post-war French economy, any repayment would be in non-convertible francs, which could only be spent in France. But plans were already afoot to open a post in Paris, and as New Zealand's representative Jean was instructed to secure at least partial repayment 'to buy, furnish and stock up a Legation.'[2] She needed no second bidding and within three months of her arrival she had negotiated a sum of 80,000,000 francs, which was more than enough to buy and furnish a splendid embassy.

Jean's shopping spree, for which she has earned the eternal gratitude of all subsequent chatelaines of No. 9 Rue Léonard de Vinci, did not stop at the 35,000,000 francs that she paid for the house. Arm in arm with her best friend, Lorna McPhee, who was also working in Paris, she would head off

---

* The Legation was upgraded to an Embassy in 1957.

New Zealand's most beautiful Embassy. The Grand Salon at the Residence in Paris.

for the celebrated auction house at the Hôtel Drouot to find furnishings and Persian carpets. Between them, they located the immense rug which still graces the *grand salon*. They also bought the concert-size Pleyel grand and dozens of exquisite wine glasses. As well as her own purchases, Jean picked up some pieces from the previous owner, the Princesse de Béarn, such as the Louis XVI chairs and the priceless damask curtains. Similarly, she was shrewd enough to employ the Princess's chef, who was reputed to be one of the best in Paris. The house was made for entertaining and within a few days of moving in, Jean had thrown her first party – a reception for 400 guests – all of whom were amply accommodated in the *grand salon*.

No great diplomatic hostess is complete without an impressive Residence and in Piera's case she was returning to a building in which she had always longed to live:

> *I loved that house from the word go because I had known it when I was a young diplomatic wife … It was such a marvellous and dignified place … like something out of a bygone era, with a back staircase and a front staircase, and special ironing rooms and sculleries. I used to think that I could stay in the house always, and never go out.*

She also had the benefit of being the first Ambassadress to have the run of the whole building. Until 1975, the warren of rooms on the upper floors had served as offices and the Ambassador and his wife had lived in the apartment on the first floor. But Piera's arrival coincided with New Zealand's entry to the OECD, whose headquarters are in Paris, and to accommodate the enlarged staff a new office had been built at the end of the garden, leaving the Ambassador in sole possession of the Residence.

During her first few days, Piera explored the house from top to bottom. In the cavernous basement kitchen, the evil-tempered Vietnamese cook was glowering. Piera suspected him of doing his own shopping out of the housekeeping money and she asked him to produce receipts. 'If you say that to me again, I'm leaving,' he said, knowing full well that she was giving her first lunch party that day. But Piera did not stand for any nonsense, 'So I said it again and he left.'

After that she found Daniel who had trained as a pâtissier's *garçon*. According to Piera he was 'a funny little fellow', but his éclairs were sublime and he turned out to be a wonderful cook. He and Piera soon settled into a comfortable daily routine: 'In the morning I'd go and discuss things; who was coming and what we might have' before he headed off to the markets resplendent in his Davy Crockett hat. In the depths of the house, she also discovered the wine cellar, full of legendary vintages that had been carefully laid down in the early days of the Legation: 'I can still remember the smell … musty, earthy and warm.' But by far her most important discovery was high up in the roof where a vast attic, strewn with cobwebs, ran half the breadth of the building. With light streaming in from the skylights, it was a painter's garret like no other.

So Piera's double life began: 'It was all a question of organising yourself … and if I want to do something, I'll find some way of doing it.' As Ambassadress, she entertained constantly with formal lunches and dinners for French officials as well as larger diplomatic occasions involving hundreds of guests. 'We had wonderful receptions,' Piera told me, 'we'd light the fires and we had a special team of waiters who came in to help.' Many others can vouch for her hospitality. The New Zealand pianist Jeffrey Grice describes giving a recital in the *grand salon*. It was a black tie occasion followed by a reception and Piera pulled out all the stops. 'They were extraordinary hosts,' Jeffrey recalls, 'and they put on great receptions.'[3]

In addition to their formal entertaining, the McArthurs were inundated with house guests. With a forty-roomed house in the XVIième, it was hard to turn anyone away. But as soon as she had discharged her hostess's duties, Piera would escape to her studio in the attic, where she entered a world of excitement and colour that she never wanted to leave: 'But if I was still painting at five o'clock, then it was time to put down my paint and my brushes and get washed and cleaned up to go to a National Day at six.' In Paris the diplomatic round is relentless and in addition to daytime engagements, she and John went out night after night.

As they moved among the well-groomed throng that makes up Parisian high society, Piera observed the sea of faces with a painter's eye: 'I was flooded with visual opportunities and it was up to me to take out of them what I wanted … I've always been interested in people and the diplomatic world is all about people.' Like every artist, she drew inspiration from her surroundings and, over the months that followed, she covered page after page of her sketchbook with people and scenes from her diplomatic life.

Piera was not working in isolation. On her earlier posting she had met a New Zealand painter named Douglas MacDiarmid, who had been living in Paris for decades. Unlike Piera he was already an established artist, whose canvases could be found in all of New Zealand's major art collections, and she approached him with considerable trepidation. Apart from her hours in Bustamente's studio, she had no formal training and no idea what Douglas would make of her work. But he put her at ease immediately. 'Show me what you've got in your folder', he said. She watched anxiously as he leafed through her carefully selected portfolio. 'Would you give me some lessons?' she asked. Douglas looked up. Like Bustamente, he had seen at a glance that she could draw. 'Good heavens no,' he said, 'but I'd be happy to paint with you.' It was the start of an extraordinary friendship, which continues uninterrupted to this day.

Despite his protestations, Douglas was a marvellous teacher:

> He was an educator in the truest sense of the word … and he didn't
> try to force any of his own forms of expression on you …He helped to
> bring out what you were about … He'd come and look at what I'd been
> doing and then there would be a lot of discussion. But he never said
> 'Put this here' or 'Put this there' … It was never 'work', but more a great
> exchange of ideas.

He was also an invaluable guide to the Parisian art scene, and before long Piera was treading the time-honoured path to the *salons* at which emerging artists submit their work to a rigorous panel of judges. Many do not survive the cull, but Piera was accepted and from there she graduated to her first solo exhibition in Paris.

Piera McArthur at work in the attic with her artistic mentor, Douglas MacDiarmid, Paris c. 1977. (By kind permission of Piera McArthur)

Piera's show on the Ile Saint-Louis marks her astonishing leap, in the space of less than three years, from that first epiphany in Santiago to her emergence as a professional artist. But she continued to live in dread of being perceived as one of the many amateur dabblers who frequent the diplomatic world. 'Being an ambassador's wife could have prevented people from taking my work seriously,' she told me, and in her dealings with galleries and artists in Paris, she went to great lengths to conceal her diplomatic connections.

Nearly forty years later, when her pictures grace the walls of public buildings and private homes the length and breadth of New Zealand, no one could doubt either her professionalism or her commitment. But her riotous romps of colour and line have always been controversial. In a review of her work in 2005, T.J. McNamara sums it up: 'McArthur's work is certainly not to everyone's taste, but there is nothing else quite like it.'[4]

Piera's style defies definition. Her spontaneity has been likened to Dufy and her rhythms to Jackson Pollock, suffused with a unique blend of humour and dash that reflects her personal vision. Perhaps the closest that she has come to explaining her creative processes is in the introduction to her exhibition, 'The Painter's Enigma':

'The Ambassador and his wife going in to dinner'. Diplomatic social life features frequently in Piera's paintings. (By kind permission of Piera McArthur)

To paint with integrity is to listen to an inner voice (if indeed you are lucky enough to have one!). Some may call this voice 'instinct', and how much to hone and refine it or let it emerge unbridled, is the painter's enigma. Authenticity does not necessarily suffer from discipline …
At the same time, it should be added that fashionable trends should hold no sway over the genuine imperious urges of a painter … There is a further dilemma to consider – imagination points to endless ways of expressing any one given theme. Heart, eye and intellect are all involved. Time and time again you must fail in order to succeed – but the search is glorious and when all is said and done, you alone can know how it has to be.

Few diplomats have had the good fortune to serve twice as Ambassador to France, but in 1983, after brief interludes in Wellington and Brussels, John was reappointed to Paris. To Piera it felt like a homecoming. '*Vous avez été en vacance, Madame?*' the Algerian street sweeper on Rue Léonard de Vinci enquired politely, swirling the water into the gutter with his long broom. Piera smiled. 'I suppose you could call it that.' Their two years in Brussels had been pleasant enough, but she was glad to be back in Paris.

She hurried up the street, running through her list of tasks. A French Minister was coming to dinner and the cook had already left for the markets. She headed for the florist to pick up the roses, diving into the *chocolatier* on the way for a box of her favourite crystallised orange to serve with the coffee. Her mind was buzzing; the Papal Nuncio was also coming and she must remind John to ask him to say grace. Then there was the wine, which John would have to taste. No detail could be left to chance, but once she had seen to everything, she could get back to the glorious painting of a string quartet that she was working on in the attic. Tomorrow she would show it to Douglas and everything would be just the same as before, or so it seemed to Piera, little guessing that one of the worst crises in New Zealand's diplomatic history was lurking just over the horizon.

Lying on its side in Auckland's Waitemata Harbour, the converted trawler looked like a beached whale. The stern was almost completely submerged, but the bow was above the waterline and beneath the band of rainbow stripes the name was clearly visible: *Rainbow Warrior*. On 10 July 1985 a member of the French External Intelligence Service, the DGSE, placed two underwater charges on the hull of the main protest vessel belonging to the international environmental organisation, Greenpeace. The DGSE's intention was to sabotage Greenpeace's planned protest against French nuclear testing in the Pacific by sinking the *Rainbow Warrior*, but things went horribly wrong. In

Piera McArthur meeting Pope John Paul II during her second term as Ambassadress in Paris, Rome mid 1980s. (By kind permission of Piera McArthur)

the second blast a Greenpeace photographer died, setting in train a murder investigation that eventually led to the desk of the President of France.

In New Zealand reactions were outraged, and a long battle for justice ensued at the heart of which was the Embassy in Paris. It was an ugly fight, which grew still uglier when the so-called 'honeymoon couple', Alain Marfart and Dominique Prieur, were sentenced to jail in New Zealand. The French government tried every means to extract them, including the threat of trade sanctions, which transformed John's formerly civilised exchanges with the Quai d'Orsay into unseemly slugging matches. Both the Embassy and the Residence were surrounded by barricades and at the height of the affair a mob gathered in the nearby square and marched down Rue Léonard de Vinci. Forewarned by the police, Piera closed all the shutters overlooking the street and retreated with the household staff to an upper landing, from where they could hear the shouts of the protesters as they stormed past. The sinking of the *Rainbow Warrior* cast a pall over New Zealand's relations with France. But Piera's affections never wavered and when the time finally came to leave Paris, she (like Hemingway)* consoled herself with the thought that she could feast on its cultural riches for ever.

---

*   Ernest Hemingway: 'If you are lucky enough to have lived in Paris as a young man, then wherever you go for the rest of your life it stays with you, for Paris is a moveable feast.'

Piera in her Wellington studio, 2010.

(*Victorious,* Alumni News, *Summer 2010*)

The McArthur's last posting was to Russia*, where Mikhail Gorbachev had become Head of State and the downfall of Communism was imminent. For Soviet artists, Gorbachev's reforms had brought liberation from the tyranny of Socialist Realism and for the first time since before the days of Stalin, they were enjoying artistic freedom. In this highly charged atmosphere, Piera's exuberant style and subversive humour spoke straight to the hearts of the Russians and early in 1990 she became the first New Zealander to have a solo show at Moscow's legendary New Tretyakov Gallery.

Within the diplomatic community, Piera's artistic debut caused quite a stir. This was no low-key affair, but rather an invitation from the Soviet Union of Artists to mount a major exhibition of one hundred paintings and graphics. 'Well, I must say, you've got balls,' said one colleague. No diplomatic wife had ever done anything quite like it and, according to Piera, the Americans were so put out that they quickly rustled up a little display by their own Ambassador's wife – on quilting.

Piera's exhibition was a blockbuster. 'I had a marvellous show,' she told me, 'the Russians loved my work … and they simply adopted me.' After the grand opening, the artists gave a party for her: 'They put on a great spread

---

*   New Zealand had re-opened its Embassy in Moscow in 1973.

of *zakuski* and sausages … It was in somebody's apartment and on the wall there was a sepia coloured photograph of the Tsar and his children … My host shook his head and muttered "We shouldn't have done it". Afterwards she was inundated with letters, including an outraged missive from two academicians in their eighties calling her a *huligan izkustvo* – an artistic hooligan – which she treasures to this day. But there were many more letters saying 'this is how we should have been painting.'

In her ninth decade, Piera paints as vigorously as ever. Her diplomatic role is long over and for the past twenty years she has been able to devote herself full-time to her painting. But although the artist now reigns supreme, her diplomatic past is ever present in her work. Parties and people abound. Drinkers, diners and dancers, sometimes clothed and sometimes nude, stream across her canvases as she portrays the affront of a hostess or the loquacity of a guest in a few deft brushstrokes. For nearly forty years, this was Piera's world. It was a life that she loved and in many of her paintings, amidst the whirl of Parisian high society, she has included a portrait of the artist.

CHAPTER 10

The Sun King of Nuku'alofa

'When the King came for dinner the first thing you had to do was borrow the special chair,' said Janine, 'and the King would see it and head straight for it.'[1] In his prime, King Taufa'ahau Tupou IV of Tonga weighed thirty-one stone and no ordinary chair could hold him. But the British High Commissioner had acquired an outsize chair of reinforced steel which he would lend to his diplomatic colleagues.

At six foot five, the King came of giant stock. His mother, Queen Salote, stood six foot three and weighed over twenty stone and her father, King Siaosi Tupou II, had also been a huge figure. During the Coronation in London in 1953, Queen Salote's great size gave rise to the famous quip that the diminutive Sultan of Kelantan, who was riding in the same coach, was 'her lunch'. But in Tongan society the colossal height and girth of the ruling family only added to their prestige and were seen as potent symbols of their absolute authority over their subjects.

In 1976, when Don and Janine Hunn arrived in Tonga to open New Zealand's first High Commission, the reins of government were still firmly in the hands of the King. He personally appointed the twelve-man Cabinet and presided over a Legislative Assembly that consisted of nine 'nobles' chosen by their peers, and nine 'commoners' who were elected by the people. It was hardly a democratic system, but in a nation that had been dominated by chiefs and nobles for hundreds of years, the King's 90,000 or so subjects accepted his role as part of the natural order. Like the Christian God, whom they had embraced so readily in the nineteenth century, he was an all-powerful and beneficent figure whose rule was divinely ordained.

Tonga was the third post that Don and Janine had been asked to open in seven years. After coping with the *coup* in Chile (on top of setting up the office in Fiji), they were supposed to be enjoying a comfortable posting in Brussels. But Soviet overtures to the newly independent Kingdom of Tonga had caused a flurry in Wellington. As far as Prime Minister Muldoon was concerned, the 'Reds' were trying to get into New Zealand's backyard and the best way to prevent them was to establish a High Commission in the Tongan capital of Nuku'alofa.

The Hunns had been in Brussels barely eighteen months, but Muldoon was not a man to be gainsaid and, after purchasing a top hat and a morning suit, Don set off to become New Zealand's first resident High Commissioner in Tonga, leaving Janine to sort out the family. As Tonga had no suitable secondary schooling, the Hunns' two children were packed off to boarding schools in New Zealand, which was a country they scarcely knew. There thirteen-year-old Martin was teased almost as mercilessly for the excellent French that he had picked up in Brussels as he was for his 'English' accent.

Much to Janine's relief, they did not have to look for a Residence. The King had already allocated them a beautiful wooden house with deep verandas that had been sent out from England in the 1880s. Despite the tropical heat, it was always cool inside and in honour of Janine a new kitchen had been incorporated into the main building to replace the old one in an outhouse.

Janine's first audience with the King took place a few days after her arrival. With a resident Diplomatic Corps of only three missions, she had no other wife to ask for advice. The long-serving British High Commissioner was a bachelor and the Ambassador of Taiwan (with which New Zealand had no diplomatic relations) had come to Tonga without his wife. 'So I just had to wing it on protocol', she told me. When the Hunns were ushered into the Throne Room, the King was sitting on a high-backed wooden throne with the Queen a few inches lower beside him. Clad in a knee-length Tongan *tupenu*, with a traditional mat wrapped around his hips, he was an immense figure. Quaking inwardly, Janine lowered herself 'very carefully' onto one of the two chairs that had been placed in front of the throne.

The Queen seemed rather less daunting, but just as Janine was plucking up courage to address her, an extraordinary being came into her line of vision bearing a plate of fruit cake. Bent double he crawled in front of the throne, thrusting the plate high above his head: 'A giant paw came out and His Majesty took a piece.' This was one of the Palace servants who, like all Tongan subjects, was obliged to keep his head below the level of the King's.

*Don and Janine
Hunn hosting their
first Waitangi
Day party in
Nuku'alofa. Janine
is doing her best to
conceal her cigar,
Tonga 1977.*

(By kind permission of Don and
Janine Hunn)

As foreign dignitaries, Don and Janine were among the few people in Tonga
who did not have to enter the royal presence on their knees.

Once the ice was broken, Janine and the King chatted happily: 'He was
very easy to talk to and he was always full of extraordinary ideas about how
he was going to make money for the Kingdom.' But their favourite topic
was cooking and before long he and Janine were swapping recipes. 'He was
a really keen cook,' Janine said, 'and I got him all sorts of things like chilli
sauce, which I took round to the Palace. He used to cook on Sundays, after
church. He'd go into the kitchen and cook me batches of scones, which
would arrive at our house and our cook, Liliani, would announce, "These
scones cooked by King Taufa'ahua Tupou IV".'

The Queen, too, proved eminently approachable. Constantly surrounded
by her court ladies, she loved to escape with Janine who, as the wife of a
High Commissioner, was quite as much of a novelty to her as royalty was
to the Hunns. 'I'd arrive at the Palace,' Janine told me, 'and she'd hop into
the car … I think she enjoyed the freedom of getting out … She couldn't go
into a shop, so I would drive her down and get her whatever she wanted.'

Far removed from the rumblings of feminism, Janine regarded ferrying the Queen around the dusty streets of Nuku'alofa as part of her job. For her, diplomatic networking and 'good works' were still the accepted tools of the trade and, inevitably, she ended up helping the Queen with her favourite charity.

It was the British High Commissioner who first suggested to the Hunns that they should invite the King to dinner. As an old-school diplomat, who drove around Nuku'alofa with a Union Jack fluttering on his Mini Moke, Humphrey Arthington-Davy had a wealth of local knowledge and was an invaluable source of guidance to successive New Zealand diplomats. Despite their shared interest in cooking, however, Janine found entertaining the King quite a challenge. As well as borrowing the reinforced chair, she had to summon a full-scale military band, which played the national anthem when the King arrived and again when he departed. During the interval, all the musicians had to be provided with beer and pies, which they ate sitting in the garden. The guest list was tricky, too. Tongan protocol prevented the King from eating with his subjects, so all the other guests had to be foreigners. Another complication was the Royal Taster, who arrived with the King's motorcade and went straight into the kitchen to taste his food. Once the Taster had completed his task, the King's food would be placed before him. 'He would start eating immediately,' Janine said, 'which meant that he'd usually finished by the time the rest of the table had been served.' Given that this was the usual routine, the King cannot really be blamed for the unfortunate misunderstanding that occurred on a later occasion, when he helped himself to the entire contents of a large bowl of whitebait that had been intended for the whole table.

In Nuku'alofa almost the only people of sufficient rank to invite the King to dinner were the envoys of Britain, New Zealand and Taiwan. Well-briefed on the King's gastronomic interests, the Ambassador of Taiwan had arrived with a superb Chinese chef, who cooked the best Asian food in the Kingdom. But thanks to the political stand-off between New Zealand and Taiwan, his legendary repasts were out of bounds for Don and Janine. Without diplomatic relations neither of them could entertain the other, and as the Royal couple enthused over their latest delicious meal with the Taiwanese, the Hunns could only listen enviously. In the end, the Queen took pity on them and persuaded the Ambassador to lend her his chef for a special dinner to which Don and Janine were invited, while the Taiwanese remained tactfully at home.

Although two of the three members of Nuku'alofa's minute Diplomatic Corps were debarred from official contact, in the course of their diplomatic duties the three envoys rubbed shoulders constantly.* Every time the King travelled they had to stand in line to welcome and farewell him at the airport. Janine also recalls being summoned regularly to sing hymns around the oil wells, which some Texan adventurers had persuaded the King would be the salvation of his cash-strapped nation:

> Whenever they found a likely spot, the King and the whole Court would attend and the three members of the Diplomatic Corps had to put on their morning suits and top hats and sing while the drilling was being done …It might have been something like 'Oh God our help in ages past' and then a Minister said some prayers.

Wesleyan missionaries had done a thorough job in Tonga, starting with the conversion of the founder of the Tupou dynasty, who took the name of 'Siaosi' (the Tongan version of George), in honour of George III, while his wife became 'Salote' in honour of Queen Charlotte. As George Tupou I, the King established a constitution whose biblical language still reflects the enduring influence of the missionaries. Even in today's revised edition, Tonga's citizens are sternly reminded that 'the Sabbath Day shall be kept holy' which in Humphrey's case led to severe reprimand for picking bananas on Sunday.

Almost the first thing that Don and Janine were asked on their arrival was which church they attended. 'We didn't go to church,' Janine explained, 'and there was a bit of muttering about that. So we said that we had our own religion and that we practised it at home.' The Hunns had bought a little sailing boat and while the Tongans were singing their hearts out in church, they would sneak off across the bay for picnics. But although the King and his family were staunch churchgoers, Don's and Janine's lack of piety was never held against them. Quite as non-judgmental as the original islanders who earned Tonga the affectionate nickname of 'The Friendly Islands', the Tongan Royals accepted the Hunns – sins and all. Thus, although the King never smoked or drank himself, this did not prevent him from slipping Janine a box of cigars from President Marcos, which he knew she would enjoy smoking.

For all its devout Methodism, the Court at Nuku'alofa was far from stuffy. After a year in London the King's daughter, Princess Pilolevu, had

---

*   As Tonga's only diplomatic wife, Janine usually accompanied Don on these occasions.

developed a passion for disco dancing and before long Don and Janine found themselves bumping and grinding to the strains of 'Saturday Night Fever'. Even the elderly Humphrey joined in the fun and later he was persuaded to throw a disco party in the offices of the British High Commission.

Another regular duty was feasting, which took place whenever there was an important visitor. Seated on the ground, in front of long trays piled high with food, the guests of honour would have first choice. Seafood and roasted pig were always the main delicacies, accompanied by taro, sweet potatoes and yams. But interspersed with these would be layer upon layer of marinated fish, chicken and mutton and tropical fruits in abundance. Like everything in Tonga, feasting is a hierarchical process and as soon as the chief guests had finished, their places would be eagerly taken by others, right down to the humblest citizens.

When the Queen and Prince Philip arrived on the *Britannia* in February 1977, the grassy field beside the Palace was spread with *tapa* cloths and thousands attended the feast. A photograph of the occasion shows King Tupou beaming at his Royal guests, clad in an impressive uniform adorned with military orders. Queen Mata'aho is more quietly dressed, but her strong, handsome features are equally smiling and she and the King radiate warmth and dignity. In accordance with Tongan protocol, the two sovereigns and their consorts sat beneath a canopy of palm fronds, while the Hunns and other members of the court sat nearby. History does not relate how much was eaten. But hundreds of baskets of food were donated and many of the little black pigs that scamper around Nuku'alofa would have ended up on the spit that day.

Apart from disco-dancing and feasting, the New Zealand High Commissioner had more serious duties. Among them was the oversight of a long-running aid project to improve the local banana crop. This had consistently failed to meet export standards, but Don got short shrift when he voiced New Zealand's dissatisfaction. 'If you think it's so easy,' said the Tongan Director of Agriculture, 'get an acre of land and grow them yourself.' It may have been a throwaway line, but Don picked up the gauntlet. Within twenty-four hours, he had leased a plot of land and registered himself and Janine as banana growers. In Nuku'alofa's close knit community, the news spread like wildfire and five others, including the Directors of Agriculture and Research, took up the challenge.

It was 30°C in the shade when Don and Janine set out for the grove of coconut palms where they were planning to plant their bananas. With sweat

King Taufa'ahau Tupou IV of Tonga and Queen
Mata'aho receive Queen Elizabeth II and the Duke of
Edinburgh at their palace in Nuku'alofa, 1977.

(From photo collection of Don and Janine Hunn)

pouring down their faces, they cleared the thick undergrowth in preparation for the 560 seedlings to which they were entitled under the Aid Programme. The Residence gardener came along too and over the next couple of months they created a model plantation, for which they even got an EEC subsidy. They also raked up the leaves and mowed the grass, and once the seedlings had been planted the whole area took on an appearance of park-like beauty. Lovingly tended by the Hunns, who were following the instruction manual from New Zealand meticulously, the bananas soon burst into luxuriant leaf.

By this time the other competitors were feeling decidedly rattled. Their plantations looked nothing like the Hunns' one and it was hinted that the Hunn's success was largely due to the contributions of the landowner's cows. Meanwhile, as the first clusters of tiny bananas began to appear, Don and Janine were weeks ahead of anyone else with the back-breaking work of spraying and fertilising. When the magnificent crop of Lady Cavendish bananas was eventually exported to New Zealand, and the Hunns received a handsome cheque, there could no longer be any question about who had won the contest. In terms of confirming the widely held suspicion that most

The banana growers relax. Don and Janine Hunn enjoying a trip into the Tongan countryside. Late 1970s. (By kind permission of Don and Janine Hunn)

of the donated fertiliser was being used for other crops, Don had made his point. But the other growers were furious and in terms of diplomacy, it was one of the biggest banana skins of Don's hitherto unblemished career.

As diplomatic relations between New Zealand and Tonga sank to an all-time low, the Hunns decided that the only solution was to give a party. The Queen was invited and in full view of the great and the good of Nuku'alofa, the cheque for the High Commission bananas was handed over to the Red Cross of which the Queen was President. Her Majesty graciously accepted the cheque, the guests were wreathed in smiles and the friendship between the two nations was restored.

Ironically, New Zealand's plan to save the Tongan economy with bananas was no more successful than the oil wells of the Texans – or the curious fish sausage that the King had thrust on Don at his credentials ceremony. By the 1980s, Ecuadorian bananas were flooding the world market and the fledgling Tongan banana industry dwindled to nothing. But, thanks to the sweated labour of Don and Janine, the High Commission's plantation continued to produce superb bananas for many years to come. Bananas were not the Hunns' only legacy. Despite the ire of the other banana growers, their warm relationship with the King and Queen had never faltered and paved the way for the lasting friendships that successive New Zealand High Commissioners and their wives later formed with the royal couple.

After four years in Tonga, Don and Janine were looking forward to returning home. They had done five back-to-back postings without a murmur, but when the Ministry sent them to Canberra a few months later, both of them had had enough. Don resigned from the Ministry and went on to pursue a successful career in the State Services Commission of which he later became the Head. The reign of King Tupou IV ends rather less happily. Beset by rogues and swindlers, he lost much of his wealth and, as thousands of Tongans took to the streets to demand greater democracy, he also forfeited his authority over his people. But he never lost their hearts and when he died, after a forty-one year reign, the official announcement that 'The Sun has set in the Kingdom of Tonga' spoke eloquently for their grief at his passing.

CHAPTER 11

Foreigner

*I had never been to New Zealand before. When I think back to that
I find it quite amazing. One would never do that now – just go with
somebody without having any clue of where you were going to end up
… I found it quite hard because it was winter … All the houses were
cold and I'd never been cold inside a house in my life. I'd certainly never
been cold like that in Moscow.*[1]

Greta and Chris met at the New Zealand Embassy's Social Club in
Moscow, which in 1977 was one of the few places in the Soviet Union where
diplomatic staff could let their hair down. Located in the basement of the
Embassy, at the end of a dilapidated passageway, the Club consisted of a
long, narrow room with a bar at one end and a dartboard at the other. It
was not a glamorous setting, but for young Western diplomats, who were
under constant surveillance by the Soviets, it was a popular watering hole.
Bachelors were in short supply and a photograph taken at a party in March
1977 shows Chris holding forth to an audience of three admiring women.
Sitting close beside him is Greta. Her smile radiates happiness and their
comfortable intimacy makes the two women perched on either side of them
look like interlopers.

Greta worked at the Netherlands Embassy and as a national of a 'friendly'
country she was a welcome guest at the Social Club. 'All the younger,
unmarried people would meet there,' she told me, 'it was a whole single
world. The Australians and the New Zealanders were far more social than
we were and I thought it was great fun.' For a single girl, life in Moscow was
very restricted. Despite Brezhnev's supposed policy of détente, the tensions
between the Soviets and the West were as great as ever and the activities

of the KGB were at their height. Phones, houses and cars were bugged and the staff of Western embassies had to take elaborate precautions to avoid being compromised. Greta was never allowed to travel by herself: 'You had to travel in even numbers, either two or four, and one would never sit next to a Russian on a train.'

Socialising with ordinary Russians was strictly forbidden. The only locals that Greta ever met were government officials or the Russians who worked at the Embassy, with whom relations were necessarily cautious. Domestic staff were equally suspect. At the New Zealand Embassy, the office cleaner was a well-known KGB operative, whom the British Embassy had fired after she had staged 'a spectacular attempt'[2] to seduce one of their most senior officers. Disappointingly, she never made more than a half-hearted pass at New Zealand's Ambassador, Jim Weir.

After the closure of the Legation in 1950, New Zealand had no diplomatic representation in Moscow for the next twenty-three years. But at the instigation of Norman Kirk's Labour government, the Mission was re-opened in 1973 with the aim of developing trade. By the time Chris arrived as Second Secretary four years later, the Soviet Union was a growing market. But the diplomatic relationship had not been helped by the notorious Sutch case in 1974, when the former public servant, Bill Sutch, was charged with passing government information to a member of the KGB at the Soviet Embassy in Wellington. His trial for espionage dominated the New Zealand media for months and, although he was eventually acquitted, the new Prime Minister, Muldoon, who was deeply suspicious of the Soviets, declared him 'guilty as sin.'[3]

Neither Chris nor Greta found much to admire in the Soviet system. In his *Letters from Moscow* Chris's boss, Jim Weir, notes that unlike their predecessors in the 1940s, the young New Zealanders at the Embassy had little time for Communism. For Chris, writes Weir, the Soviet Union represented 'institutionalised inefficiency' and a 'pervasive cynicism.'[4] Greta, who had arrived in Moscow a year earlier, was equally unimpressed: 'I thought it would be totally different and very interesting … But when I arrived I was afraid that I'd made a terrible mistake. It was all so drab and grey.' Their romance changed everything. Within a few weeks of meeting, Chris and Greta had fallen in love and were living in a world of their own.

When Chris set out to collect Greta from her office for a game of squash, he was muffled in a heavy overcoat with his trademark Lenin-style cap pulled well down over his face. As he pushed through the first set of double doors

Chris Smithyman hamming it up for a group of admirers at the New Zealand Embassy Social Club in Moscow, 1977. Greta Keur (later Smithyman) is 2nd from the left. (From Jim Weir's Letters from Moscow, Hodder & Stoughton Ltd., 1988)

to the Netherlands Embassy, he was set upon by two men who tried to drag him back on to the street. He lashed out in self-defence and his heavy watch struck one of his assailants on the nose. Blood sprayed everywhere; then he was seized by the scruff of the neck and hauled outside. In the struggle, the back seam of his overcoat split and his briefcase burst open, scattering his papers over the pavement. From her desk, the receptionist watched in horror and called Greta's office.

Greta appeared on the scene just moments after the attack. When I asked her how it had affected Chris, her only comment was that 'it was certainly something a bit different.' But in a diary entry made several days after the incident, Jim Weir is more specific: 'I hadn't realised till this morning how badly Chris had been shaken.'[5] Brutal beatings up by the KGB were not uncommon. Their usual victims were local dissidents, but foreign diplomats were also harassed and an ugly attack was later made on two couples from the British Embassy. Fortunately for Chris, the New Zealand colleagues who had dropped him off at the Embassy saw the fracas and came rushing back to help. Splattered with his attackers' blood and proclaiming his innocence loudly, Chris finally managed to extract his diplomatic ID from an inner pocket. The onslaught halted as abruptly as it had started and the two men melted away. With admirable *sang-froid*, Chris and Greta proceeded with their game of squash which, not surprisingly, was won by Greta.

Although the whole incident lasted for less than five minutes, as an act of violence against a New Zealand diplomat it could not be left without redress.

In the minds of those who witnessed the attack, there was never any doubt that the perpetrators were officially sanctioned. One of the 'heavies' had been the uniformed militia man who was supposed to be on guard at the Embassy, while the other had emerged in mufti from a car parked opposite the entrance. As Weir was in Finland, the task of delivering a strongly worded protest to the Soviet Chief of Protocol fell to his newly arrived Deputy, Daniel Richards. He delivered it the following morning, but his note was rejected outright. Chris, so the Soviets claimed, 'resembled a criminal sought by the police.' Moreover, he had struck an innocent militia man in the face and the Embassy was requested to take 'disciplinary measures'[6] against him. Leaving his two-page note pointedly on the table, Daniel beat a dignified retreat.

Back in Wellington, Muldoon was having a field day, summoning the Soviet Chargé to his office and trumpeting his displeasure to the press. Although not quite on a par with the Sutch case, the incident aroused widespread outrage and gave Muldoon yet another opportunity to vent his spleen on the Soviets. What he never revealed, however, was that Chris's call at the Netherlands Embassy was not, as he claimed 'on official business',[7] but rather a lovers' tryst.

After a tense four-day stand-off, during which both Chris and Greta feared that he might be forced to leave, the Soviets produced an apology. As everyone had suspected, it had all been 'a monstrous mountain'[8] made out of a molehill, for which Chris's fashion sense was largely to blame. The Netherlands Embassy handled numerous enquiries from turbulent Soviet Jews and, with his untidy red beard and peaked cap, Chris had been mistaken for a Jewish dissident. According to Daniel Richards, he even tucked his trousers Russian-style into his boots. Over a glass of beer at the Club, Weir ribbed him gently: 'You know if you go around this place looking like Lenin ... you're bound to get into trouble.'[9] When Greta's car was broken into a few weeks later, Chris must have wondered if he was being targeted. 'A professional job', notes Weir, 'and the lass's new winter coat and Chris's briefcase had gone.'[10] Fortunately, the briefcase contained nothing more sensitive than Chris's language notes.

Despite these trials, Greta and Chris were supremely happy in Moscow. Like all tough postings, it was a place where the Diplomatic Corps formed a close-knit group and they were part of a lively circle. In common with her New Zealand counterparts, Greta would have lost her job on marriage, but as soon as her posting had finished, she and Chris got married in her home town in Holland. A few months later, they set off for New Zealand.

The New Zealand Embassy in Moscow: the Mindovsky Mansion (said to have been built by a merchant for his mistress). (Moskovskie Osobnyaki, Moskovskie Uchebniki, Moscow 1997)

Chris and Greta Smithyman on a visit to the writers' colony at Peredelkino, Moscow 1978.
(By kind permission of Greta Keur)

It was mid-winter when they arrived and Chris's modest wooden villa, perched high above Wellington harbour, boasted no such luxury as central heating. Battling the full blast of the 'southerly busters', Greta often longed to be back in Moscow with its wealth of opera and ballet and their cosy group of friends. There everyone had been a 'foreigner', but in Wellington she was the only outsider and she had never felt more isolated: 'People seemed to talk a lot about Muldoon. But as I didn't know anything about New Zealand politics … I often felt very left out.' In her cosmopolitan homeland they did things differently: 'In Holland people make sure in social situations that everyone is happy and if someone was just sitting there feeling left out, you'd try to talk about something else.' But Wellington was still an inward-looking place and even when she began to understand what was being talked about, Greta was struck by how seldom people asked her about herself: 'For at least the first year, I was always hoping that we would be posted somewhere so that I could escape.'

Inevitably, she gravitated to other foreigners: 'All my best friends seemed to be people in the same situation … Other European wives married to New Zealand diplomats, French and Belgian … and we all felt a bit the same.' Once she found a job, life became easier and later, after the birth of her first baby, she began to meet the neighbours. In time, she also realised that she had married into an extraordinary family. In Moscow, Chris's surname had meant nothing to her, but in New Zealand her father-in-law, Kendrick Smithyman, was a well-known figure, whose poetry formed part of the country's literary canon. Chris's mother, Mary Stanley, was an equally gifted poet. Gentler and more intuitive than her husband, she was always a support to Greta, but her health was already failing and their acquaintance was fleeting.

When their second child was four months old, the Smithymans were posted to the New Zealand High Commission in Delhi. After three difficult years, Greta welcomed the prospect of returning to diplomatic life. As Assistant High Commissioner, Chris would have considerable representational responsibilities and she was looking forward to playing her part as a diplomatic wife and hostess. A photograph of the family taken shortly after their arrival in Delhi shows them seated outside a spacious white bungalow, with a staff of four in attendance. Greta looks relaxed and smiling. Running a large household held no fears for her and, with two small children, she was enjoying having live-in babysitters. She and Chris had been thrown straight into a whirl of diplomatic engagements representing the High Commissioner, who was still waiting to present his credentials. Chris's diplomatic career was going well and as they sat in the back of the official car, with the New Zealand flag flying proudly on the bonnet, they must have felt that it was a taste of things to come.

At first, Greta thought that Chris's headaches were stress related. They had started before they left Wellington, when the packing up was taking its toll and the baby was waking them at nights. But in Delhi the symptoms became more disturbing: 'He discovered that he couldn't remember things like the access code to the Chancery … Or he couldn't remember the word for his wristwatch.' As Chris grew increasingly unwell, they made an appointment at the hospital. The news was devastating. 'When they discovered that it was a brain tumour … I felt my whole stomach sinking,' said Greta, 'The world seemed to be coming to an end, but because of the children, I had to keep going.'

Within two months, Chris and Greta and their children were heading back to New Zealand. Chris was due to see a specialist and they travelled with a couple of suitcases, expecting to return. They never did. Instead they found themselves holed up in a cramped service apartment that had been rented for them by the Ministry. 'It was awful,' said Greta, 'and the worst thing was that we couldn't get back into our own house.' They had let their house fully furnished and the tenants were refusing to leave. With the doctor's warning that 'anything longer than three months would be a bonus' ringing in their ears, it looked as if Chris might never return to his own home. 'So he made a little book for me,' said Greta, 'with all the things that I needed to know – like where he kept the borer bomb.'

With a sick husband and a fretful baby, the apartment was becoming unbearable and after a couple of months they moved to a sparsely furnished rental property, which was all they could afford. 'In the beginning we had nothing,' Greta told me, 'we didn't even have a proper washing machine.' But at the Ministry the news had spread and day by day Chris's colleagues would arrive at the door, bearing plates of food and 'spare' pieces of furniture. To help keep the wolf from the door, a job was found for Chris: 'The Ministry gave him something he could manage … rather than just staying at home.' Nevertheless, money was tight and looking ahead, Greta wondered how she and her children were going to survive: 'So I learnt typesetting and I got an evening job … I worked from four to twelve and I would get home at almost one o'clock. Then I couldn't sleep straight away and the baby would wake at six. In the end, it became too much and I couldn't keep it up.'

Despite the doctor's prognosis, Chris lived for another two-and-a-half years. Eventually the tenants were prevailed upon to leave and the Smithymans were able to return to their own home, where they built on a much-needed extension. When Chris died aged thirty-six, the only instruction that he left for his funeral was that 'he didn't want a fuss'. But the response to his death was overwhelming. Messages poured in from New Zealand's posts all over the world and hundreds attended the service in Wellington. In the many tributes, Greta and the children were not forgotten. 'We grieve with the living as well as for the dead', wrote the historian, Keith Sinclair, who had

Greta today. She has never regretted her decision to return to New Zealand.

(By kind permission of Greta Keur)

known Chris since he was two days old. Nor could he resist referring to Chris's unique distinction 'of being assaulted by two Russian agents.'[11]

After Chris's death, Greta found herself in limbo: 'I didn't know what to do.' The children felt equally lost and Chris's little son would try to fill his father's shoes by striding round the house with his briefcase. Early the following year, she let her house and returned to Holland. At first, life seemed reassuringly familiar. Both the children went to local schools and within a few months, her daughter had forgotten her English. But, as time passed, Greta realised that something vital was missing: 'It just didn't feel right to be in Holland. It was as if I had cut off everything from Chris and all the people who knew him and could talk about him.' To her family and friends in Holland, Chris was a little-known figure, who had appeared briefly at the wedding with an uncharacteristically well-groomed beard. But in New Zealand, his memory was cherished by a host of friends who had loved his warmth and exuberance: 'So I thought about it and I decided to come back.'

On her return from Holland, Greta looked at Wellington with new eyes – from the mighty sweep of the harbour to the graceful curve of the hills. Even the boisterous winds, that she had once found so trying, now seemed more like an affectionate buffeting. Above all, however, she was back with those who had stood by her during her darkest days and were now her closest friends: 'I received lots of help … I felt so lucky that Chris had such good colleagues who were not only nice when he was alive, but also when he was no longer there.' When a group from the Ministry turned up at her house with paint brushes, Greta welcomed them with open arms. Clad in tattered shorts and workmen's boots, the cream of New Zealand's Diplomatic Service spent a whole day swarming over her rusty roof 'knowing that it would have been on Chris's agenda and that I could not pay for it.' As she made the coffee in the kitchen, Greta listened to their lively banter. She smiled to herself. Nothing had changed since those early days. It was almost as if Chris was there. They were still talking New Zealand politics and they were still making jokes about Muldoon. But the big difference was that she no longer felt like a foreigner.

Greta has never regretted her decision to return to Wellington, where she lives happily to this day.

CHAPTER 12

Penny's Garden

Ever since Papua New Guinea had gained its independence in 1975, law and order in Port Moresby had deteriorated. By the time Phillip and Penny Klap and their two little blonde-haired daughters arrived in March 1978, gangs of 'raskols' were roaming the streets and break-ins were rife. But as the new Trade Commissioner at the New Zealand High Commission, and an employee of the Department of Trade and Industry, Phillip was not entitled to one of the well-guarded houses provided by the Ministry of Foreign Affairs. Instead, he and Penny rented a rambling property on the edge of a reserve with a large, unfenced garden.

During the 1960s and '70s, relations between diplomats and trade commissioners were often strained. Part of the problem was that the trade commissioners were answerable to a different department. Personalities and petty jealousies also played a role. But the main trouble arose from the tendency of the diplomatic officers to regard their commercial colleagues as lesser beings, who were incapable of mastering the subtleties of international trade policy. In reality, New Zealand's Trade Commissioner Service has a far longer pedigree than its Diplomatic Service and an illustrious roll of honour. But despite this, the interdepartmental turf-war persisted and was only resolved in 1988, when the Ministry took on fifty trade policy staff from the dismantled Department of Trade and Industry and changed its name to MERT.*

Happily, few of these rivalries filtered through to the wives, who were all in the same boat. Trade commissioners network and entertain quite as much

---

*   Ministry of External Relations and Trade.

as diplomats and at an overseas post their wives play similar roles. The only difference is in the guest lists. But with the additional burden of hosting visiting businessmen, the wives of trade commissioners work harder than most. In her letters to her parents, Penny refers constantly to being 'flat out shopping and cooking' for the numerous New Zealand businessmen whom Phillip brought home for dinner. Most of them assumed that the hospitality was 'on the government' and occasionally Penny lets her exasperation show: 'I am sick and tired of the off the cuff comments about public servants "being kept" by the NZ taxpayer.'[1] Like his diplomatic colleagues, Phillip had an allowance for entertaining local contacts, but this did not include the dozens of meals that he and Penny produced for visiting Kiwis. Few bothered to show their gratitude. 'Never so much as a bunch of bananas', Penny notes sadly.

Within a few days of moving into her new home, Penny told her parents that she had decided to plant a vegetable garden:

> On Saturday morning, a couple from the office took me to one of the two supermarkets here … Meat is frozen and refrozen and the vegetables are awful. Carrots are soft and brown and the one zucchini (at 60 cents) was dry through … The frozen foods are exorbitantly priced too …so the sooner we can grow our own the better … I will find out all I can and start a vegetable garden as soon as possible.

Three months later, she was able to report that her Chinese cabbages were 'shooting up' alongside beans, silverbeet, tomatoes, peppers and aubergines. The watermelons were also ripening and pawpaws were dripping from the trees. By this time, the wet season was over and the weather was at its best. 'You would love it' she tells her parents, 'the bougainvillea is out everywhere with frangipani, hibiscus and orchids and other exotica as well.'

The wealth of fruit and vegetables was matched by an abundance of wildlife. By day, stick insects and praying mantis streamed across the veranda; geckos darted up the walls and 'beautiful, big iridescent green beetles' foraged among the undergrowth. After dark, the garden became alive with moths and bats and the roar of cicadas. But Penny did not find all the wildlife so desirable: 'There is a rat infestation in the roof, families and families of them … and we also have huge cockroaches, which run all over the children at nights.' Dishes had to be washed instantly 'or else you have a seething swarm of ants.' For the mother of an intrepid two-year-old 'who prods everything', the venomous snakes and bird-eating spiders were even more alarming. By far the greatest health risk, however, came from the mosquitoes. No spraying had been done since independence and whenever

Penny Klap tending the flowers on the balcony of her house in Port Moresby, 1978. (By kind permission of Phillip and Penny Klap)

the humidity was high, the mosquitoes descended like a plague on the city.

According to Penny, the house was in 'utter chaos' when they arrived. The roof leaked and during their first tropical storm the rain poured into the hall between the girls' bedrooms. The décor was in equally bad shape and the list of things that needed fixing ran to over two pages. But Penny was philosophical: 'Although a few things need to be done, other than that, we are very lucky indeed to have so much space' – and at least the security arrangements looked satisfactory: 'Our house is so well protected with bars everywhere and a very efficient burglar alarm that can be heard for miles.' Two weeks later, they had their first break-in:

Phillip will have mentioned our burglary at 4.00am. The alarm certainly is incredible and they must have taken off like rockets as the kitchen window was open … and the dining room window downstairs at the same time, so there must have been 2 or 3 of them. The police took 1½ hours to turn up!

A second break-in followed:

But this time the police arrived within 5 minutes of ringing. 5 cars and hordes of police – at 2.30am and 3 houses in a row were attempted. But they got away …. They always break in with a group, so thank heavens the alarm is so loud. It scares the hell out of them and they take off. Otherwise we would be frightened to death.

The following day, 'a few extra precautions' were taken and Penny was assured that the only way that anyone could enter the house was 'to smash down one of the 8 doors (all glass).' As Phillip was about to leave on a six-day business trip to the outer islands, she asked the domestic staff, who lived in a 'boy house' in the garden, to sleep downstairs. She also moved the two little girls into her bedroom, where she could lock the door.

In her letters home Penny tries to give the Papua New Guineans the benefit of the doubt:

> Like anywhere, the hardcore criminals are a minority and in general the Papuans are delightfully friendly ... Seeing the conditions, it's not surprising what is going on. There are so many coming down from the Highlands, not educated enough to get jobs, with no money and no homes, which obviously leads them into trouble – just like anywhere else in the world with similar problems ... It is horrifying to see the attitude of most Australians here. They treat the locals like dirt.

But her faith in the host nation took a knock when the couple they had employed started stealing: 'We've been completely taken for ride ... People told us not to be too kind, but we felt that they had been here too long and were getting slightly embittered.' The couple had lasted for less than a month and their departure created a major problem:

> It is depressing living in a locked up house during the day, but now no-one else is here, you just have to. At 7.30 am, the other day, I was going to hang out the washing when a man silently appeared upstairs. Their usual excuse for getting inside is that 'they are looking for work' ... and being barefoot you never hear them ... The moment we go out, people appear. We came home at 7.00pm last night and several characters shot down our drive – probably trying to get in, as well as pinching from the garden.

Penny struggled on alone, but within a few weeks it had become apparent to both of them that, with Phillip's frequent business trips, she had to have someone living in. After a fruitless search for another couple, the reappearance of Mango (who had originally worked for their predecessors) seemed like an answer to prayer. Less than five foot tall, and clad in nothing but a pair of shorts, he belonged to one of Papua New Guinea's most warlike tribes, the Kukukuku. The Kukukuku had an unrivalled reputation for ferocity and Penny boasts that her new houseboy 'is feared by all around'.

Mango soon proved his worth by killing a monstrous lizard 'with huge head and fangs' in the garden. Later, he helped Penny to track down a bird-eating spider with 'a body the size of a man's hand' that had been terrorising

The Klaps' Kukukuku houseboy, Mango, displays a snake that he has killed in the garden, Port Moresby, 1979. (By kind permission of Phillip and Penny Klap)

the girls in their bedrooms. By the end of the year, he had caught another five. He also excelled at his watchdog duties – with the help of a bow and arrow.

Bows and arrows were banned in Port Moresby, but at Mango's request Penny had purchased him a black palm bow from a tourist shop with a selection of lethal-looking arrows. In the hands of a Kukukuku, a bow can be deadly and Mango only had to appear on the veranda for would-be burglars to flee. Meanwhile, to dispel any doubts about his marksmanship, he spent his spare moments shooting pigeons off the treetops, hitting them neatly between the eyes.

Between his household duties, Mango worked on a vast new vegetable patch that extended well into the reserve. Penny could see at once that he was an intuitive gardener and before long he was producing enough fruit and vegetables to feed a small army. She, meanwhile, was cultivating a growing collection of miniature orchids, which Mango and his fellow Kukukuku brought her as gifts from the uplands of Sogeri. Over time, her garden became a place of pilgrimage: 'Even the famous NZ author who has written a wonderful book on PNG orchids has visited', she tells her parents proudly.

As well as tending the garden, she and Mango spent many hours in the kitchen. Trade was booming and the stream of hungry (and thirsty) businessmen seemed unending. Twenty-two arrived in one week – and most of them came for a meal. Penny also cooked non-stop for official dinners and receptions. During the first New Zealand trade fair in Port Moresby, the catering took on almost industrial proportions:

> *We had an enormous group here at home on Saturday afternoon …*
> *I cooked frantically all day and turned out ten different dishes for the*
> *buffet … The last left at 03.00 am. Incredible. Then last night, Tuesday,*
> *we had 16 again. The children were away in the morning, so it was a*
> *clear run for me … We have got 150 on Friday evening … and I am*
> *catering for yet another mob for dinner afterwards.*

When the guests finally departed, Penny would fall into bed exhausted. The next morning she and Mango would do the cleaning up together. As they worked side by side at the sink, Mango boasted to her of his exploits:

> *Mango has fought and killed and has showed me his arrow wounds*
> *…'Look – you see – through here – and out there.' He tells me that he is*
> *a very good warrior … 'We best people, best strongest fighters in Papua*
> *New Guinea' … and that he can build a kunai grass house and make a*
> *club and a bow and arrow.*

He also told Penny that his father had been a cannibal, whose smoked corpse sat in a cave high up in the mountains.

From her long conversations with Mango, Penny began to understand the tyranny of the local 'wantok'* system, whereby those with jobs are obliged to support countless relatives from their earnings. As the number of warriors sunning themselves on her lawn increased, Penny realised that Mango was feeding most of the 60-strong Kukukuku community in Port Moresby from her garden. But as far as she was concerned, it was a fair exchange. Along with the fruit and vegetables, the Kukukuku had taken her household under their protection and when a 'raskol' armed with a long steel rod ambled into the garden and sliced the top off her beautiful frangipani tree, their response was instantaneous: 'We yelled out to Mango … and within seconds we had 8 Kukukuku streaking up the hill behind him.'

Early in August, Penny collapsed:

---

* 'Wantok' is pidgin for 'one-talk' which, in a nation with 841 different languages, has come to mean someone from the same village.

*Friday I felt simply dreadful, but kept going … My temperature was 40°
… and the nurse at the laboratory taking my blood sample took one
look at me and said you look far too ill to be looking after your littlies
(and they too looked awful) … I had high fever for six days … It felt
as if my head would just explode apart … with relentless headaches 24
hours around the clock.*

Engrossed in her gardening, Penny had barely noticed the sinister whine
of the black and white mosquitoes that carry dengue fever. By the time she
saw a doctor, she was far too ill to be evacuated to Australia. According to
Phillip, she was unable even to walk to the bathroom and her parents had to
send up a nurse from New Zealand to look after her. It took her six months
to make a full recovery.

In the meantime temptation, in the form of a good-looking girl from the
Chimbu tribe, had entered Mango's garden. She was living with him in the
'boy house' and he assured Penny that they were going to marry: 'Missus me
gat meri. Mi and meri live her now.' But as Mango tended his bananas and
planted a crop of peanuts, trouble was brewing over his new girlfriend. Her
'wantoks' hailed from Mount Hagen, the most violent place in the country,
where warring tribesmen in face paint and feathers were still fighting each
other with axes:

*Some very rough diamonds from Mount Hagen want her back … They
arrived here at 02.00am this morning and tried to break in. Mango
chased them all away waving a huge machete, threatening to kill them.
We woke up having heard the commotion and Phillip flew out of bed to
see Mango in the moonlight with them all. He had the presence of mind
to open the window and set off our alarm, which woke up the entire
area and they took off.*

A few days later they came back:

*This morning we were woken by a huge truck screaming up the drive
with 12 to 14 Mount Hagen rascals … one or two with bush knives …
They made a feeble excuse about looking for a 'brother' and Phillip sent
them packing. They backed flat out down the drive, making an almighty
mess and knocking down our favourite plants and trees … We were so
worried that they had come to attack Mango, who was not there … or
to break into our own home … So we quickly locked ourselves inside
and called the police. We got their number plate, but the police arrived
far too late.*

When Mango returned, he was full of his usual braggadocio. Penny's heart sank: 'He says if any rascals appear he will kill them … and then there would be "pay back" and the relatives would come and kill him.' As neighbouring tribes, the Kukukuku and the Chimbu had been fighting over women since time immemorial. For the next two months, Mango spent his evenings 'stalking around like a cassowary bird, with his black palm bow larger than himself and an arrow poised in readiness.' The Mount Hagen 'raskols' never reappeared, but the Chimbu girl turned out to be a thief and in the end she was Mango's downfall. More and more items went missing from the house and eventually Penny had to tell them both to leave. Mango's 'wantoks' promptly produced a replacement and on his last morning six of them turned up to remove him from the 'boy house'. Mango, however, had no intention of going quietly:

> All hell was let loose … He went berserk and with a two foot bush knife, he hacked the entire garden to shreds, all our banana trees, paw paws, kau kau and abaca … While his wild little figure was hacking away … he was silhouetted against an enormous bush fire, which came over our hill with intense speed, the wind blowing strongly our way. Suddenly we had a high wall of flames … The house became like a furnace and I grabbed photos, files, teddy bears and girls and took off down the hill. Two fire engines arrived and all the Kukukuku fellows began fire-fighting, slashing down the high grass and trees, amidst the drama of the lone figure of Mango … Then a miserable incident occurred as several fellows got stuck into Mango calling him a 'bighead'.

Perhaps it was just as well that, a few days later, the whole family set off on an idyllic visit to the picturesque Milne Bay region, where they stayed with the family of a local friend, Morris Alaluku, whose wife, Zen, was Phillip's secretary at the High Commission.

Back in Port Moresby, several Kukukuku came and went before Penny settled on an older man named Gabiaye, whom she describes as 'a happy character and immaculately fussy'. Under his care, the garden gradually recovered, but it proved an unsettling period for the family. After less than two years, the landlord announced that he wanted the house back. With the chronic shortage of housing in Port Moresby, it looked for a time as if they were going to have to move into a scungy hotel on the beach. But after weeks of searching, they came across a charming white-washed house with which they immediately fell in love. To Penny's joy, it already had a little vegetable patch and a garden full of huge rain trees, which would provide an ideal environment for her orchids.

Mango's successor, Gabiaye, with Annabelle (left) and Nicola (right). The Kukukuku would have killed to protect the children, Port Moresby, c. 1980.

(By kind permission of Phillip and Penny Klap)

On the day of the move, she and Gabiaye and the recently appointed 'garden boy' carried dozens of tiny orchids over to the new garden. Within minutes of their arrival, the two Kukukuku had shinned up a tree to pick a coconut, which they shared with Penny and Phillip and their children. It was a sign of welcome and good luck and the six of them sat down to eat it as companionably as a family. Despite the dramatic departure of Mango, the bonds between the Klaps and the Kukukuku had become stronger than ever, not least because Penny and Phillip had been willing to give them a second chance. Penny infinitely preferred these diminutive warriors to the more sophisticated coastal people, who were 'too sly and too clever', and whenever possible she would recommend them to her friends. In return, the Kukukuku gave her their ferocious loyalty.

Less colourful but steadier than Mango, Gabiaye was proving equally conscientious as a bodyguard. Installed on the veranda with a bow and arrow, he would be up for most of the night whenever Phillip was away. He also had far more control over his 'wantoks', who now appeared only at weekends. They still helped themselves to the fruit and vegetables, but with Penny's encouragement Gabiaye was now selling most of the surplus at the market and putting the proceeds towards his annual airfare home. Even with the protection of the Kukukuku, security remained a problem and in the new house Penny felt more vulnerable than ever: 'Our bedroom and the children's are so unsafe, all at ground level and there are no bars … Compared with all the other Embassies, we are very badly off. Everyone else has high fences and security guards.' Belatedly, 'a huge barred area' with locked gates was built around the house, but only after the bedroom doors had been forced on countless occasions.

Whenever their Kukukuku protectors were absent, the Klaps were plagued by prowlers:

Thursday evening: Phillip is sitting outside with his wooden police baton. Gabiaye and his wantoks have gone out tonight and a rascal has somehow got in. Our gates are locked and the dogs have gone berserk, but he has disappeared down the bottom of the hill, into the long grass and trees. We have no phone as the cable has been cut, so Phillip has turned the outside security lights on … Goodness knows how this fellow has got in unless he has cut the cyclone wire, or the chain of the padlock.

The 'raskols' were becoming bolder by the day and cutting the phone lines was their latest ploy.

In other ways, Penny's life was becoming increasingly enjoyable. The expatriates led a lively social life and Penny's letters are full of references to receptions and dinners or to the diplomatic wives' 'Sandwich Club', which hosted monthly lectures and lunches. Inevitably, 'good works' also reared their head:

Today I began my voluntary work at the General Port Moresby Hospital. What a shock. I had never seen the children's ward and although I had heard plenty, I still had not envisaged it to be such a shock. Even more so, realizing that one's own child might end up there …

The stench was unbelievable (I rushed out and was sick in the gutter). The ward, built of corrugated iron, is a disgrace and the walls are black with filth – or red with betel nut … The little ones are bandaged up naked, sleeping on the floor, or a bed, if they are really lucky … The children in traction are unable to move, wee-ing and lying in their own doings. None are even washed down … and they are often covered in skin disease.

All the linen had been stolen, but although the goal of Penny's volunteer group was to make 300 sheets and pillowcases, washing the children and providing them with food soon became their top priority. A prime mover in the project was a courageous expatriate woman named Janey, who was a full-time social worker at the hospital. She and her Australian husband had been living in Port Moresby for seventeen years and, despite being knocked out cold by one her patients, she had a deep love and respect for the Papua New Guineans. In her letters, Penny describes Janey as 'the heart and soul of the hospital' and they became close friends.

Thanks to her art school training, Penny had also found a part-time job at the National Museum, where her task was to make drawings of over 300 priceless artefacts, dating back from 3500 to 7000 years. Like many others, she was captivated by Papua New Guinea's astonishing cultural diversity and she tells her parents that if she could have her life over again, her dearest wish would be to become an anthropologist.

When she was not fundraising for the children's school or giving swimming lessons, Penny busied herself with edging and paving the flower beds and tying her orchids to the rain trees, to keep them moist during the long dry season. Pottering amongst her flowers and vegetables she tried not to dwell on the many horror stories that were circulating around the expatriate community. In the preceding weeks scarcely a day had passed without some fresh act of violence. Burglary had always been endemic, but guns were a new phenomenon and when the deputy at the New Zealand High Commission was held up at gunpoint on his own veranda, the upsurge in crime became impossible to ignore.

That same evening, Penny had a close call returning home alone from the theatre:

> I was driving along the one-way road along the coast when I was overtaken by a utility full of very fierce and unsavoury drunks. They slowed down until we were crawling at 5 miles an hour and finally they stopped and got out. I was petrified and as I was trapped between the steep hill and the sea on a one-way road, I started to drive backwards, flat out around the corners along the pitch dark coast.

A terrifying game of cat and mouse followed. The coast road was her only way home and even when she tucked in behind some other cars, the men were waiting for her. In the end she outwitted them: 'I put my flickers on 'turn right' and they took off, turning right first. I put my foot down and tore straight ahead and went back home in a complete circle simply terrified.' When she got home, Gabiaye upbraided her roundly: 'Missus you no go out at night, too many rascals, and they catch you and rape you and cut your throat.'

Penny was considerably shaken, but what happened a few weeks later was far worse:

Janey's three daughters are the latest victims. Thirty odd rascals appeared at their house and asked to be let in. They threatened to axe the door down so Suzanne, the eldest aged 14 let them in. They gave the girls a terrible time for two hours. Suzanne was dragged out into the bushes and raped by two of the gang while others watched … Then they were after Andrea and Anna (9 years and 6 ½ years old), but Suzanne pleaded and pleaded with them to leave the girls alone. While they were emptying the house and stealing all they could, Andrea crept into her parents' room and rang the police. She pleaded with them that many people were in the house and raping Suzanne. But they never came.

As they had done for many years, Janey and her husband had left the girls with their household staff, but they were no match for a gang of thirty. At 7.00 a.m. the next morning Penny had a call from Janey, who was crying hysterically. She went straight around to the house, which by this time was swarming with police. The girls were in a terrible state and the parents were heartbroken. Not long afterwards, Janey and her husband packed up and left for Australia.

For Penny, the whole affair was a re-enactment of her worst nightmares. Like her diplomatic counterparts, she regarded the social round as part of her job and night after night she and Phillip entrusted their two little daughters to babysitters. Everyone had warned her against leaving the girls with a male, but after months of agonising she had concluded that they were safer with Mango (and later Gabiaye) than they were with anyone else. Both men would kill to protect them, she reflected uneasily, and had Janey's staff been Kukukuku, the rampage of rape and pillage would also have been a bloodbath.

In the wake of these events, Phillip and Penny thought hard and long before accepting an invitation to attend a 'Sing Sing' in a remote township in the Highlands. But it was the chance of a lifetime and once she had arranged for the girls to stay safely with friends, Penny was bursting with excitement:

On 23 October we fly together to Mount Hagen to stay with Andy Flower and the three of us are going off into the bush all week, camping in the villages with the locals … We could not be with a better person as Andy has a marvellous feeling and understanding for the people here and is highly regarded by the locals.

Their host was a pioneering New Zealand businessman and an experienced traveller in the Highlands, with whom they would have no fears about security. Their six-day journey by 4-wheel-drive was an unforgettable

The experience of a lifetime: Penny Klap on a trip to the Highlands, Mount Hagen 1981. (By kind permission of Phillip and Penny Klap)

experience, but the climax of the trip was their arrival at Koroba, where the 'Sing Sing' was to take place:

> *The excitement was unbelievable. Truckloads of up to 50 or 60 people piled high, singing and screaming at other groups. The town was alive with gaiety and incredible colour … Late in the evening, Ken, the teacher walked us around the school compound … pitch dark except for the glow of the fires with the throbbing of drums everywhere, singing and excitement, bare thighs …*

> *We peeped inside a few houses filled with people crouched low chatting and singing. In the dark I discreetly watched the amazing care and attention given to preparing the headdress and face paint for the Sing Sing, like preparing for a wedding … The men preen like peacocks and are the king pin in their attire, imitating their famous Bird of Paradise.*

By 5.00 a.m. the following morning thousands had gathered, and when the Deputy Prime Minister arrived, he was given an uproarious welcome. For the more remote tribes, this was a rare chance to bend the ear of a leading politician and an elaborate programme of festivities had been planned in his honour. Surrounded by a multitude of feathers and headdresses, Phillip and Penny were part of a small group of expatriates, most of whom were teachers or missionaries. Meanwhile great rain clouds had gathered and, as the Deputy Prime Minister rose to speak, the heavens opened. Mindful, no doubt, that the unsealed roads would become impassable, he shrugged his shoulders and announced that he was leaving:

> With that, the crowd went mad ... The Minister was hustled off the truck and into his car ... They made the first bridge just in time. As the stampeding clans ripped off their headdresses, the sky was simply black with thousands of arrows at their fury at not having government representation at an event that had taken them two years to prepare ... and we nodded in approval ... The people – then in hundreds – broke up the 2 bridges, so the rest of the Minister's party was trapped.

Phillip and Penny watched from a prudent distance, but although the rain stopped by lunchtime, the exuberance of the morning had vanished and the 'Sing Sing' had ended.

On their return to Port Moresby, the Klaps began to focus on their departure. During these final weeks, Penny's garden was at its most beautiful. The beds were a riot of tropical flowers and the trunks of the rain trees were smothered with exquisite orchids. The vegetable patch was equally prolific, producing lettuces, aubergines, peppers, tomatoes, cucumbers, beans, custard apples, melons, pawpaws and ginger. 'Not bad!' Penny notes with satisfaction, 'also mint, marjoram, parsley and spring onions, all difficult to grow.' The garden had been her salvation and she would be sad to leave it. But a far greater sorrow would be parting from the Kukukuku.

Over their three years in Port Moresby, Phillip and Penny had become like parents to the whole Kukukuku community. In his memoir, *What a Life!* Phillip describes leaving Port Moresby as 'the first of some highly emotional moments in our family lives.' After a tearful farewell with Gabiaye and his wife and daughter at the house, he and Penny were astonished to find that all the Kukukuku had come to the airport to say goodbye. Phillip describes the scene:

> Being Kukukuku, they walked straight through the police and the customs checks to the exit hall, where the women sat down on the floor in a circle talking to the girls with tears in their eyes, while the men just stood and stared at us. I found Gabiaye standing aside ... and he grabbed my hand and held it.[2]

As the Klaps headed out onto the tarmac, the Kukukuku followed them and when the plane started taxiing down the runway, they ran beside it waving. Fighting back the tears, Penny and Phillip never said a word to each other until they reached Sydney.

CHAPTER 13.

The Abolition of Slavery

When I married a New Zealand diplomat in 1970, I had no idea that my future life would be governed by a set of regulations known as the *Overseas Service Handbook*. In my case the full import of the *Handbook* took some time to sink in and I continued to park illegally and behave with gay abandon for several years to come. But although my conduct fell far short of the 'exemplary standard'[1] required, there was one regulation which not even I could ignore. This appeared under the innocent heading of 'General Instructions' and it debarred diplomatic wives from working.

I first became aware of it the day after we had returned from our honeymoon. Smartly dressed for my new job, I stared at my husband of one week with disbelief. He smiled sympathetically: 'Sorry, darling, but I think it's against the rules.' He scooped up his briefcase and headed off for the Embassy. Tears of frustration streamed down my face as the empty days stretched ahead. But frustration soon turned to anger. What right had my husband's employer to stop me from earning my living and anyway, why hadn't I been told? I was, of course, being completely unreasonable – or so my mother said. As a diplomatic wife, it would be quite improper for me to work and my real job was giving dinner parties.

The Ministry's *Handbook* leaves no aspect of a diplomat's life unregulated. It also includes the reassuring statement that should the diplomat be so unfortunate as to die *en poste* 'necessary funeral expenses not exceeding the cost of preparing and returning the body to New Zealand may be met at official charge.' Moreover, after her husband's death, the bereaved spouse could look forward to '21 days commencing from the day after the date of death' on overseas allowances before reverting to her widow's pension.

Marriage to non-New Zealanders was discouraged and a dim view was taken of divorce: 'An officer who becomes involved in a divorce suit … may, at the discretion of the Minister of Foreign Affairs, be called upon to resign.'[2]

At the time of my marriage, the fate of the wives was determined by two short passages. The first merely stated that a wife could not accept employment on a posting 'without first obtaining the permission of the Head of Mission'. But the sting was in the second: 'As the wives of diplomatic and consular officers at overseas posts are expected to make a full contribution to representational activities it is unlikely that they will in many cases be in a position to accept gainful employment'.[3] This terse statement (with its attendant caveats) effectively ruled out the possibility of working and obliged the wives to devote all their energies to networking and entertaining.

The widely held notion that it was 'improper' for a diplomatic wife to take paid employment probably originated from Article 42 of diplomacy's founding document, the Vienna Convention. This states that 'a diplomatic agent shall not in the receiving State practise for personal profit any professional or commercial activity.'[4] But although this makes the position of the diplomat quite clear, no such prohibitions apply to his wife. Nevertheless, until the late 1970s, most governments believed that it was incompatible with the dignity of a diplomat for his wife to work. In the absence of any legal basis for this restriction, the more cautious members of the Ministry in Wellington took care to present it simply 'as an expression of our views',[5] but a note written by veteran diplomat Lloyd White in the 1960s typifies the outlook of the period:

> I am fairly strongly opposed to diplomatic wives working … Activity in the 'good works' field is all right, but employment even part-time could bring discredit on our Service … The wife's duty should be to assist her husband and I will need some convincing otherwise.[6]

In 1964, the discovery that a junior wife at the Embassy in Bangkok had taken a job without seeking permission beforehand provoked an agitated exchange of memos. Legally, the Ministry could do nothing to stop her, but the First Secretary was waiting to pounce: 'What I did decide when I found out … was that if ever she ducked any representational obligation (e.g. a lunch at the Residence) and if this was clearly because of her job, then I would have to intervene.'[7] Fortunately for the wife in question, this never happened. At other posts a handful of brave souls followed suit – usually as teachers or typists.

In the United States, however, the Women's Liberation Movement was becoming a major political force and was gaining millions of adherents, including in diplomatic circles. As an increasing number of diplomatic wives began demanding the right to work, the Ministry looked on in dismay: 'We are becoming a little concerned at the tendency of wives of diplomatic officers with representational responsibilities to "opt out" as it were, by taking full-time employment … [and] we are beginning to wonder where the line can be drawn.'[8] But the Movement was unstoppable and by early 1973 the diplomatic wives and the women officers of the Ministry had formed a powerful alliance and were preparing for battle.

When Jean McKenzie was promoted to Minister in Paris in 1955, New Zealand became one of the earliest countries to be represented by a female Head of Mission.* Yet despite this promising start, the Department's (and later the Ministry's) treatment of its female staff was far from equitable. All too often, well-qualified women were sidelined into minor positions in administration or protocol. Similarly, for those who aspired to a career in diplomacy, the practice of labelling female recruits 'Research Assistants', while their male counterparts were known as 'Diplomatic Trainees', was particularly galling. The requirement for female staff to resign on marriage, on the assumption that they would then be 'unpostable', was also bitterly resented, as was the implication that their loyalty to their husbands would interfere with their loyalty to their jobs.

From the pages of correspondence citing their mistreatment, it is clear that the Ministry's women officers already had ample grounds for complaint. But their hand was considerably strengthened by joining forces with the wives. The two groups were not natural allies. At diplomatic posts wives and career women sniped at one another regularly. On this occasion, however, the fact that some of the wives were themselves former staff members may have prompted the show of unity. Furthermore, for the more militant wives, the emergence of a redoubtable champion in the form of Pat Caughley, the female Secretary of the newly formed Foreign Service Association, presented an ideal opportunity for them to challenge the Ministry.

With the liberal-minded Frank Corner as the new Secretary of Foreign Affairs, the women had picked their moment well. Equally fortunate for the wives was the timing of the US State Department's famous 'freedom proclamation', which had been issued in 1972 and acknowledged, for the first

---

* Britain did not appoint a female head of mission until 1973, but the US appointed a woman ambassador in 1933 and the Soviet Union appointed its first female ambassador in 1923.

time, that a diplomatic wife was a private individual on whom the Foreign Service had 'no right to levy any duties'. Hailed as a triumph for the Women's Movement, the State Department's directive turned the traditional view of the wifely role on its head. American wives were now permitted to have their own career interests 'be they academic, professional, family or avocational' and could choose whether or not to participate in entertaining.[9] Equally revolutionary was the ruling that a wife's representational activities (which in the US had long been regarded as crucial to promotion) would no longer be evaluated as part of her husband's efficiency rating.

Unlike the State Department, the Ministry had never formally assessed a wife's performance. But in an era when most diplomatic wives accepted their representational role unquestioningly, a wife's social skills had always been a factor in determining a diplomat's suitability for a post. With the advent of feminism, however, women's attitudes had changed dramatically and for younger wives, with professional aspirations, the Ministry's expectation that they would peddle their charms (and their cooking) to further their husbands' careers was quite as demeaning as the ban on working.

Writing many years later, a younger wife describes her 'considerable despair' as she struggled to keep her academic career alive during a posting to Brussels: 'Loneliness, which is anyway an occupational hazard of being married to a diplomat, is intensified by shutting yourself up in a study or a bedroom for a substantial part of every day.' Evenings spent accompanying her husband to 'an endless series of professionally derived cocktail parties and dinners and see people lose interest in you when you turn out not to be a useful contact' only increased her sense of isolation. Already professionally disadvantaged by their frequent moves, she never considered her husband's diplomatic role 'to be also my job.' In her view she was there 'to keep him company' and get on with her own career. 'And if that means fewer cocktail party appearances it's a small price to pay.'[10]

The women's Bill of Rights to the Ministry took nearly a year to complete and when early drafts were circulated to staff, they elicited some trenchant comments:

> *That a married officer should be able to perform his representational functions satisfactorily if his wife is living with him but not willing to cooperate is inconceivable ... Both the man and the woman are well aware of the traditional obligations likely to be placed on them ... and it is unwise of them to marry if he proposes to follow that career unless they are both prepared to play their part.*

The position of a woman marrying the average New Zealand farmer seems to me an almost exact parallel.[11]

As a prime mover of the submission, Pat Caughley wrote a tactful acknowledgement to the (male) officer in question: 'I was delighted that the arguments presented caught your attention and stimulated a series of counter-arguments' – and then demolished his case.[12]

From Washington, where he had just become Ambassador, Lloyd White wrote a predictably outraged response:

If the diplomatic wife does not wish to do what is expected of her, this must inevitably have a deleterious effect on her husband's career … If she takes the further step of wishing to lead her own life and have her own job … this negates the reason for giving her diplomatic privileges and other benefits including the occupancy of a house bought or rented at great expense by the Government on the assumption that it will be used by both husband and wife for the advancement of New Zealand's interests in the country of posting …

If the United States Government is silly enough to issue such a policy statement, that is no reason why New Zealand should follow suit.[13]

But many others supported the submission and in December 1973, when the final version was put up to Frank Corner, it included the ominous rider that 'the resolution of the problems … may well determine whether a number of officers will see their future as lying within the Ministry or outside it.'[14]

For the women officers the outcome was a significant victory, resulting in the redress of many of the inequalities that had previously disadvantaged their careers. For the diplomatic wives, however, the Ministry's response fell well short of the 'freedom proclamation' for which they had been hoping. Unlike their American sisters, they were still not liberated 'to do their own thing' regardless of their husband's status. Nor were they going to be let off the hook socially. Entertaining was part of the job, so the Ministry insisted, and 'if diplomatic officers are to make the full contribution expected of them … they will, in the Ministry's view, in most cases find their wives' support not only helpful but essential.'[15]

The question of employment was also still far from resolved (although the Ministry did pronounce itself willing 'to examine with sympathy'[16] any amendments to the *Handbook*). In most countries, taking a job meant forfeiting diplomatic immunity, which in some places could be highly risky. In others, the host nation might withhold its permission – or present so many bureaucratic obstacles that potential employers gave up the struggle. Over time many of these difficulties have been resolved either by reciprocal agreements or by less formal Dependant Employment Agreements, but these have often taken decades to negotiate.

In the short term, however, for the small group of wives who had spearheaded the campaign, the Ministry's response was bitterly disappointing. It is hardly surprising therefore, that Marguerite Scott's well-intentioned attempts to enlighten them on etiquette and protocol went down like a lead balloon. On the vexed subject of entertaining, the wives fought on and by 1977 the Ministry had managed to reconcile all parties with a skilful rewording of the *Handbook* that avoided any hint of compulsion, while maintaining that wives could 'contribute a good deal to the effectiveness of New Zealand representation' if they wished.[17]

Throughout Europe, similar confrontations were taking place. In Germany, a fiery article on 'the revolt against unpaid service for the Foreign Office' appeared in Bonn's *General-Anzeiger*. 'Don't marry a diplomat if you want to make anything of your life' one wife is cited as saying.[18] In London, the growing assertiveness of Britain's diplomatic wives was reported in the *Times* under the heading of 'Dippy Wives', accompanied by a photograph of some imposing-looking women: 'Neither staff, ministers, nor Whitehall's permanent secretaries can afford to ignore the massed battalions of the Diplomatic Service Wives' Association', notes the article, which was reporting on a meeting between the Foreign Office and the DSWA Committee: 'They are nice, charming, quietly formidable women with a touch of traditional memsahib's steel ... [who] would be difficult for any foreign secretary to gainsay.'[19]

Thanks to the State Department's vigorous Association of Foreign Service Women, diplomatic wives were also making headlines in the US. In July 1979, a lengthy article in the *Washington Post* reported on the demands of wives to be reimbursed for their hours of unpaid labour – a cause that was later taken up by Marlene Eagleburger, the wife of one of the most powerful men in the State Department. Later that year, the Iran hostage crisis and the plight of the hostages' families highlighted the grievances of diplomatic wives still further. 'I received not one iota of support from the State Department', said Penelope Laingen, whose husband, Bruce, was the senior diplomat in Tehran and spent 444 days in captivity: 'I have given my whole life to this service and have come up with nothing.'[20]

Shortly after her husband's release in early 1981, Penelope Laingen was one of a group of high-powered US diplomatic wives who aired their views in a full-page feature in the *Washington Star*, claiming that 'the pay ethic has become the only viable form of recognition for work performed.' At Georgetown University, the Institute for the Study of Diplomacy leapt on the bandwagon with a symposium entitled 'Diplomacy: The Role of the Wife', which was described by an academic at the Institute as 'the sexiest thing we've done'. [21]

Two wives from the New Zealand Embassy in Washington attended the panel discussion at Georgetown. One of them was Moina Simcock who, as a young and inexperienced wife in Delhi, had shouldered a heavy round of representational duties without demur. But a letter to 'dear Mama' not long after the symposium reflects her change of heart: 'I have been working very hard with official entertainment duties. Far too hard. Such efforts are not appreciated these days. I shall have to cut down and do something for myself.'[22] Later she became one of the first head-of-mission wives to commute between her husband's overseas post and a job in Wellington.

In 1984, the US media's interest in disgruntled wives reached an all-time high when a forceful article by Marlene Eagleburger appeared in the *Washington Post*. 'Mrs Foreign Service Deserves to Be Paid Too' she wrote, 'in the Foreign Service, dinners, luncheons, etc. are weekly business … It always amazes me … that people outside the Foreign Service look upon this part of Foreign Service life as glamorous and exciting. In reality it is 80 per cent plain hard work.' [23]

The *New York Times* picked up the story and a flurry of articles and interviews followed. Although a system of payment had been in place for some time in countries like Italy and Japan, reactions in the US had always been mixed. As one wife put it in an earlier article: 'I love my husband and I like to support him. To pay me $3 an hour for pushing canapés around puts me in the category of a waitress.' Another asked 'How do you grade it? Her mushrooms aren't good, but her chicken salad is marvellous?'[24] After months of debate, the proposal went nowhere. Instead, the State Department started looking at creative ways of providing employment for wives at its overseas posts.

This neat in-house solution, which sidesteps the problem of immunity, had already been adopted by several countries. But thanks to an outmoded government regulation banning husbands and wives from working in the same office, New Zealand was well behind the play. Writing from one of the world's toughest posts for wives, a desperate husband (who describes his wife as 'a bloody good administrator') could barely conceal his exasperation:

> *Here in Riyadh employment opportunities for female spouses are, as you might have guessed, minimal. The usual barriers of language and local preference are reinforced here by official and individual attitudes to women unlike anything experienced in the West for at least a century ...*

> *Because of that most Western countries in Riyadh (except ours) have a policy of promoting within their missions employment opportunities for spouses. The Australians, Canadians and British will employ any of their spouses who wish to work. The US Embassy ... has divided many support jobs in half to create jobs (part-time) for double the number of women.*[25]

By the mid-1980s, equal rights to employment had become a top priority for governments worldwide, with women being the greatest beneficiaries. Within the Ministry, several female officers were appointed as Heads of Mission and the lot of the wives was improving steadily. Opportunities for them to work at overseas posts were on the increase and participation in official entertaining was now deemed by the *Handbook* to be 'a matter for the spouse to decide'.[26] In addition, thanks to persistent lobbying, the Ministry had long since changed its stance on 'family reunion' and diplomatic children were now able to spend every school holidays with their parents. But for the small group of younger women from whom most of the momentum for change had come, the struggle was far from over. Their sights were set on forming a spouses' association and a throw-away line at the end of a letter in support of the association suggests that among the freedom-fighters emotions were still running high: 'How many of us are alcoholics, neurotics or emotional cripples? What might have prevented this?'[27]

The Spouses' Group took several years to materialise. In the meantime, the Foreign Service Association did its best to fight in the wives' corner – with mixed results. In 1986, a much-vaunted 'Spouse Survey' produced a disappointingly low response rate as well as some stinging criticisms:

> *Your 26 page survey was largely a summary of the whingeing and carping of a small minority of Foreign Service spouses ... On the one hand the group wants 'freedom' from the 'burden' of involvement in entertainment ... and, on the other to be molly-coddled by the Ministry from the cradle to the grave ... In just a few short years, it seems, we've*

gone from a HOM's wife asking a junior officer's wife to wash the former's smalls, to a present day spouse expecting his or her smalls to be laundered by the Ministry ...

The FSA should exhibit a certain resolve and clarity of purpose in distinguishing between what are legitimate concerns, and what is unhinged drivel.[28]

The writer's claim that the survey represented only the views of a 'small minority' had more than a grain of truth. Scattered at posts across the world, the wives were a fragmented group and now that the ban on working had been lifted, many of them had lost interest in the cause. But indifference was not the only factor. Apart from a few individuals like Marguerite Scott, there was also a major ideological divide between the older and younger women. In a spirited memo written at the very outset of the struggle, Pat Caughley had foreseen this problem:

Those whose emotional commitment is to the present situation are not expected to acknowledge that New Zealand society has loosened up since the Second World War ... Senior wives at overseas posts, who have had to put up with restricted freedom in the past, and are in a position to command the services and subordination of junior wives are unlikely to voluntarily relinquish their power ...

Naturally the more senior officers in the Ministry and their wives are not going to be willing to acknowledge that their behaviour might be irrational, or unacceptably authoritarian. To deflect any implied criticism, they will counter the questions raised ... by appealing to the 'sacrosanct' traditions of diplomacy whereby wives are expected to curtail their own interests by devoting themselves to charitable work within a tightly organised hierarchy of diplomatic wives ... The charitable activities of diplomatic wives are one of a number of leisure outlets; <u>not</u> a vital component of New Zealand foreign policy.[29]

But Pat's memo does not tell the full story. The senior wives' attachment to the status quo was not simply based on a desire to lord it over their junior colleagues, or pique at seeing the devaluation of a system to which they had dedicated their lives. On the contrary, with years of diplomatic experience under their belts, they genuinely feared that some of the more extreme positions taken by the younger women could run counter to the wives' interests, depriving them not only of spacious housing and domestic staff, but also of the opportunity to play a unique role of which they, as junior wives, had little understanding.

In her 2005 research paper, 'Soft Power in Global Politics', the Auckland academic Tania Domett spells out what the senior wives were talking about: 'Social functions and networking play an important role and indeed are a defining feature of diplomatic relations ... Through their participation in social events, which they often host, diplomatic partners become important players, and the private sphere an important site within global politics.' Citing a feminist perspective, Domett adds: 'the home, which is "the domain of the wife" ... is seen as the place where trust and confidence between diplomats can be cultivated' in which partners are 'key political players.'[30]

Nothing in Domett's learned paper would have come as any surprise to the senior wives, who were well aware of the highly focused agenda that lies behind diplomatic networking and entertaining. But as the Women's Movement roared on, all they could do was wring their hands and hope that in their quest for liberation and 'empowerment', the younger wives were not going to destroy one of the pillars of diplomacy.

By early 1987, the Spouses' Group had finally begun to take shape, with a representative on the FSA Executive and a programme of regular meetings. After that, matters progressed rapidly and within a few months the Ministry had agreed to establish a new position which would at last give the wives an official point of contact through which they could voice their concerns. For the dedicated group who had worked so tirelessly for the wives' cause, the appointment in April 1988 of the first Family Liaison Officer was a proud achievement. But by this time the passion of the early struggle had gone and the front line had moved elsewhere.

Today working wives are the norm. Less entertaining takes place at home and as a result houses are smaller and domestic staff are fewer. But in other ways, the worst fears of the senior wives have not been realised. At senior levels, wives still look after visiting dignitaries and may (if they are so inclined) continue to play the age-old games of diplomacy; at junior levels the household chores are more equally shared, but quite a number of wives still dress up and give dinner parties. Given their ongoing involvement, one might ask if the wives have really been liberated from servitude. The answer is emphatically yes. In the past diplomatic wives were the unpaid minions of the state, who were forbidden to work and whose representational duties were obligatory. Now their service is voluntary and they are free to pursue a career. Contrary to what many believed, however, the debate was never about supporting their husbands. It was about having the freedom to choose.

CHAPTER 14.

Supping with the Ayatollah

Women's rights were the last thing on my mind when our plane touched down in Tehran in late January 1984. It was my husband Richard's first posting as Ambassador and all my thoughts were focused on making the best possible impression on arrival. Clad in a suitably Islamic outfit, with my head decoratively draped in a shawl, I sailed down the aircraft steps towards the little group of Iranian officials who had come to meet us. Stretching out my hand to the most senior-looking member of the group, I treated him to what I hoped was a dazzling smile. Ignoring my outstretched hand, he looked straight past me and stepped forward to greet Richard.

Smarting from the insult, I headed towards the large black car that was waiting to take us to the terminal building. But a rough push from one of the lesser officials redirected me. 'This car is not for you', he said, and indicated a battered station wagon, into which I was unceremoniously bundled. From there I was driven to an airport lounge where the only other wife at the Embassy, Mary Bedkober, was waiting to greet me. Richard, meanwhile, had swept past me in a posse of bearded men and was being plied with tea and cakes. It was a brutal introduction to the Islamic Republic of Iran.

As the men sat laughing and talking around a coffee table, Mary and I stood by ourselves, conversing in undertones. When I recounted what had happened, Mary shook her head in disbelief. 'Surely somebody must have warned you that Iranian men are forbidden to shake hands with women in public – or even to make eye contact', she said. I listened with dismay. So the blunder had been mine. This was our second posting to Iran and I had thought I was well briefed. But our first posting had been under the Shah

Our first posting to Iran was under the Shah. Watched nervously by her husband, the author chats to the Shah's Prime Minister at New Zealand's first Waitangi Day party in Tehran, 1976. From left to right: Ambassador Bruce Brown, Prime Minister Amir-Abbas Hoveyda, Foreign Minister Abbas-Ali Khalatbari, Richard Woods, Joanna Woods.

and it had never crossed my mind that the Iranian Chief of Protocol would cut me dead at the airport.

Once the diplomatic niceties had been completed, Richard and I were driven to our new home in the northern suburbs. We sat in the back of the official car in stony silence. Nothing that I felt like saying was for the ears of the Embassy driver. Nor could we talk freely in the house. The only way we could have a frank discussion was to go for a walk in the garden. Still choking with indignation, I barely noticed the route, but as the iron gates to the Residence swung open, I saw two men standing in the shadows. Their guns were slung casually over their shoulders and they stared at us, unsmiling, as we passed. These were our guards, who were supplied by the Iranian government, but they looked more like gaolers to me.

That first night I lay awake for hours, fretting over my gaffe at the airport and the realisation, after talking to Mary, that I had seriously underestimated the severity with which the heavily armed Revolutionary Guards enforced the *hejab*. Within my house and garden, and those of my friends, I could dress as I pleased, but once outside the gates I would have to wear either

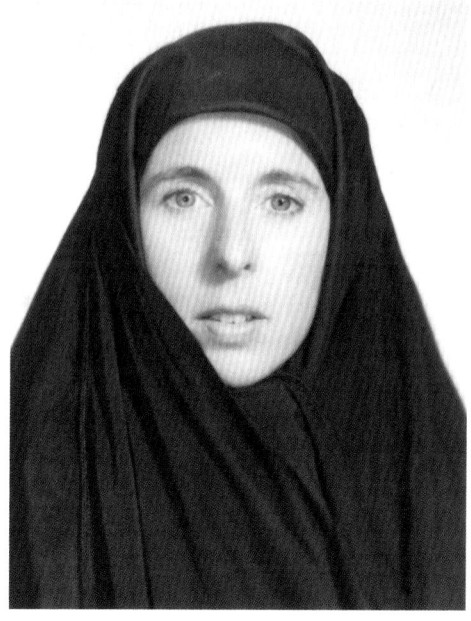

*Things were rather different under Khomeini.
The author in a* chador. *Tehran 1984.*

the all-enveloping black *chador* or its more convenient counterpart, the *ruhpush*, with every wisp of hair concealed under a headscarf. Make-up was also suspect and I later heard appalling tales of Iranian women whose lips had been slashed by razors or whose fingertips had been filed to pulp to remove the varnish. My greatest protection was my diplomatic ID card and I never ventured from home without it. Yet despite the well-established conventions of diplomacy, in a confrontation with the Revolutionary Guards, my diplomatic status would not necessarily have saved me – any more than it had the American hostages.

It was now three years since the release of the Americans, but for the embattled Diplomatic Corps in Tehran, the hostage crisis continued to cast a long shadow. In the face of considerable adversity, the diplomatic community formed a tightly knit group that swapped information constantly. Security was a major concern. Two European ambassadors had been shot and although both had made a full recovery, no one had any illusions about the inviolability of diplomatic personnel or premises. After the Islamic Revolution in 1979, many countries had recalled their diplomats and, of the five Anglo-Saxon nations, New Zealand was the only one that had reappointed an ambassador. The Americans and the Canadians had closed their Embassies, the British were operating under the Swedish flag and the Australians had downgraded to a Chargé d'Affaires. But all of them were in a very different position from New Zealand. Thanks to Britain's entry to the EEC, New Zealand was fighting for its economic life and Iran was about to become its second largest market for butter and its biggest market for lamb.

After a broken night, I awoke to find the Pakistani butler standing beside our bed with tea on a silver tray. In his white top, he looked just like a hospital orderly and I never got used to his presence in our bedroom. Sipping a cup of tea, I contemplated my surroundings. The house was sumptuously appointed in the opulent style of the previous regime. The floors were marble and all the bathroom fittings were gold – although much of the plumbing had ceased to function. It belonged to some wealthy Iranians who, like many other supporters of the Shah, had fled during the Revolution. Thankful to have found a good tenant, the landlord had let it cheaply and thrown in his own Louis XV-style bedroom suite as an added inducement.

My most urgent task was to find some food. The kitchen cupboards were bare and the scant meal that we had eaten the previous evening had been produced by a quick whip round the other staff at the Embassy. After breakfast, the cook and I set out for the local bazaar which I remembered as a colourful market overflowing with food. It had changed out of all recognition and I returned home close to despair with a kilo of stunted carrots and half a dozen kidneys. When I asked about the shops, the cook gave a hollow laugh. 'Nothing but empty shelves, Ma'am,' he said, 'all the food has gone to the Front.' Iran was fighting a war and while the civilian population was subsisting on meagre government rations, the army was marching into battle on New Zealand butter and lamb.

By the time we arrived in Tehran, the conflict with Iraq had been raging for nearly four years. Tens of thousands of Iranians had died and all over the city their death was glorified in outsize murals of the Ayatollah and lurid scenes of the Front. On my regular route to the Embassy, I passed a painting of a dying soldier whose leg had been severed by a mine. Blood gushed from the wound and his shattered femur protruded from the stump realistically. Iraqi mines were decimating the army and in the absence of any mine-clearing equipment, the Iranians had been sending waves of volunteers across the minefields. Many of them were young boys who had to be roped together in lines to prevent them from fleeing. But by far the most telling

The house felt like a gilded cage. The New Zealand Residence in Tehran, 1984.

evidence of the slaughter was at the cemetery of Behesht-e Zahra. There blood-red water gurgled from a fountain and row upon row of fresh graves stretched as far as the eye could see.

Once we started calling on our diplomatic colleagues, I rapidly discovered how the other wives managed their housekeeping. Everyone ordered their supplies from a Danish firm that specialised in duty free shopping, which they supplemented with whatever they could find in the markets. Since Iranian officials were forbidden to mix with women, diplomatic entertaining veered wildly between stiff all-male lunches at the Residence (when I had to hide upstairs), and evening parties with other diplomats at which the wives exploded into their finery and conjured miracles out of their store cupboards. Driving home at nights we soon learnt to stop for the young boys manning the road blocks. They were backed up by men from the local *Komiteh*, who trained their guns on our car as the driver wearily explained that under the Vienna Convention they had no right to search a diplomatic vehicle. Sometimes he prevailed, but on several occasions we had to submit at gunpoint.

Despite these distractions, the time hung heavily on my hands. Our children were far away at boarding school and in an attempt to find something more purposeful than bridge or coffee parties, I looked for a job. Apart from a few clerical positions in the embassies, work for foreign women was almost non-existent. Eventually I tracked down some English teaching, but when it emerged that I would lose my diplomatic immunity, I had to abandon it. I also embarked on a journal, but even here I was thwarted. My personal jottings, so it seemed, had to be as veiled in discretion as I was and they were shipped home by diplomatic bag in tightly sealed envelopes. Trapped in a gilded cage, in the midst of a hostile city, I was becoming increasingly despondent – when a chance introduction changed everything.

Manijeh did not fall into any of the usual categories of Iranian women whom I had met since my arrival. She belonged to the old Turkic aristocracy and she regarded both the Ayatollah and the Shah as upstarts. But her disdain for the previous regime had not prevented her from working for the Shah's government and, as Director of Tribal Affairs, she had spent months travelling in the remote areas of Iran championing the cause of the nomads. 'Maybe she would let you ride her horses', said Louise Firouz, who was another legendary figure and had made the introduction.

Manijeh was living just outside the city in an isolated villa surrounded by a walled garden. There she kept a few mares and a magnificent black stallion. Apart from her horses and a few acres in Hamadan she had lost everything in the Revolution, but even in her reduced circumstances she had the bearing of a feudal khan. I looked at the horses admiringly. 'Why don't you buy one?' said Manijeh, 'the National Stud is planning an auction and I could help you to choose something good.' My heart leapt. After the stifling atmosphere of the Residence, the thought of roaming the hills on horseback seemed like heaven.

Over the next few months, Manijeh and I became firm friends and whenever I could I would escape from the tedium of my marble palace to sit and drink tea with her. Despite her limited means she held court to a stream of visitors, mysterious figures from a timeless Iranian world that few diplomats ever saw. During the Revolution, she had been lucky to escape execution. 'They were idealistic then and they took the trouble to question me,' she told me later, 'but now it can be so quick.' I understood only too well. The notorious prison at Evin was not far from our house and late at night we could hear the firing squad.

Not all the company Manijeh kept was appropriate for the wife of a foreign envoy. On one occasion, when I turned up unexpectedly, she met me with a quizzical smile. 'You're going to see something that will shock you,' she said. My imagination ran riot. They must be having an orgy, I thought, following her upstairs to the sitting room. Two men were sitting beside a brazier passing a pipe between them. A ball of gummy resin was sizzling in the bowl and, from the sweet smell of the smoke, I realised that it was opium. Manijeh sat on the carpet watching my reactions. 'Over a certain age,' she said, 'opium is good for you. In fact His Imperial Majesty used to supply it free to elderly addicts ... who made a huge profit by selling it.' She poured me a glass of tea and with a lordly gesture indicated to the two men that it was time for them to leave.

The horse auction did not take place for many months and in the meantime our two sons flew out for the school holidays. Before their arrival, I struggled to think of things to do with them. Cinemas and theatres were closed and all public amusements were banned. Even cassettes and videos were illegal and had to be smuggled into the country. Furthermore it was high summer and the boys, then aged twelve and thirteen, were not allowed to wear shorts or T-shirts that would expose their arms and legs in public. But my worries were unfounded. After the rigours of an English boarding school, they revelled in the luxury of the Residence, basking for hours by the swimming pool and drinking endless glasses of coca-cola.

Even an outing to the Shah's palace proved an unexpected success, as we peered into the late Shah's cupboards and gaped at Farah Diba's shoes. But what the boys really liked was the guns. At the road blocks they looked at the Kalashnikovs in awe and stared with undisguised envy at the busloads of volunteers that drew into our local petrol station. With their guns and their martyrs' headbands, many of the volunteers were the same age as the boys. 'Cool,' said our younger son admiringly, as the buses headed off for the Front. The pump attendant smirked. 'Next stop paradise,' he said.

By the time the auction was announced, several other diplomats had also decided to buy horses, including a Norwegian friend named Inger who became my closest riding companion. Like everywhere else, the National Stud was heavily guarded by the Revolutionary Guards, but the auction had been deemed a gala day and a huge crowd had been allowed into the grounds to see the fun. As foreign women, Inger and I were the objects of intense curiosity. On Manijeh's advice, Inger bought the Shah's favourite hack, a beautifully schooled gelding which the revolutionaries had overlooked. Much to the disgust of the crowd, I bid on a skinny grey filly which went for a few hundred rials. The locals thought she was a very poor choice for an ambassadress, but I knew better. Manijeh had shown me her bloodlines and she came from priceless Arabian stock. 'She will be beautiful,' Manijeh told me, 'and she will go like the wind.' Her name was Ramesh, which means 'cheerfulness' or 'singing for joy', and over the next four years, she brought me hours of happiness.

Throughout our first year the war was little more than a distant backdrop, but in March 1985 the conflict came closer to home. In the early hours of the morning, Richard and I were awoken by a deafening explosion. We rushed to the bedroom window expecting to see a huge crater in the garden. What we saw was the sky ablaze with tracer bullets backed up by heavy gunfire. Iran had just launched a massive new offensive on Iraq and in retaliation the Iraqis had despatched two jet fighters to bomb Khomeini's compound, which was about a kilometre east of the Residence.

Throughout the day, the city was in an uproar. Baghdad Radio was breathing fire and brimstone and no one knew when the Iraqis would come back. Late in the afternoon, Richard and I went to see the nearby apartment block that had been hit. It was a sobering sight. All that remained was rubble, surrounded by a carpet of broken glass that had been blasted from the neighbouring houses, causing horrific injuries. Two nights later the Iraqis returned and we were awoken by yet another explosion. The walls of the house trembled and from further away to the west came a series of dull thuds. For a split second, there was a stunned silence before the sky erupted into a frenzy of rockets and tracer bullets. From my bedroom window, I scanned the sky for some sign of the enemy and far above the anti-aircraft fire I saw the Iraqi planes – two tiny dots of light climbing towards the stars.

After this second attack, many of the diplomatic wives left. Feeling slightly absurd, Richard and I spent the night on mattresses in the basement, where we were half suffocated by the fumes from the central heating plant. Of course nothing happened, but over the next two weeks the Iraqis returned regularly. By this time thousands of Iranians had fled the northern suburbs, where most of the bombing was targeted, and our neighbourhood had become a ghost town. But statistically, so Richard assured me, the chances of our house being hit were extremely small. Nevertheless, the tension of lying in the dark waiting for the bombs to fall was starting to take its toll.

My greatest concern was the boys. They were supposed to be joining us for the Easter holidays, but if the air raids continued for another couple of weeks, I would have to fly out instead. As I agonised over what to do, the decision was taken out of my hands by an announcement on Baghdad Radio that as of 17.00 hrs the following day, no civilian aircraft would be safe in Iranian airspace. Mayhem followed as people fought tooth and nail for the last seats out and we did not stand a chance of getting a ticket.

That afternoon, to distract my thoughts, I drove out to the stables where I was keeping Ramesh. As Manijeh had predicted, with proper feeding, she was growing stronger and more beautiful by the day and before long I would be able to start riding her. After grooming her dappled coat, I started home

Envoy's wife near Tehran explosion

By NZPA staff correspondent PETER O'HARA

TEHRAN, June 17. — Joanna Woods, wife of the New Zealand Ambassador in Tehran, was about 20m from one of the blasts which have hit the Iranian capital during Iraqi raids over the weekend.

Mrs Woods was visiting the young filly she keeps for a hobby near Tehran's bleak Grey Mountains when her car shook and flames erupted nearby.

She was protected by a wall from the explosion and saw the crater left by either a rocket or bomb from one of the Iraqi jets which fly high out of range of Iranian fighters.

Shrapnel from Iranian anti-aircraft fire has fallen on the roof of another New Zealander's house in Tehran and provided some souvenirs of the war.

Like embassy staff, Mrs Woods figures the odds are that she has come about as close to the bombing as she will get.

The Iraqi attacks during a recent three-week campaign were believed to be restricted to a handful of explosions each day in a capital of around eight to 10 million people.

There is no sign of the war ending. On the contrary millions marched chanting pro-war slogans in Iran during a recent visit by a New Zealand trade delegation.

Anti-aircraft fire which is supposed to protect the city cannot reach the Iraqi fighters, and nor can the F-24 aircraft which the Iranian Air Force sends up.

From that height the bombing is very random but there have been attempts to knock out the Ayatollah Khomeiny's house.

The vicinity of the home of Iran's leader can be seen from New Zealand Ambassador Richard Woods' official residence. It is in a direct line across the base of the mountains at a similar panoramic elevation to that which the Tehran embassy residence enjoys.

The Evening Post's coverage of my lucky escape. June 1985.

in the dusk, bumping along the unsealed road in my second-hand Honda Civic. The car shuddered violently. My first thought was that someone was taking a shot at me, but as I jammed my foot on the accelerator, about a hundred yards to my right I saw a great arc of soil curving into the air, engulfed in a wall of flame. I braked and stared at it uncomprehendingly while a group of children ran away screaming.

Shortly after I got home, I received a call from the Turkish Ambassador. He was offering me the last seat on a Turkish charter flight that was airlifting some Japanese workers before the Iraqis closed the airspace. I accepted it thankfully. The next morning on our way to the airport, Richard and I revisited the road to the stables and found a large crowd inspecting the two deep craters which had been made by the Iraqi rockets. They had fallen on either side of the road and by some miracle I had passed between them unscathed.

By June the Iraqi threat had receded. The airlines had resumed their flights and I was able to return to Tehran, where I became involved in a new venture. 'I'm ringing about the Diplomatic Ladies' Group,' said Caritas, who was the wife of the Greek Counsellor, 'we'd like you to become the next President.' My heart sank. This was the first I'd heard of a Ladies' Group and I had no desire to become its President. I suggested a string of more suitable candidates. 'I've tried them,' replied Caritas, 'and they've all turned it down.' Since my arrival in Iran the Group had been in recess, but some enterprising wives had decided to revive it and once I had accepted my fate as President, I became fired with enthusiasm.

Nowhere could the need for a diplomatic wives' support group have been greater. Excluded from any social contact with Iranian officials and their wives, our skills as hostesses and networkers counted for nothing. Even in our own homes, we were banished from official lunches and dinners. At one point, the Iranian Ministry of Foreign Affairs demanded that screens should be erected at diplomatic receptions, so that the diplomatic wives could not be seen. Fortunately this particular episode was short-lived, but at our first New Zealand Day reception (which we never repeated) the officials who attended made a point of ignoring me. As foreign women, we also attracted the constant attentions of the Revolutionary Guards on the streets. Indeed, some of the more timid wives were so frightened that they never left their houses without their husbands. For most of us, daily life in Tehran had little to do with diplomacy. It was about survival.

Within a few weeks we had formed a committee and devised a programme. The options were extremely limited, but our visits to the Carpet Museum and the Botanical Gardens were a resounding success – and the display of aerobic dancing by the staff of the British Interests Section brought the house down. Before long the Group had gathered wives from every diplomatic mission in Tehran and had nearly doubled its membership. It also expanded to form several interest groups, including a lively book club. At the end of the year we decided to record our activities by publishing a magazine. For the front cover we used a painting of a sea of veiled women and for the back page, the secretary of the committee, Nicky Chaplin, and I went down to the local photographic studio and had our pictures taken in black *chadors*.

With a growing number of friends and interests, I was starting to feel quite at home and, like millions of Iranians, I was learning how to live with the Ayatollahs. As diplomats, we needed permits to travel beyond forty kilometres of Tehran, but during the boys' long summer holidays Richard had discovered a little-known short cut to the high mountain valley of the Lar, which enabled us to enjoy glorious camping trips without recourse to the authorities. We also made some adventurous expeditions deep into the Alborz mountains to visit the ruined castles of the Assassins. On one trip, we were joined by the BBC's veteran foreign correspondent, John Simpson, and I have a photograph of him cooling off in a muddy stream in his Y-fronts. Even our cavernous Residence had become more bearable after the purchase of a colourful Pakistani *shamiana*. Scattered with carpets and cushions, it formed an exotic pavilion on the terrace, in which we ate all our meals from May to September. The garden was full of roses and on summer nights, when the sky was studded with stars, it seemed as if nothing had changed since the days of Omar Khayyam.

Nevertheless, once the boys had returned to school, the house seemed unbearably empty. The Ladies' Group occupied a certain amount of my time, as did foraging for food. But in between my other tasks, I spent hours riding over the hills. Far from the roar of the traffic and the predatory Revolutionary Guards, it felt like another world. The local people seemed untouched by the Revolution and as they strolled between their orchards and gardens, they greeted me amiably. Sometimes, in a stretch of woodland, I would come across an old man with a long white beard. His eyes had the faraway look of a mystic and he wore a faded green hat covered with stars.

By this time Ramesh had grown into a graceful, snow white mare, whose paces were as smooth as silk. 'On a true Arabian,' so Manijeh had told me, 'you can drink tea from a cup and saucer without spilling a drop'. She was also the fastest horse for miles around and when I raced her against Manijeh's stallion, she left him standing. Since the air raids Manijeh had moved far out into the countryside, where she had built a mud-brick barn to house her growing number of horses. Inger and I stabled our horses nearby and Manijeh's barn was one of our favourite destinations. In winter we would sit in her little room, snugly furnished with saddlebags and kilims. In summer she received us out of doors, enthroned on a wooden platform beneath a canopy of poplar leaves.

The Iraqis had not raided Tehran for months, but the lull was too good to last and early in 1987 Mary Bedkober's successor,* Judith Paulin, had the closest call of any wife in New Zealand's diplomatic history:

---

*   Irvine Paulin had succeeded John Bedkober as the Commercial Counsellor at the Embassy.

The noise of the jets was so deafening that I thought they were coming through my front door and then there was the most enormous explosion … The glass around our interior courtyard shattered … I don't recall the sound of breaking glass because there was such a tremendous noise.

Except for the Pakistani houseboy and his wife and child, Judith was alone when the bomb fell:

We rushed downstairs and went into a room that had been officially designated the 'bomb shelter' … [where] we sat for 30–40 minutes … Eventually I went upstairs … People were dazed. There was silence and dust everywhere. It was really hard to see, people sort of emerged out of the dust. I sat outside on a wall. I was quite traumatised, but I don't think it really sank in until about an hour later … when I just burst into tears.[1]

The two Iraqi jets had swooped in from the south in broad daylight, flying so low over the northern suburbs that the trees were flattened by their downdraft. As usual, they were aiming for the Ayatollah's compound and one of their bombs landed a hundred metres from the house occupied by Judith and her husband, Irvine, which was only a block away from the Residence. 'We were very lucky', Irvine told his parents, 'a second or two more on the button and the pilot would have hit our house'.[2] At the time Irvine had been out in the car and it was not until he got through the roadblocks that he discovered what had happened to Judith.

The force of the explosion shook the whole neighbourhood and thirty-six hours later, when Richard and I returned from home leave in New Zealand, we found the Residence staff still in a state of shock. Our usually well-groomed butler opened the front door with his hair sticking out like a halo holding an evil-looking piece of shrapnel, which had fallen in the garden. Compared with other houses in the area, our damage was minor; the blast had blown in the windows and doors and lifted one of the French windows off its hinges. But Judith's narrow escape and our twisted window-frames were grim reminders of our vulnerability. That night I found it hard to sleep and at dawn a distant thud signalled another air raid. As I flung open the window to look for the planes, Richard handed me one of the plastic hard hats that had been sent to us by the Ministry. We had laughed when they arrived, but after fingering the jagged edges of the shrapnel, they no longer seemed so ludicrous.

For many months my father's illness had been hanging over our family like a dark cloud. In late May 1987, I travelled to England to see him,

Even on horseback, I had to observe the hejab. *The author on Ramesh, Tehran 1985.*

but when my mother and I took him to hospital for treatment, we never imagined that he had less than twenty-four hours to live. 29 May 1987 was one of the worst days of my life. Early in the morning, I heard the news that Nicky's husband, Edward, who was a diplomat in the British Interests Section, had been kidnapped the previous day. He had been dragged from his car and beaten by six heavily armed men before being bundled into a jeep. Since then there had been no news of him. I felt sick with dread. Less than four months earlier, Terry Waite had vanished without trace in Beirut. Many believed that he was dead and the thought that Edward might suffer a similar fate preyed on my mind like a nightmare.

Edward's abduction was front page news and as further details emerged during the day, my anguish for Nicky increased. She and their three-year-old daughter and seven-week-old baby had been in the car when it was rammed and had witnessed the beating. The attack had taken place on a stretch of road that Richard drove daily to the Embassy and I could envisage the scene vividly. Later that day my father died and the shock and sorrow of his death banished everything else from my mind. But shortly before I went to bed, I heard that Edward had been released. His captors had been the Revolutionary Guards, who were avenging the detention of the Iranian Vice-Consul in Manchester for shoplifting.

When I returned to Tehran in June, nearly all my closest diplomatic friends had gone. In the aftermath of the kidnapping, the staff of the British Interests Section had been reduced to one and as a result of a 'satirical' piece on Australian television, both the Australian Consul and the Trade Commissioner, whose wives were key figures in the Ladies' Group, had been expelled. In July, a further outrage shook our beleaguered community. The French Embassy compound in Tehran was put under siege, trapping the only French wife, Estelle Torri, who had just given birth to her first baby. Initially no food or supplies were allowed in and it was suggested to the Italian Ambassador, whose Embassy was next door, that he might throw a few cartons of milk over the wall to her. After weeks of negotiation, Estelle and her baby were allowed to leave. But her husband and his diplomatic colleagues continued to languish in their encircled compound for many months to come. In the meantime, both the Saudi and Kuwaiti Embassies had been sacked, while the Diplomatic Corps stood helplessly by wondering who would be next.

When I first mentioned the idea of a moonlight picnic to Louise Firouz, she laughed me to scorn. 'You diplomats are crazy,' she said, 'the whole god-damned place is blowing up and all you can think about is moonlight picnics.' But my suggestion was greeted enthusiastically by the younger members of the Diplomatic Corps and on the appointed night a great stream of diplomatic cars, groaning with food and drink, bumped its way along the stony track to Manijeh's barn. It was pitch dark, but Manijeh, who had donned a long white robe and a turban in honour of the occasion, had built an enormous fire which illuminated the whole area. When everyone had arrived, she signalled to the wild-looking Afghan boys who looked after her horses to open the doors of the barn. A dozen Arabians thundered out into a rough corral where they galloped in tight circles, plunging and snorting, before crashing through the fences and disappearing into the darkness. I turned to Manijeh in dismay, but she never batted an eyelid. 'They'll come back', she said.

As the fire died down, the moon rose, bathing the surrounding hills in a silver sheen. The ground was spread with carpets and the women flung off their *hejab*, emerging into the moonlight in their flimsy summer dresses like butterflies. The wine flowed. No one had remembered to bring any water and the party was growing merrier by the minute when two enormous trucks lumbered down the track piled high with bales of alfalfa. Manijeh swore vehemently. It was the winter feed for her horses and it had to be unloaded that evening. The two drivers swung down from their cabs and stared at the revellers in astonishment. With the scantily clad women and the wine, they must have thought they had been transported to paradise and they squatted down happily with a plate of kebabs while the party continued noisily.

By the time Manijeh called for volunteers to unload the bales, few of the reclining males felt like responding. Louise and I swarmed up the back of the first truck, followed by one of the Afghans, and started hurling down the bales. Some others tackled the second truck and amidst cheers of 'Up Afghanistan' a furious contest ensued. Louise and I lost by a narrow margin, but the bales were unloaded in record time and the two drivers drove off into the night grinning from ear to ear.

Three months later we left Iran.

I never saw Manijeh again, but we corresponded for many years. When she died in 2001, the nomads came in their hundreds. They buried her in the foothills of the Alborz, not far from her mud-brick barn, and at her funeral they brought her Arabian horses, richly caparisoned, to pay their last respects at her grave.

CHAPTER 15.

The Official Companion

Beside the campfire, two young women were dancing, one dark-haired and vivacious, the other fair with a winning smile. As they danced, they were belting out Dinah Lee's 'Do the Blue Beat', while the crowd cheered and stamped appreciatively. Both the girls were good dancers and everyone was enjoying the show – all except for Ed, who sat glowering in the shadows: 'He was furious … It was just good fun, but he didn't like it. Maybe he thought we were drunk.'[1]

At over 3000 metres in the Mingbo Valley, Louise Hillary and June Mulgrew may well have been a little light-headed, but they were certainly not drunk. After years of waving their husbands off on expeditions that lasted for months on end, in early 1961 they had finally been invited to join the party and they were celebrating. But although Ed had given the 'Ladies' Expedition' his blessing, in the all-male world of high altitude climbing he was not at all sure that his wife and her friend should be strutting their stuff to an audience of Sherpas. The Sherpas, however, saw nothing amiss. Singing and dancing around the campfire were part of a long tradition and their own women were quite as feisty as June and Louise.

The close friendship between June and Louise had started four years earlier, during their husbands' sixteen-month trip to Antarctica, which had culminated in a dash to the Pole on three Massey Ferguson tractors. The two women had much in common. For all its apparent glamour, marriage to serial adventurers like Ed Hillary and Peter Mulgrew was no bed of roses and holding the fort at home, with only the occasional letter or radio contact from their husbands, required very special qualities. Neither of them had been to Nepal before. 'It was a huge plunge for us,' June told me, 'because our children were small and we were away for a long time, which was quite hard.' Ed was leading an assault on the world's fifth highest mountain, Makalu, and some of the climbers' wives had joined the group for the 180-mile walk into the base camp: 'I didn't have any idea what I was letting myself in for. But I was young and fit and I'd done a lot of skipping and walking.'

To the delight of the wives, the hillsides were ablaze with rhododendrons and orchids. 'More than anything it was the flowers that made our days so wonderful', Ed wrote later, as he and his fellow climbers saw 'the old familiar route' through the ecstatic eyes of the women.[2] But when the party reached base camp, the mood became less upbeat. The only form of transport back to Kathmandu was by single-engine plane from the perilous airstrip at Mingbo and Louise was far from happy. 'She was very, very frightened of small planes,' June recalls, 'and she was in a state of collapse.' The ten-seater aircraft was already loaded to capacity and June was put on the floor and tied down with a piece of rope: 'The pilot said "if anything happens just pull the rope".'

We were at about 15,000 feet ... There were two rocks behind the wheels and they just pulled these out and the plane took off down this very rough airstrip and fell off the edge ... Ed came with us, but Peter stayed behind and he told me later that he'd never felt so physically sick as when he watched that plane take off.

For Peter, far worse was in store. A few weeks later, less than two hundred metres from the summit of Makalu, he collapsed with pulmonary oedema. Semi-conscious and hallucinating, he was carried down to base camp, by which time his hands and feet had become severely frost-bitten. From there he was flown by helicopter to Kathmandu, where he spent several agonising months in hospital, surviving on two-hourly painkilling injections of pethidine. June flew up from New Zealand to be at his bedside and to administer his injections: 'I'm not a nurse, but I'd learnt a lot from sticking hypodermic needles into oranges.' On his return to New Zealand, both Peter's legs had to be amputated.

Ed accompanied the Mulgrews on their journey home. He and June were already friends, but this was the first time that he had seen her out of a social context. As he watched her coping calmly and patiently with Peter through an endless succession of flights, he saw 'a very different June'[3] from the light-hearted young woman who had danced beside the campfire. A photograph taken in an ambulance at Auckland airport shows the trio – Ed larger than life as usual, Peter grinning defiantly and June with a brave smile.

Peter and June Mulgrew in an ambulance on their return to New Zealand after Peter's disastrous attempt on Makalu. Ed Hillary had flown with them from Nepal, Auckland 1961. (The Press)

The Mulgrews and the Hillarys dining together at an Auckland restaurant, c. 1963. (Robin Mulgrew)

During Peter's long convalescence, as he struggled to master his prosthetic legs and battled with an addiction to pethidine, June often had to pick up the pieces. Photographs of them at the time – including in a good-looking foursome with the Hillarys at an Auckland restaurant – underscore Peter's indomitable spirit and June's rocklike support. Three years later, she and Peter were among the select group of close friends who became founder members of the Himalayan Trust, which Ed had formed to support his programme of school, hospital and bridge-building in Nepal. But for Peter, returning to the Himalayas only highlighted his new disabilities, and to combat his frustration he transformed himself into a world-class sailor and a successful businessman. Somewhere along the line, however, his personality changed. The ongoing pain was taking its toll and by the early 1970s Ed was finding that the easy-going companion of earlier days was often 'grumpy' and 'aggressive'.[4]

In late March 1975, June was surprised to find Louise and her parents waiting to meet her at Kathmandu airport. June had become an enthusiastic trekker and she and her elder daughter had just flown in from the mountains to catch an onward connection to New Zealand. It was a distressing encounter. 'Louise was crying,' said June, 'which was unusual for her' and she was already worrying about the flight to join Ed at his latest hospital project a few days later. Unlike Louise, June had never been bothered by light aircraft: 'I've done a huge amount of flying in small helicopters and I'm very fatalistic … Once they shut the door, that's it.' Louise's purpose in coming out to the airport that day had been to ask June to witness her signature on a new will; looking back, June is convinced that she had some sort of premonition. On 31 March 1975 Louise and her sixteen-year-old daughter, Belinda, boarded the same single-engine aircraft in which June and her daughter had travelled from the mountains. But someone had left a locking pin in one of the wing flaps and the plane crashed moments after take-off. It exploded in a ball of fire and there were no survivors.

'It was so preventable,' said June, 'and I think that is what devastated Ed more than anything else.' In his various autobiographies, Ed records his feelings about Louise's death unflinchingly: 'I knew it was all my fault – Louise had hated flying in small planes, but I had ignored her fears. This feeling would hang over my head for ever.' One of the worst moments was returning to New Zealand: 'Our house was just like an empty tomb … and I didn't care too much if I lived or died.'[5] Less well documented, however, is his struggle with an ongoing depression that dogged his life for the next six years.

Throughout this anguished period, June was living through a nightmare of her own. Her marriage to Peter had become increasingly unhappy and by the time he was killed on Air New Zealand's ill-fated sightseeing flight to Antarctica in November 1979, they were already estranged. Never much of a ladies man, it took Ed some time to realise that June was as lonely as he was. But after a few companionable dinners and some long walks on Auckland's Piha beach, their relationship deepened. 'Peter had died on Erebus and Louise had died in the Himalayas,' said June, 'and we were simply looking after each other … Being married or not being married didn't seem to matter.' For Ed, however, this was a turning point and the moment when the black despair, which had been haunting him ever since the death of Louise, finally began to recede.

The call from recently elected Prime Minister David Lange came as a complete surprise. It was August 1984 and he was thinking of re-opening the New Zealand High Commission in Delhi.* Would Ed be prepared to go as High Commissioner? Ed's mind raced. The idea certainly appealed to him, but with his building projects in Nepal and his fundraising tours to finance them he already had more than enough commitments. And what about June? Later he admits to being 'a little scared to ask her to join me in case she turned me down.'[6] But, much to his relief, June made the suggestion herself.

With a lordly disdain for the Ministry's regulations, Lange swept aside their unmarried status. June was to be Ed's 'Official Companion' and, as the first officially recognised partner of a New Zealand Head of Mission, she was to be treated exactly like a wife. Much to June's amusement, many people in Delhi assumed that 'Official Companion' was some form of decoration and invitations would arrive for her with the letters O.C. after her name: 'They all knew that we weren't married. But it was never an issue. They just took us at face value and because Ed was Ed, doors just seemed to open.'

On her arrival in India in March 1985, June's most pressing task was to re-establish the Residence. By this time the High Commission had been closed for three years and although the Government had managed to rent back the original Residence, it had deteriorated badly in the interim. With its Lutyens-style façade and magnificent lawn, June could see the potential of the house and she set to work at once, driving around Delhi in the small car that Ed had bought for her, chasing up fabrics and furniture. Not many diplomatic women drove themselves, but June had been running her own trekking business in Nepal and, after driving 'a mini-ute with a brick under the seat and one gear' in Kathmandu, the streets of Delhi seemed pretty tame.

---

* In 1982, the New Zealand High Commission in Delhi was closed by Robert Muldoon as part of a cost-cutting exercise.

Another major undertaking was recruiting the household staff: 'There were about eleven of them … A couple in the garden, a washing man, a sweeping man and a couple of bearers. So the numbers just mounted up.' She also found a good cook 'who could do everything from Chinese to Pavlova.' Unlike many of her counterparts, June was often in the kitchen 'passing through or talking, so the house was never divided between 'them' and 'us''. She also kept a close eye on the detail: 'I would make sure that what was being served was what I had said – I didn't want custard on the beetroot – and I would know if the water wasn't being filtered.'

In Delhi high society, the Raj was still very much in evidence and for diplomatic dinners hostesses would dress their staff up in turbans and insist that they wore white gloves. But June had no time for such airs and graces: 'I thought it was rather insulting to imply that their hands were not clean, so they just wore their white uniforms.' In other respects, however, her official parties were quite as vice-regal as those of her peers: 'The scale of the entertaining was extraordinary … and I was fortunate in having a background of white table napkins and doing things nicely, so I knew what to do.' Formal dinner-parties of up to forty-eight guests usually took place indoors, but for larger occasions June would pitch a brilliantly coloured *shamiana* on the lawn and bring a band of musicians from Rajasthan to play on the veranda.

Some of her happiest memories are of the children's parties that she gave at Christmas – often when her family were staying:

We had conjurers and all sorts of magicians, and camels with saddlebags full of presents from Father Christmas … It was great fun, although having things like an elephant in the garden put these parties on a rather different scale from the parties I had given for my own children at home.

My mother came over too. She was eighty-five, but we still got her on the back of an elephant … Those were really good Christmases – the best ones I've ever had, I think … One of my granddaughters was proposed to by the Maharajah of Baroda. She was ten at the time and she told him that he was too old.

Despite her skills as a hostess, June was thankful to find a mentor to guide her through the intricacies of coffee mornings and charity work: 'I'm not a committee person, but because diplomatic wives are supposed to do this sort of thing, the wife of the Australian High Commissioner, Nicky Feakes, took me in hand.' The Delhi Commonwealth Women's Association proved to be a unique experience that she 'wouldn't have missed for anything':

> *It was full of very sophisticated Indian women, who carried their jewellery around in their handbags because they didn't dare leave it at home … They were all strong women, shouting and bossing. After my first meeting one of the women from the British High Commission came up to me and said, 'Don't worry, it gets worse.'*

Despite the uproar, the Committee's fundraising functions were always 'amazingly successful' and with its enormous lawn ideally suited to large-scale entertaining, the New Zealand Residence (and its occupants) were always in high demand. But unlike most of their diplomatic colleagues, Ed and June had heavy responsibilities elsewhere because, in addition to representing his country on a grand scale, Ed had made a lifelong commitment to the Sherpas:

> *I think we must have kept up our fundraising for the Himalayan Trust while we were in Delhi because we had to keep the money coming in, and for that we'd have to go overseas for Ed to lecture … He was used to these huge trips, but I always remember feeling tired when I got back – and there was still everything else to do … Then in another six weeks, we'd be off again. Ed had itchy feet and as soon as he got back from one trip, he'd be in his study planning the next one.*

June, meanwhile, would be flat out organising menus and guest lists for the next burst of official entertaining.

As the conqueror of Everest, Ed's duties extended far beyond the diplomatic round in Delhi: 'He was invited to things all over India …We went to schools and all sorts of other interesting places – often to open them. Everyone knew who he was, which was an amazing situation to be in … You can't really imagine what it was like.' Similarly in political circles, Ed had the status of a national figure and when he fainted at a school prize-giving, a sympathetic note arrived from the Prime Minister, Rajiv Gandhi, the following morning. But despite such marks of friendship, Ed and June never got to know the Gandhis well: 'We met them, but we never had them to dinner – it seemed all too apparent that he was at risk.' Ever since Indira Gandhi's assassination in 1984, Rajiv and his wife, Sonia, had been surrounded by heavy security: 'Every time we went to a function at which Rajiv was present, all the diplomats were frisked and there would be a row of guards with their fingers on the trigger.'* The only time that Ed and June saw Rajiv without a bullet-proof vest was when he made an official visit to New Zealand.

---

*   Rajiv Gandhi was assassinated by a suicide bomber in 1991.

The charming Lutyens-style bungalow that June Mulgrew restored to its former glory. The former New Zealand Residence in Delhi, c. 1986. (By kind permission of Priscilla Williams)

The formal dining-room at New Zealand's new, purpose-built High Commission in Delhi. Much of the furniture and tableware came from the former Residence and was chosen by June Mulgrew, 1990. (Trends Magazine)

Straddling so many different worlds, June admits to a certain detachment: 'Despite being part of diplomatic society, I don't think we were terribly swept away with cocktail parties. We went to them because we had to.' The people who mattered most to them were the Sherpas and in May 1986, when Tenzing Norgay died suddenly in Darjeeling, they never considered not attending his funeral. At the time, Nepali factions in Darjeeling were conducting a violent campaign for a separate state in West Bengal. But it would have taken more than a few militants to deter Ed from farewelling the man with whom he had shared the glory of Everest. To allay official concerns, they travelled with an army escort: 'We were stopped by protesters several times. But as soon as they saw Ed, they just waved us through.'

To his own people and the wider Nepali community, Tenzing was a hero and the elaborate Buddhist ceremony was attended by thousands:

> The funeral itself was amazing … Everyone sat around the pyre on sofas, having picnics … There was no mourning. Believing in reincarnation makes such a difference … The pyre was shoulder-height and built up like a table. It was alight and melted ghee was thrown over the body to help it burn. Then they wait for the skull to crack, which means that the spirit has gone.

Towards the end of their posting, Ed and June were summoned to a very different conflagration. In February 1989, the famous Tengboche Monastery at the foot of Everest was burned to the ground. It was the main religious centre for the Sherpas, who immediately turned to their greatest champion for help. As soon as they heard the news, Ed and June caught the first plane to Kathmandu and took a helicopter up to Tengboche. Some of the most precious artefacts had been saved, but the building was a smouldering ruin. According to June, electricity had just been installed 'without anyone giving them any idea how to handle it.' The water was at the bottom of the valley and when the fire started 'it just went straight up.' Rebuilding would cost thousands of dollars, but Ed and June added it to their already groaning portfolio of fundraising causes and within four years a new monastery had risen from the ashes.

By July 1989 they were saying their farewells. When the packers descended on the Residence, June watched in dismay as they wrapped all her precious cups and glasses in newspaper and tossed them over their shoulders: 'But nothing was broken. After that it was all put in a big container and two buffaloes came along with a wagon to take it away.' On their return to Auckland, Ed and June moved back into their separate houses. After four

A serene presence who helped Ed Hillary to overcome his depression. June Hillary with her dog 'Dorje', late 1990s. (News Media)

and half years under the same roof, both of them felt rather lonely: 'It was my daughters who suggested that we should get married. "Well Mother, what else would you do?" Ed was delighted to fall in with their plans and on 21 December 1989, June exchanged the designation of 'Official Companion' for the title of Lady Hillary.

A further honour lay in store. In the 1990 birthday honours, June was awarded the Queen's Service Medal in recognition of her efforts in refurbishing the Residence. Her reactions were suitably modest: 'When I was given the QSM, I thought that I must be the only person in the world who has been awarded a medal for just enjoying myself.' But it raised a few eyebrows in the Ministry and shortly afterwards a letter appeared in the *Evening Post*:

> *Sir, I am a diplomatic spouse. For several years, along with many, many other spouses I have given up career opportunities and family links, have packed up possessions, torn children from schools and friends, and left homes to the tender mercies of the uncertain to follow a diplomatic officer to a post. Dozens of women to my knowledge have helped to set*

up posts – have taken on much of the establishment and outfitting of new buildings, homes and offices.

They have done it in unknown territory where New Zealand has never been represented before and they have done it efficiently and effectively. How many of them have ever been recognised, much less rewarded?

I do not for one moment begrudge Lady Hillary her recently awarded QSM; I know from experience how well she deserves it and I am deeply pleased that a spouse's vital role has been valued as an asset at long last.

But I fail to see how Lady Hillary is in any way different from the unnamed others who have done no less.[7]

The writer was Gillian Green, who was a leading member of the Spouses' Group, and on the basis of the citation for June's award, her comments are more than justified. Many of us have refurbished several Residences – not to mention staff houses and offices. But the real reason for June's award had very little to do with choosing curtains or re-covering the chairs. It was to thank her for looking after Ed.

CHAPTER 16

The Reluctant Diplomat

Jill's admiration for the Red Cross dates from the late 1960s when, spurred on by the media coverage of the war in Biafra, she made her first application to work for them. As a student nurse, she was turned down, but the desire to be part of one of the great humanitarian organisations of the world never left her. 'I've always had a sense of wanting to contribute something to the community,' she told me, 'and I've always been a bit independent … determined to be able to cope on my own and to create my own life.'[1] For her, the prospect of being a junior diplomatic wife at a large post held few attractions and when her husband, Tim Caughley, was posted as First Secretary to the New Zealand High Commission in Malaysia, she leapt at the opportunity to work at a Red Cross hospital on the war-torn borders of neighbouring Thailand.

The long-running crisis on the Thai-Cambodian border had its origins in the unspeakable horrors perpetrated by Pol Pot and the Khmer Rouge. But it was the Vietnamese invasion of 1978 that prompted tens of thousands of Cambodians to flee across the border into Thailand. Many arrived in the last stages of starvation and, as the stream of refugees grew to a torrent, a mass of makeshift camps sprang up around the Thai border town of Aranyaprathet, where the fugitives died in droves, of dysentery, malaria and misery.

By the time Jill arrived to work at the purpose-built camp at Khao-i-Dang in 1985, conditions had improved enormously. The camps had been standardised, with proper sewage and water, and dozens of international relief agencies had set up hospitals and schools. But the situation was far from stable. As well as sheltering thousands of refugees, the Thais had become reluctant hosts to large numbers of Khmer Rouge fighters and other resistance groups, who were still engaged in violent clashes with the Vietnamese within a few kilometres of the camps.

Overjoyed to be nursing for the Red Cross, Jill never gave a thought to her own safety: 'When I got to Khao-i-Dang, I didn't sleep for a month. I was absolutely blown away by excitement. This was what I'd wanted to do for a long time ... It was the best kind of nursing that I have ever done and the most rewarding.' Working in a surgical hospital, where most of the patients were war wounded, was a new experience for Jill: 'When I arrived, I was really quite worried that my practical skills were a bit rusty ... In New Zealand I'd been working as a tutor ... and many of my colleagues had worked in intensive care or in A & E.' But an upsurge in the fighting on the border soon brought her up to speed:

> You could hear the battles in the distance and you could even see the sky lighting up ... When that was going on I knew that we probably had a few hours to get ready before we had to absorb the war wounded. We would receive radio information about their impending arrival as they passed through the checkpoints on the border ... Sometimes when the fighting became very loud, I did worry a bit. We would hear explosions, shooting and landmines going off and then receive the consequences ...

> There were some pretty gruesome injuries – you'd see someone coming in with both legs blown off ... But things were dealt with so well and so rapidly – and it helped being able to patch up people whom you would have thought had no chance of survival.

Jill's photographs bear witness to the severity of the injuries: a heavily bandaged land mine victim lying on a blood-splattered stretcher; a pair of men duelling with their amputated stumps, and a boy with a two-inch bullet in his head which had miraculously failed to kill him. One photograph shows Jill attending to a wounded man. Lean and tanned, in her regulation blue trousers and white T-shirt, she is absorbed in her task and quite unaware of the presence of the camera. In the background, the flimsy structure of the Hospital is all too apparent:

> It was really just a bamboo construction on a concrete base ... The hospital kitchen, which we used to refer to as the 'bunker' ... had a large table in it and was surrounded by walls about waist high. We were told to go there in the unlikely event of rocket fire landing on the hospital.

The nearby fighting was not the only threat. Within the camp, smuggling and theft were rife and, despite the throng of foreign aid workers, it was

Jill Caughley in action with the war wounded at Khao-i-Dang. Thailand 1985.
(By kind permission of Jill Caughley)

not immune to violence. Jill can recall 'a few hand grenades being thrown around' and several people being injured. At the height of the influx from Cambodia, Khao-i-Dang had a population of 160,000. Later the numbers were greatly reduced, but as the only camp from which refugees could be resettled to a third country, many were desperate to gain access to it. 'The camp was guarded by Thai soldiers,' Jill told me, 'we had to have passes to enter and leave, and it was fenced with barbed wire like a prison.'

Like most of the aid workers, Jill and her colleagues lived in nearby Aranyaprathet: 'I shared a bungalow with three others … and we were bussed into Khao-i-Dang every day.' Except when she was on night duty, she worked from eight to four: 'After that we'd come home and have a shower and then we could go out for a meal.' Thanks to the international aid agencies, 'Aran' had a booming nightlife. In his book *The Quality of Mercy*, William Shawcross refers to 'a M*A*S*H-type atmosphere' with doctors and nurses strolling into restaurants 'in full medical regalia, even though the hospitals in which they worked were over twenty miles away.'[2] No doubt professional vanity played a role. Saving lives is a heady business and according to Shawcross thousands of lives were saved at Khao-i-Dang. Jill certainly felt the adrenalin buzz of being at the cutting edge of international relief work, but she also experienced the downsides:

Once a week we'd go on night duty for twelve hours and there'd be just the theatre team, the surgeon, the anaesthetist and the theatre nurse with one ward nurse. It could be quite a hell of a night sometimes, especially if there'd been some fighting …

In intensive care, where we would care for our sickest patients, there was no extra technology, just a few more eyes to watch over them. Our hospital had the basics: a small blood bank, laboratory, and an X-ray machine. Then there was the operating theatre and two other wards. We kept everything locked … to prevent pilfering, whether by the staff or the patients … Everything had a value in the camp.

One of Jill's most unpleasant experiences happened during night duty when she and the three-person theatre team were the only expatriate staff in the hospital:

I was out in the ward where people were crying out in pain for medication. As I was unlocking the dispensary, a guy – an amputee – had crawled out of his bed and came in behind me and hit me with his crutches on the back of the knee. He was angry because I hadn't given him any pain relief. It was actually quite frightening … I suppose I could have been whacked on the head … I remember waking up my colleagues … They did a double shift and if they weren't operating, they were sleeping … They wouldn't have heard anything.

In accordance with its founding charter, the Red Cross accepted everyone and many of Jill's patients would have been Khmer Rouge.

At the end of her six-month assignment, Jill returned to Kuala Lumpur. But in diplomatic circles she felt like a misfit; few of the other wives understood what she had been doing and she found her experiences hard to talk about. Khao-i-Dang was constantly in her thoughts and within a few months she was back there. On her second tour of duty, she felt far more confident. During her earlier mission, she had learnt a lot from her colleagues, especially from the Head Nurse, fellow New Zealander Philippa Parker, whom she describes as 'an amazing woman … a straight talker, no nonsense and incredibly dedicated.'

When the fighting tailed off at the onset of the rainy season, Jill set up a teaching programme. 'I was keen to see that the Khmers* had an opportunity to learn a bit about nursing,' she told me. The hospital employed quite a number of refugees, mostly as porters or nurse helpers, but anyone with medical qualifications was also eagerly recruited. One of these was a

---

*   Cambodians

Cambodian doctor named Haing S. Ngor, who worked in the hospital in 1979 and later won an Academy Award for his performance in *The Killing Fields*. The last scene of the film was shot at the Red Cross hospital in Khao-i-Dang and, during Jill's second mission there in 1986, the Wellington Red Cross invited her mother to the New Zealand premiere so that she could see where her daughter was working.

Early in 1987, only a few months after she and Tim had returned to Wellington, Jill accepted another six-month mission with the Red Cross. Well aware of how much his diplomatic postings had cut across her career, Tim was always 'very understanding and supportive'. Moreover, during her time in Thailand, he had been able to visit her regularly. 'He came for my days off,' said Jill, 'so that he could see the situation for himself and meet my colleagues.' But her next assignment was to a hospital on one of the world's most lawless frontiers, where it would be far less easy to visit.

Jill's new charges were the Mujahideen, the so-called freedom fighters of Afghanistan, who for the past eight years had been resisting the Soviet invasion of their country. Like the Cambodians, they were the victims of a global power struggle which, in the case of Afghanistan, had pitched the US-supported Mujahideen against the might of the USSR. In addition to the Americans, the Mujahideen had other supporters, especially in the Arab world. Among them was an austere Saudi businessman named Osama bin Laden, who was channelling billions of dollars to the resistance and had just set up an innocent-sounding organisation called 'The Base' for which the Arabic is 'Al Qaeda'.

Despite the heavy casualties on both sides, the Soviet-backed government had debarred the Red Cross from operating inside Afghanistan. Instead, the Pakistani Red Crescent Society* had been obliged to set up a string of first-aid posts along the border, while the International Red Cross opened a 100-bed surgical hospital forty kilometres away in Peshawar.† But, as the New Zealand surgical team in Vietnam had also discovered, Jill soon found out that distance was no deterrent to the wounded:

> *They all seemed to know about us and they came from the depths of Afghanistan by any form of transport they could find. Those who could walk came on foot; others came by mule or were carried by friends and family. They even came in wheelbarrows. I learnt to listen for the crunch of the gravel outside the front entrance, which invariably*

---

* Red Crescent is the name used by the Red Cross in Islamic counties.
† A second hospital was established in Quetta.

heralded the arrival of a patient ... Often just a heap of clothing in a cart ... After days – even weeks – on the road, their wounds would be already festering and sometimes they would be beyond help.

The hospital was located in an old post office building, whose brick walls and lofty portico looked reassuringly solid after the bamboo structures of Khao-i-Dang. But as the incoming Head Nurse, Jill had little time to savour her new environment. Even before she and her predecessor had completed their handover, Soviet planes had carried out a savage bombing raid on the refugee camps just over the Pakistani border. Seventy to eighty casualties arrived on the first night and by the following day a tent had been erected in the garden to house the overflow:

The medical staff were working flat out for several days and all leave was cancelled. We also had a visit from the Prime Minister of Pakistan, Muhammed Khan Junejo, who came to see the wounded and thank us for our efforts ... I remember doing a quick clean up to give some semblance of order after the chaos.

In the middle of all this, Jill received a message that the New Zealand Ambassador to Iran (who was also accredited to Pakistan) was turning up with his wife to pay a call. Understandably, her memory of our visit is hazy, but I will never forget it. Clad in her Head Nurse's white coat, Jill met us at the front entrance. 'I expect you'd like to see the women's room,' she said. The small ward for women and children was crammed to bursting point, with a coffin lying in a corner. Jill caught my glance. 'We lost that patient this morning,' she said. We moved on to the operating theatre, which was a large room divided by a sheet, where the two theatre teams could operate simultaneously. One of the teams was in action and as I peered through the door, I saw a yellow, gangrenous arm being lifted away from a male torso. Jill closed the door briskly and hurried us on to see the men.

The men's wards were full of bearded fighters attended by male relatives. Later I asked Jill how the men reacted to her:

Because I was a foreigner, I think they regarded me as an honorary male. I also think that our caring role was respected ... As Head Nurse, I was often on call in the evenings, or sometimes I would just want to check on a particular patient whom I wasn't too happy about. I suppose it was my nurse's instinct ...

It became my favourite time because I'd find all the men talking in their wards or sitting in the garden telling tales of bravery ... I remember

Jill Caughley as Head Nurse at the Red Cross Hospital in Peshawar, 1987. (By kind permission of Jill Caughley)

Below: Despite the language barrier, communication was never a problem: Jill Caughley with some of her Afghan patients, Peshawar 1987. (By kind permission of Jill Caughley)

looking down from the balcony and seeing the patients and their relatives praying on the concrete slab in front of the hospital, with their shawls spread out as prayer mats and the Red Cross flag* flying behind them. It never failed to move me.

Professionally she was far less hands-on than in Khao-i-Dang:

My role was more supervisory and involved lots of liaison … We did medical rounds every day in the intensive care area … but the medical plan and the nursing care were carried out by the very capable Pakistani and Afghan nurses.

One of her most challenging tasks was explaining to relatives that they needed to donate blood: 'Patients in other hospitals tended to buy blood in the bazaar – terrifyingly unsafe … and if the blood hadn't been used, they would ask for it back!' Obtaining consent for surgery, especially for an amputation, could also often take days of discussion: 'We weren't always successful, but we had to respect their wishes.' She also spent much of her time remonstrating with the hordes of visitors – 'almost always male and Afghan fighters' – in an attempt to keep down the numbers.

A further contrast with her previous job was the sense of isolation. At Khao-i-Dang, all the humanitarian agencies had been grouped together in the camp, but in Peshawar the international community was spread across the city: 'What made me nervous was that people carried guns and there was a lot of firing, particularly at nights.' With no street lights, driving back alone to her lodgings could be a nerve-racking experience. On a couple of occasions, the front wheel of her car went into one of the deep gutters beside the street. Some 'good guys' lifted her out. But things could have ended differently. Peshawar was a wild place and unescorted women were fair game. There were also times when she got indecent phone calls and feared that men were watching her.

After the Soviet withdrawal in 1989, many of the Mujahideen whom Jill and her fellow workers struggled so hard to save joined the ranks of the Taliban, who continue to wreak war and bloodshed on their countrymen. Yet when I asked Jill how she felt about having soothed the brow of the Taliban, her reply could have come straight from the Red Cross Manual: 'It is not for us to pass judgement … Help is given with impartiality and in accordance with need.'

---

* The Red Cross flag was displayed prominently to protect the hospital from attacks by Soviet aircraft.

In reality, Jill's feelings were more complex and after three bloodstained missions, she was nursing some wounds of her own: 'I was angry about what soldiers were doing to each other, and to the innocent civilians who get caught up in it.' On her return to Wellington, as part of the new job that she had just taken with the New Zealand Red Cross, she joined in some army exercises. It proved a healing experience: 'The soldiers would come up and start talking to me, and it was then that I realised that these guys are just as human as humanitarian workers. They care about suffering too and they care about the pain they inflict.' All the same, Peshawar was her last frontline assignment and in 1991, when Tim was appointed as New Zealand's Representative to the Cook Islands,* she went with him.

To this day, Jill stills cringes with embarrassment at the thought of their arrival on the outlying island of Rakahanga, when she, Tim and the Deputy Prime Minister of the Cook Islands were borne aloft, like colonial overlords, on a wooden platform carried by eight strong men. Worse still, by some mischance, their first official visit to Rakahanga – aboard the RNZN frigate *Southland* – had coincided with the arrival of a group of New Zealand journalists. As the Representative to the Cook Islands and his wife rode by in state, seated on a floral sofa, the cameras clicked furiously. The islanders had insisted on carrying them into the village. But no one at home would believe it and, when the photo duly appeared in the *New Zealand Geographic*, the Caughleys were teased mercilessly.

Apart from this unfortunate incident, however, and being banished to sleep in the sick bay on the *Southland* (which had no facilities for women), Jill was finding her first experience of being a Head of Mission's wife surprisingly enjoyable:

> The Cook Islands were a perfect place for us to be initiated and we had the great privilege of integrating into the community, which we mightn't have done anywhere else … We were the only diplomatic representatives … so there was an expectation that we would go to everything. There were always seats for us at the front. On an island like Rarotonga with a population of 9,000, there was no getting away. Everyone knew who you were … It was like living in a goldfish bowl.

Even their high visibility never troubled Jill unduly. She could always retreat to their garden, which was large enough to get lost in, and she was enjoying socialising with the Cook Islanders: 'The usual protocol was that you'd be

---

* During their posting, Tim's title was changed to High Commissioner.

dragged on to the dance floor to make a fool of yourself.' When she and Tim turned up at the local night spot, the whole island heard about it: 'I think Tim was probably the first New Zealand Representative to go to the "Banana Court" ... but it was just part of the Friday night flow of things ... and we'd feel like some dancing.'

Jill was also discovering that diplomatic entertaining could be fun:

> We had a wonderful cook ... I'd brought all my cook books with me and we tried to use things that were grown locally ... So my Greek coconut cake rapidly became a Rarotongan coconut cake – with coconut from the trees in the garden. The lemons came from the garden too ...There was a blackboard in the kitchen where I'd write up the menu with a reference to the page in my cookbook ... We had huge feasts for all sorts of occasions ... We hardly ever used the dining room. When the Cook Islands Cabinet came to dinner, we put tables on the veranda ... You can be informal and still honour the occasion.

With New Zealand only a short flight away, visitors came in droves. But after running a 100-bed hospital, Jill was hardly going to be fazed by a few houseguests and before long she was, once again, looking around for work.

Since leaving Peshawar, her professional interests had shifted. Through her reading of the latest humanitarian literature, she had become persuaded of the vital role of public health education. The front line was no longer only the battlefield, but also in the home, against domestic violence and health disasters like HIV/AIDS, and before her departure to the Cook Islands she had attended the first Red Cross conference in the Pacific on HIV/AIDS. In the ultra-conservative Cook Islands such issues as sexually transmitted diseases, or violence and rape, were barely mentioned – let alone addressed by public health programmes. But the actions of one courageous woman changed everything and enabled Jill, for the first time in her married life, to combine her skills as a health practitioner with a meaningful contribution as a diplomatic wife. In the process, she also gained the distinction of being the only Head of Mission's wife to travel around her husband's jurisdiction brandishing a packet of condoms.

Shortly after Jill's arrival in Rarotonga a female rape victim took the unprecedented step of appearing on Cook Islands television to tell her story. 'It was incredibly brave of her,' said Jill, 'and a group of Cook Islands women said "we've got to do something about this".' The outcome was a nationwide 'Stop Rape and Violence March' and the formation of the Women's Counselling Centre, Te Punanga Tauturu, to combat domestic

Cringing with embarrassment. Jill Caughley being carried ashore at Rakahanga with her husband, Tim Caughley (left) and the Deputy Prime Minister of the Cook Islands (right), 1991. (New Zealand Geographic, no.11, Jul–Sep 1991)

violence. After months of trying to convince people that her search for work was serious, Jill was invited to join the Advisory Committee: 'It wasn't in an honorary role at all. I was very much part of the team and I learnt to do counselling there, which links to my work in war. War is such a violent act and this is all about violence between individuals.'

Far from finding her diplomatic status a disadvantage, Jill discovered that it helped to be an outsider: 'Confidentiality is always a problem in small communities,' she said, 'and people would even turn up at our house needing a bit of support … I was accepted as a helper and a carer.' From then on her life took off:

> *Our house was always full of Cook Islanders. We had various health related activities there, the Food and Nutrition Committee, fundraisers for the Women's Counselling Centre and netball with the Health Department teams. And then of course, spontaneous parties, as well as all the representational functions, most of which ended up dancing on the front lawn.*

A photograph of Jill hosting a group of her fellow health practitioners, decked like goddesses in white dresses and floral wreaths, captures the gaiety of the Cook Islanders and the close friendships that Jill enjoyed with them.

By this time she was also working for the Ministry of Health, where she participated in a couple of workshops to the outer islands. Subjects like HIV/AIDS and unwanted pregnancies had finally come out of the closet and accompanying Jill and her colleagues on the tiny plane to Aitutaki was a wooden box, containing a carved figure known as 'Tangaroa', who was magnificently erect and had been specially made so that Jill could demonstrate the use of a condom. The party included both the Secretary of Health, George Koteka, and Ngapoko Short, then Director of Nursing. But in true Cook Islands style the mood was far from serious:

> As soon as we arrived, we found a box of mangoes specially put aside for us. So we travelled to wherever we were staying in the back of a truck eating mangoes … and if we spotted a tree laden with mangoes …we'd get out and there would be George with a stick, shaking the tree, while Ngapoko and I caught them.

As a fellow nurse, Ngapoko was one of Jill's greatest allies and she later became the first woman to be appointed the Director of Health of the Cook Islands.

In October 1992, when the Pacific Arts Festival was attracting thousands of visitors from the outlying islands and elsewhere to Rarotonga, Jill was closely involved with the health promotion: 'We did quite a lot of sexual health promotion too … We were mainly concerned about unwanted pregnancies … although I think I was a bit naïve not to see these gatherings as a very natural way to mix up the gene pools.' On sparsely populated islands such as Pukapuka, the male interest in new blood is so keen that visiting female aid workers have to barricade themselves into their bedrooms. But inculcated with the principles of the Red Cross, Jill refuses to be judgemental: 'You can't make assumptions about people's sexual activities,' she told me 'and often we, as outsiders, can't even begin to understand the complexity of small communities.'

Inevitably, Jill's beloved Red Cross continued to play an important role in her life. As a lawyer, Tim was able to help the members of the Cook Islands Red Cross Society to draft their constitution, while Jill invited them to hold their First Aid classes on her front lawn. Many years later, when Tim had become New Zealand's Ambassador to the UN in Geneva, the Caughleys gave a party for the President of the Cook Islands Red Cross,

Girls night out. Jill Caughley (2nd from right) entertaining some of her Cook Islands friends at the New Zealand Residence in Rarotonga, c. 1993. (By kind permission of Jill Caughley)

who was attending the International Red Cross Conference. All the other Pacific Island delegates attended, many of whom were old friends of Jill's. It was a nostalgic evening: 'Out came the ukeleles' and they sang all the old songs of lost loves and farewells that had been so much part of their lives in Rarotonga.

For Jill, living in Geneva, the headquarters of the Red Cross and the hub of the humanitarian world, felt like a homecoming. There, too, she found fulfilling work and, a reluctant diplomat no longer, she even joined the Diplomatic Spouses' Group – although she could never quite bring herself to attend their coffee mornings. Looking back over her career, Jill's comment that she 'had to keep re-inventing herself' would strike a chord with many diplomatic wives. But she has no regrets about her diplomatic role: 'It's a privilege to represent one's country … and whenever I've been forced to change tack because of postings, usually something very good has come out of it.' Formal entertaining and diplomatic networking were never high on her agenda, but in her contacts with other nations, her love of humanity has served her just as well.

CHAPTER 17

Couped up in Paradise

Thanks to her meticulous records, Barbara can still recall what she cooked for dinner on 15 April 1987: fillet of beef, lemon chicken, minted peas and mushrooms, green salad and rice, followed by a choice of passionfruit or grapefruit sorbet. It was a buffet for twelve and the guests were a mixture of Fijian civil servants and army officers. Among them was the swashbuckling number three in the Royal Fiji Military Forces, Sitiveni Rabuka, with his wife, Suluweti.

As a second secretary at the New Zealand High Commission in Suva, Barbara's husband Ian Hill was well down in the diplomatic pecking order. But in a small Pacific nation like Fiji, New Zealand was a big player – particularly with the military – and Ian was well plugged in with the senior officers. Barbara had first met 'Steve' and 'Sulu' a year earlier, when they attended a reception hosted by the Hills during the talks for the Military Assistance Programme. The party lasted until well after midnight and throughout the evening a stream of Fijian military took it in turns to rock the Hills' eight-week-old son, Matthew, who was asleep in his pram on the veranda. As one of the pram rockers, Rabuka found a sure way to Barbara's heart by referring to Matthew as her 'little prop forward' and enquiring tenderly after his health whenever they met. Before long he and Sulu had become regular guests. 'Steve was a charming and affable personality,' Barbara told me, and an easy dinner companion.[1]

On the day of their dinner party, Barbara and Ian, together with the rest of the High Commission, were relishing the return to normality. The build-up to the recent general election had been tense and when the long-established Alliance Party was beaten by a newly formed Labour-led coalition, shock waves rocked the country. After seventeen years as Prime Minister, Fiji's grand old man of politics, the aristocratic Ratu Sir Kamisese Mara, had been ousted by a modest Fijian doctor named Timoci Bavadra, who planned to include a large number of Indo-Fijians in his Cabinet. This had provoked an outcry among the indigenous Fijians, who feared that the Indo-Fijians would dominate the government.

But by 15 April the flash point seemed to have passed. Two days earlier, the new Prime Minister had been sworn in without incident and everyone was heaving a sigh of relief: 'The fear of racial violence can be forgotten as election hysterics', observed the *Dominion* in Wellington. 'The Fijians … are known for their patience and respect for others. Their main concern now is how the new government will safeguard their interests.'[2]

'We have revisited that evening a million times', Barbara told me, 'and could recall no indication of events to come despite deliberate probing during the evening trying to elicit our guests' reactions to the recent turn of political events. The evening was relaxed. I can remember we all sat around after dinner … discussing the outcome of the election …The general consensus was that the new government should be given time to prove itself … Conversation was open and free flowing, and I don't remember people being especially guarded in their comments.' Rabuka was sitting with Sulu on a couch opposite her. He had just taken a decision that would alter the course of Fijian history, but his demeanour betrayed nothing.

A few hours earlier Rabuka had attended a secret meeting with three military colleagues in the offices of the Methodist Church of Fiji. As cover, he took his Bible and some financial ledgers from his church with him. Appalled by the result of the election, the four men talked for several hours before concluding that the only solution was to remove Bavadra and his Cabinet with a military strike. As the Staff Officer of Operations and Training, Rabuka was by far the best placed to carry this through; moreover, both he and his companions were convinced that God had chosen him for the task. After praying for the success of their mission, the conspirators parted and, burning with 'a sense of destiny', Rabuka headed out for dinner.[3]

When Ian and Barbara arrived in Fiji in November 1985, it seemed like a tropical paradise. Barbara was seven months pregnant and having just finished a busy job as a lawyer, she was looking forward to relaxing before the birth of her first baby. They moved into one of the High Commission houses, in a lush green suburb with a garden so full of orchids that local taxi drivers added it to their 'tourist route' for passengers from visiting cruise ships. They also inherited an experienced 'house girl', who had worked for successive staff at the High Commission and took care of the housekeeping. Barbara still did most of the cooking for dinners and receptions, but after her hectic professional life in Wellington she was enjoying the casual 'island style' of entertaining. At weekends they escaped to the beaches, where Barbara found 'the balmy weather, golden sand and clear, warm water were just as wonderful as the tourist posters had promised.' The contrast with their earlier posting to the Soviet Union could hardly have been greater.

Almost a month to the day after their evening with Rabuka, the Hills were once again hosting a buffet dinner. This time Barbara was serving parmesan chicken with basil sauce, Sicilian pasta and fillet of beef, accompanied by a green salad and a vegetable risotto, and followed by a passionfruit pie. The Fijians appreciate a good meal and, when the telephone rang, she was preparing a mountain of food. It was May Kung, the locally engaged Public Affairs Officer at the High Commission. As May gabbled incomprehensibly down the phone, Barbara thought she must be joking. 'There's been a *what*?' she asked, itching to get back to the kitchen. 'There's been a COOP – a MILITARY COOP', shouted May, her local intonation accentuated by her anxiety. Barbara's immediate concern was to help her to contact Ian, who was tied up in a meeting. The full realisation of what had happened only sank in later.

Shortly before 10 a.m. on Thursday 14 May, Rabuka was seen entering the chamber of the Fijian Parliament. As he took his place in the public gallery, the new Speaker (who was also his uncle) noticed that he was wearing civilian dress, instead of his usual uniform. 'Putting on the drag' was how Rabuka described it. He was unarmed, but the members of the ten-man hit squad who had been training for the past month were carrying loaded 9-mm pistols. The larger back-up team was in full combat gear with M16 assault rifles. 'If we had to shoot to kill, we would have,' Rabuka claimed afterwards.[4]

Minutes later the hit-squad burst into the chamber. Their faces were concealed by gas marks and they were led by an officer wearing a black balaclava. Rabuka had learnt much of his trade carrying out peacekeeping duties in Lebanon and the Sinai, and the whole operation bore more than a passing likeness to a Middle Eastern terrorist attack. Like Rabuka, the members of the hit squad were wearing civilian dress, under which they had concealed their weapons as they entered the Parliament Building.

Sitting in stunned silence, the house watched as Rabuka strode down from the gallery and took up a commanding position beside the Speaker's

Barbara Hill with Matthew on the balcony of their house in Suva, Fiji 1986.

(By kind permission of Ian and Barbara Hill)

Rabuka always enquired tenderly after Barbara's 'little prop forward'. Matthew aged about 18 months, Fiji 1987. *(By kind permission of Ian and Barbara Hill)*

chair. 'Mr Prime Minister,' he said, indicating the exit, 'please lead your team down to the right.' Lining the walls of the corridor, the heavily armed back-up team was already in place: 'Mr Prime Minister, Sir, will you lead the team *now*.'[5] Rabuka's tone precluded any discussion and the Coalition members filed out of the chamber like lambs. Outside, they were herded onto trucks and taken to the nearby barracks, where they were locked in the guard room.

The execution of the coup had been faultless. Not a shot had been fired and the government had been removed from power in less than ten minutes.

Back in her leafy suburb, Barbara was feeling almost as stunned as the members of Parliament. Rumours were flying and no one knew what was happening. Fiji had no local television and the military had seized control of all the major communications outlets, including the radio stations. By mid-afternoon, the Fiji Broadcasting Commission was issuing a nationwide call-up and armed patrols had been activated all over Suva. Barbara does not remember feeling frightened: 'But it was a time of uncertainty and tension … and the possibility of violence was always present.' Her most pressing problem was what to do about all the food; while Ian was cancelling the dinner party, she and her elderly neighbour tried to save as much of it as possible. Two of the guests still turned up but Barbara, who was under strict instructions not to allow anyone into the house, could only call down to them from the upstairs veranda.

Downtown at the High Commission, the New Zealand staff were already heavily involved. Shortly after the coup the High Commissioner, Rod Gates, had received a call from a staffer at the Prime Minister's office seeking protection for Bavadra's special adviser, William Sutherland, who was a New Zealander. Rabuka was hunting him down and the building was swarming with military. 'I wanted to lock him up because my information said he was responsible for a lot of the Coalition's policy-making,' Rabuka said later.[6] 'I couldn't really say no,' Gates told me, 'and as it was daytime, I said "bring him round to the office". Someone sneaked him in … Then Sutherland said "can you find my family" … So we had him and his family in the library.'[7] When the military eventually tracked Sutherland down, they tried to gain access to the High Commission where Ian (who knew many of them personally) had the unenviable task of dissuading them from entering.

For the wives and families of the abducted members of Parliament, it was a terrifying day. 'You just can't imagine what we went through,' recalls Bavadra's wife, Adi Kuini Vuikaba, who had no idea where her husband had been taken. 'I got the children together … I thought the safest thing was not to leave the house.'[8] The Prime Minister's Residence was only 'two doors away as the crow flies' from the Hills and when Barbara awoke the next morning, she found that the action had moved to her doorstep. During the night, the prisoners had been transferred to the Prime Ministerial Residence, which was now encircled by barbed wire and under mass military surveillance.

Outside the gates the vociferous group of Coalition supporters, which eventually swelled to over a thousand, was clearly visible from the Hills' house: 'From our veranda the chanting crowd was a constant reminder of the swirling unrest. The crowd was essentially benevolent, but the fear of a crowd suddenly turning was always at the back of my mind and our garden could soon have become a pathway for escaping protesters.' The following afternoon, the military tried to disperse the supporters by lining up trucks and army vehicles in front of them and forcing them to retreat. Singing the national anthem, 'Blessings Grant O God of Nations', the crowd backed off with guns in their backs. But suspecting that the captives might be removed by stealth, they kept an all-night vigil further down the road.

Trapped at home with a toddler, Barbara felt a growing sense of isolation. 'There was no information about what was happening just streets away … The tension of not knowing was a constant stress.' Many of her immediate neighbours had already left. Two days after the coup, a rumour went round the town that the High Commission staff had been taken into custody and well-meaning Fijian friends rushed round to check on Matthew and Barbara: 'I had felt fine until then, but now I had an anxious wait until Ian got in contact with me.' All telecommunications were in the hands of the military and to add to Barbara's isolation, the local phone lines were barely functioning. Scattered across the city, the other High Commission wives were feeling equally cut off and later they were supplied with two-way radios on which they could contact the office.

Although all the families at the High Commission had been given the option of going home, for Barbara it was not an easy decision: 'The question of evacuation to New Zealand was fraught … and there was always the question of who would decide when it was safe to return.' Her father was pressing her to come home with Matthew, but at that stage she did not feel any 'immediate personal threat' and she opted to stay with Ian.

By Sunday, events at the Prime Ministerial Residence had taken an ugly turn. Rabuka wanted to split up the prisoners along racial lines, but this time his plans did not go quite so smoothly. A struggle ensued and a special squad was called in. Adi Kuini describes the scene: 'We lay on the floor, arms linked together in resistance. They dragged away the Indians and people were falling on the roadside and thrown into trucks … They had about five vans with armed guards on them.'[9] As the Indians were driven off, their Fijian colleagues fell on their knees and prayed. Outside many of their supporters believed that they were going to be shot.

At the High Commission, relations with the new regime had also taken a turn for the worse. Infuriated by Prime Minister David Lange's thunderous condemnations of the coup, Rabuka had reacted furiously to the arrival of the New Zealand frigate, *Wellington*, which was on a routine visit. 'The Fijians told us that it was an affront to have this warship down in the harbour,' Gates told me, 'and they set up a blockade of the ship'. But as a matter of principle Gates saw no reason why he and his wife, Pat, should not accept the Captain's invitation to lunch. The Hills were invited, too, and Barbara remembers a few tense moments at the checkpoint when the military discovered a sealed box in the boot. It contained all the Gates' family photo albums, which Pat was giving to the Captain for safekeeping.

On 20 May, the hijacking of an Air New Zealand 747 during a refuelling stop at Fiji's Nadi Airport raised the ante still further. At a hastily called press conference, Lange announced that SAS troops and police had been put on full alert and told reporters that if military intervention in Fiji became necessary, he had no intention of seeking 'permission'[10] from Rabuka. The hijacker was an airport employee, who had come aboard with half a dozen sticks of dynamite attached to six-second fuses. He was an Indo-Fijian and he was demanding to be flown to Libya. But his real objective was to force New Zealand to step in militarily to restore Bavadra to power.

The passengers were already re-boarding, but an alert crew member managed to disembark them, leaving only the three remaining flight crew on board. Throughout the negotiations, the hijacker held a stick of dynamite in his hand with a burning cigarette next to the fuse. At times his hands were trembling so violently that he came close to blowing the plane up by mistake, the Captain reported later. After six hours, the drama ended on a note of slapstick worthy of Charlie Chaplin. The hijacker was felled with a bottle of whisky which the Flight Engineer had purchased earlier in the duty free shop at Nadi.

Back in Suva, Rabuka was also having a bad day. (In his own account of the coup, the Air New Zealand hijacking is not even mentioned.) Having sworn in Rabuka as Prime Minister, the Governor General, Ratu Sir Penaia Ganilau, seemed to be having second thoughts and had declined to swear in his Council of Ministers. In the ensuing atmosphere of uncertainty, a mob of Fijian males went on the rampage, kicking and punching Indo-Fijians and smashing car windscreens and shop fronts. In Suva's Albert Park, they attacked a large group of Indo-Fijians who were holding a prayer meeting, before looting their way back downtown.

Holed up in Suva's Travelodge Hotel, visiting New Zealand journalists were badly shaken and on the morning of 21 May, the front pages of the New Zealand papers were plastered with headlines claiming that Fiji was on the brink of racial war. More rioting broke out the following day, which was witnessed by the Co-ordinator for Domestic and External Security, Gerald Hensley, whom Lange had despatched to Fiji. In his memoir, Hensley describes it as a day of 'random racial violence' during which 'mobs armed with clubs and bush knives' roamed through the city, smashing the windows of parked cars as they went. As Hensley hurried from the High Commission to move his car, he observed an extraordinary stand-off:

> *A file of armed soldiers moved out from the central police headquarters opposite me and across the road. They dropped on to one knee and levelled their weapons directly at the crowd. There was a tense silence in which the only sound was the click of the safety catches being removed … then the crowd silently dissolved, flooding on to the footpaths and back up the hill.*[11]

From her half-empty suburb, Barbara did her best to ignore the wild rumours of massacres and shootings, but the lurking fear of a backlash against foreigners was ever present. The house had a guard on the gate, who was supplied by a local security firm. But he inspired about as much confidence as the little card citing the relevant clause of the Vienna Convention that the wives had been given by the High Commission to read to any military who tried to enter their houses. Barbara's survival technique was to keep busy. While Ian worked long hours at the office, she spent her days making clothes for a long-awaited European trip that was looking less and less likely to happen.

Within forty-eight hours, Rabuka had persuaded Ganilau to endorse the coup. To affirm his Prime Ministership, he appeared on the balcony of the Civic Centre, 'stylishly attired in a powder blue *sulu* and flashing a wide smile', to an ecstatic crowd of 5000. According to an eye-witness account, 'the biggest roar of approval … came when he strode out right on cue as the army band played and sang "I Did It My Way".[12]

While Rabuka was consolidating his position, the members of the Coalition government were pinning their last hopes on New Zealand. Their six days in captivity had ended after a night of terror for Adi Kuini: 'Six armed soldiers with masks stormed in. They told us to move into one room … "You have to stay right there" they said, guns pointing at us all the time … Doc and I thought we were going to lose our lives … I lay with my eyes open all night, expecting to die at any moment.'[13] Instead they were all released the following evening, when the Bavadras went straight into hiding. Two days later they and their press officer, Richard Naidu, fled to the New Zealand Residence, which was being guarded by a detachment of sailors from the *Wellington*.

Encouraged by Lange's trumpetings to the press, Bavadra had sent him a message requesting New Zealand military support to restore him as Prime Minister. But it was a forlorn hope and, by the time Bavadra took refuge at the Residence, his main focus was on a risky scheme to escape by sea to his powerbase on the western side of the island. Gates and his staff also had some pretty adventurous evacuation schemes. By now, roadblocks were controlling the access to both of Fiji's airports, but from the Residence (with its kiwi-shaped pool) it was possible to reach the beach, from which staff and other New Zealanders could be ferried out to the *Wellington*. Hensley had already briefed the New Zealand journalists on how to get to the ship and in an emergency the *Wellington*'s tiny Wasp helicopter could also have been pressed into service. Disappointingly, none of these measures proved necessary. Sutherland and his family were smuggled to the airport in the back of Hensley's car and, as Suva reverted to an uneasy calm, the Bavadras were able to reach their stronghold by more conventional means.

But getting out of the country was still far from straightforward. Fijian citizens had to seek official approval to leave and when Ian finally received clearance from Wellington for his mid-tour leave, he and Barbara were dismayed to discover that under Fijian law their son Matthew, who was born in Suva, was regarded as a Fijian citizen. Elaborate documentation had to be prepared before he was permitted to accompany them which, combined with a harassing search of their luggage, turned their departure into an ordeal. It was not until they finally arrived in the charming Cotswold village of Great Tew, where people were oblivious to the troubles in Fiji, that Barbara felt the tensions of the past months ebbing away.

The country to which she returned six weeks later was very different from the tropical paradise of her first arrival. Although the beaches were still idyllic and the sea was as warm as ever, the political situation was volatile. Racial violence had become an almost daily occurrence and thousands of Indo-Fijians were leaving. Amidst travel advisories to avoid Fiji, tourism was hard hit. One of the few upsides, Barbara discovered, was that the local resorts became 'unbelievably cheap.' Similarly, as dozens of Indo-Fijian shopkeepers tried to sell their stock before they left, goods were often heavily discounted. On the other hand, the supply of imported items dwindled and Barbara often struggled to find quite basic cooking ingredients.

On 23 September, after weeks of disorder orchestrated by the nationalist Taukei Movement (including a spate of *lovo* fires with strong overtones of cannibalism), Ratu Mara, Ganilau and Bavadra finally signed a power-sharing agreement, which would have returned Fiji to democracy. The local press was ecstatic. 'Fiji is now set to walk out of the darkness and find its place in the sun again', warbled the *Fiji Times*, 'now let us walk together towards the dawn.'[14] But by now Rabuka was firmly in the Taukei camp and two days later he staged a second coup which was, if anything, even slicker than his first. During the afternoon of 25 September, the troops moved in. The newspapers were closed down; communications were seized and by 5.00 p.m. Rabuka was able to announce that he had taken control of the country. This time the gloves were well and truly off. A group of sixty soldiers ransacked Bavadra's home in Suva and he and his colleagues were thrown into Naboro Prison. Many others were arrested and gaoled. Three days later, Rabuka suspended the Constitution and on 7 October he proclaimed Fiji a republic – with himself as Head of State.

After the second coup, the atmosphere in Suva became far more menacing. For Barbara, the empty houses in her neighbourhood were a constant reminder of her isolation: 'We had security guards coming around the houses on nightly patrols and in each High Commission house a secure room was created, where families could shelter if there was a threat of a house invasion.' The Hills already had iron grilles across the windows to prevent burglaries, but now a heavy metal door with a lock was installed to the master bedroom.

Armed road blocks appeared all over the city at which Barbara was regularly questioned, although the mood was lightened by Matthew who once again made a hit with the military. 'These soldiers are my friends,' he announced, and (referring to the news clips of Lebanon that he had seen during their mid-tour leave) 'not like those nasty soldiers on Grandma's TV in New Zealand.' In happier days, many of the military had been friends and Barbara always found them courteous. Nevertheless, New Zealand's former easygoing relationship with Fiji had changed drastically for the worse and diplomatic entertaining was fraught with tensions. In a society that had become bitterly divided, the Hills had to be particularly sensitive to the combination of guests. Even so, their Fijian contacts often huddled in groups, talking in Fijian, whereas formerly they had always spoken in

Even after the second coup, paradise was not completely lost. Ian and Barbara Hill on the beach with their two children, Fiji 1988. (By kind permission of Ian and Barbara Hill)

English. 'Our role was to observe not participate,' Barbara recalls, 'and learn not to voice opinions about events or actions'.

Suva's once-smiling streets were now full of no-go areas. On one occasion, when she ignored Ian's warnings, Barbara found herself in trouble: 'Once I'd entered the street, I could sense the tension'. It was an Indo-Fijian area and the shopkeepers were all standing in their doorways in anticipation of imminent looting. 'As I was again pregnant, my solution was to stick out my stomach out and walk unhurriedly to safety on the assumption that they wouldn't assault a pregnant woman.' Fortunately for Barbara, 'it worked'.

In late November, the drama moved from the streets of Suva to her own body. At seven months pregnant, she went into premature labour. Hospital facilities in Suva had always been marginal, but since the coup hundreds of doctors and nurses had left and the baby's chances of survival were minimal. Medical evacuation to New Zealand seemed the only option and for a tense few days a request for a RNZAF plane with an obstetrics team sat on Lange's desk in Wellington. In the end it never needed to be actioned. The labour was halted and Barbara and Matthew were able to take a commercial flight back to Auckland, with a midwife in attendance. Six weeks later her daughter, Emma, was born safely in New Zealand.

After the birth (which Ian, of course, missed), Barbara returned with her two small children for a further nine months in Fiji. Unlike many wives of the previous generation, she had excellent professional qualifications and she could easily have found work in New Zealand. But it never occurred to her not to rejoin Ian. 'We certainly felt that we should stay together as a family unit,' she told me, and moreover she was quite as committed to their diplomatic partnership as he was. Nor was paradise completely lost. Despite the trials of living in post-coup Fiji, Barbara still succumbed to the timeless charm of the Pacific. 'The Pacific Island life had got under our skin,' she told me, and ten years later she and Ian returned to the South Seas to take up a rather more peaceful posting in Tonga.

CHAPTER 18

Stand by your Woman

Today the Ministry's travel advisory for Iraq reads as follows:

> There is **extreme risk** to your security in Iraq and we advise against all travel. Terrorism, kidnapping and the hostile security situation present a significant risk to New Zealanders. Any New Zealanders currently in Iraq with concerns for their safety are advised to depart.

For those who choose to ignore this advice, the Ministry recommends that 'appropriate personal security protection measures are in place at all times' and cites a chilling number of 'lethal attacks' and hostage-takings. The advisory also points out that New Zealanders are on their own: 'As there is no New Zealand diplomatic presence in Iraq, the ability of the government to assist New Zealand citizens who get into trouble is severely limited'.[1]

But when Michele Wood was posted to Baghdad in 1989, things were very different. Iraq was still regarded as a state with which Westerners could do business and New Zealand had a well-established Embassy there. Despite high hopes, however, the trade side had never taken off and by the time Michele arrived with her husband, Geoff, the diplomatic staff of the Embassy had been reduced to two, consisting of herself as Vice Consul and the Ambassador, John Clarke.

Five years earlier Geoff and Michele had met in Wellington, through the Tramping and Mountaineering Club:

> There was a party and I can remember it as clear as a bell, standing at one end of the room with about thirty people in it … The door opened and a friend of mine came in and then Michele came in … She had just come back from Italy … and something about her stood out for me.[2]

At the time, Geoff was working as a communications technician, but in 1986 he took leave from his job to accompany Michele on a posting to Mexico. In the 1980s, 'trailing husbands' were still something of a rarity who, unlike the wives, had no readymade support group. But Geoff soon found his way into the congenial, expatriate world that revolved around the British Embassy's social club. This produced some useful job offers and before long his technical skills were in regular demand at the Canadian and Australian Embassies. 'I called myself "Diplotronics", he told me, 'and I even had my own letterhead.' In between jobs, he busied himself with the household cooking and escorting their many visitors.

When the cross-posting to Baghdad was offered, he and Michele leapt at it. They were adventurous spirits and the prospect of living in 'a slightly exotic place, not just your average Western city' appealed to them. 'It was too good to refuse,' said Geoff. They had no idea what to expect and on arrival Geoff was a little disappointed to discover that the romantic desert of his dreams looked more like a scrubby wasteland. On the other hand, he was pleasantly surprised by the quality of the infrastructure. In fact, he reckoned that the road to Basra was 'quite a lot more significant' than New Zealand's State Highway 1.

Once they had moved into the little bungalow which they had inherited from Michele's predecessor, Geoff got to grips with the housekeeping. The food shopping was fairly basic, but having spent six months 'on the ice' with the DSIR* in Antarctica, he was hardly going to be troubled by an absence of supermarkets. In any case, every few months he and Michele would drive to neighbouring Kuwait with their chilly bins and shop to their hearts' content: 'We could bring back anything we wanted except bacon and pork – and we could get those in Baghdad.'

In practical terms, however, daily life proved quite a lot more difficult than in Mexico. Iraq's eight-year war with Iran had only just ended and many things were still in short supply. Technical jobs at other embassies were also harder to find. Thanks to the activities of Saddam Hussein's infamous *Mukhabarat*,† bugging and phone tapping were rife and most Western diplomatic missions had sophisticated communications systems with their own in-house maintenance arrangements. On the other hand, for the short-

---

*   Department of Scientific and Industrial Research, now part of the Crown Research
      Institutes.
†   The Iraqi Intelligence Service.

Geoff Wood in Baghdad, 1989.

(By kind permission of Geoff Wood)

The New Zealand Embassy Landcruiser in Kuwait loaded with supplies for Baghdad. Geoff Wood is at the wheel, 1989. *(By kind permission of Geoff Wood)*

staffed New Zealand Ambassador the presence of a loyal Kiwi, who was also a skilled technician, was later to prove a godsend.

Both Michele and Geoff were well aware of the regime's darker side. Despite its fine roads and Westernised educational system, Saddam's Iraq was a sinister place. Through its vast network of 'bureaus' and agents, the *Mukhabarat* had infiltrated every aspect of daily life and anyone who was unwise enough to criticise the government was brutally silenced. Torture and execution were commonplace. Internal opposition was equally ruthlessly suppressed, culminating in a genocidal chemical attack on the Kurds in 1988 under the direction of Saddam's first cousin, Ali Hassan Al-Majid, better known as 'Chemical Ali'.

As he came to know the Iraqis better, Geoff could not help admiring their fortitude: 'They had no control over their lives, but they were used to resigning themselves to whatever was going to happen … and most of them were very philosophical.' Many spoke excellent English and through their Embassy contacts, Geoff and Michele made quite a number of Iraqi friends: 'On a day to day basis, they were pretty pragmatic. They knew what they could and couldn't say.' Nevertheless, with the ever-present *Mukhabarat*, conversations were always cautious: 'Of course one avoided saying things that were contentious and might get them into trouble.' As a consular and administrative officer, with no direct involvement in political issues, Michele would not have been a prime target for the Intelligence Services. Nor did the machinations of Saddam have much bearing on her day-to-day work. But overnight the situation changed dramatically and on the morning of 2 August 1990, she and Geoff awoke to find themselves on the front line of an international hostage crisis, whose outcome depended on Saddam's every whim.

At around 4.00 a.m. on 2 August, Flight BA 149 landed at Kuwait International Airport. On board were five New Zealanders, two of whom, Henry and Daphne Halkyard, were travelling on their British passports. The plane was en route for Kuala Lumpur and, anticipating a brief refuelling stop, the Halkyards decided to remain on board. But as they were waiting for the other passengers to re-embark, the airport came under fire. In her book, *Unscheduled Stopover in Iraq*, Daphne describes what followed:

> *We hear a series of loud explosions and, moments later, engines and air conditioning are switched off. Immediately, there is an order from the captain. All passengers must leave the plane at once … There is loud gunfire and the stewardesses hustle us urgently to the exits … There are*

many armed soldiers present, whom we assume to be Kuwaitis ... After what seemed like a very long time we were led out of the airport, under armed guard to board buses which take us a few hundred yards to the Kuwait Airport Hotel ... In the foreground are twenty-seven stationary tanks ... [and] we hear gunfire and explosions intermittently.[3]

A few hours earlier, the Iraqis had invaded Kuwait and together with fellow New Zealanders Ngaire Campbell and Barry and Anne Lovegrove, the Halkyards' long ordeal at the hands of Saddam Hussein had begun.

When Geoff and Michele tuned into the BBC World Service at 6.00 a.m., they were flabbergasted: 'We did a double take,' Geoff told me, 'are we imagining this? We had no idea that it was going to happen. I don't think anyone did ... Not even the Americans.' The invasion had caught the whole world on the back foot, including the Kuwaiti Army, which was crushed within a few hours: 'Michele was straight on the phone to the Ambassador ... and then it seemed like a good idea to get down to the Embassy.' As the Vice Consul, Michele's top priority was to account for the handful of New Zealanders living in Iraq and the two dozen or so in Kuwait, most of whom were registered at the Embassy.* Meanwhile, all the phone lines to Kuwait had been cut, Baghdad Airport and the land borders were closed, and the rumour mill was working overtime.

In Kuwait's large expatriate community, anxiety levels were at fever pitch. Using unmapped tracks and Bedouin guides, convoys of cars started fleeing across the border into Saudi Arabia. But when an escaping British businessman was shot dead by an Iraqi patrol, the enthusiasm for desert crossings waned and many decided that it was safer to lie low in Kuwait. In Baghdad, the situation was deteriorating rapidly. Taken aback by the force of the UN Security Council's condemnation, Saddam had responded with characteristic deviousness and had forbidden all foreigners to leave the country – including the diplomats. By 6 August, the passengers of flight BA 149 were being divided up according to passport. Those whose countries were deemed to be 'aggressive' were put on buses to Baghdad, while other nationalities were taken to beach hotels in Kuwait. Saddam's game was obvious to everyone, but with the memory of the American hostage crisis still fresh in people's minds, nobody wanted to use the 'h' word. Instead, the *Washington Post* referred coyly to 'restrictees'.[4]

At the New Zealand Embassy in Baghdad the two-person team was working flat out. In her contribution to the Ministry's fiftieth anniversary publication, Michele describes 'going for days on end'[5] with just two to three hours' sleep. By this time Geoff and John Clarke's wife, Hong, were also helping out at the office 'contacting NZers, chasing up administrative questions and keeping the coms machines moving.'[6] As a multinational naval blockade began to assemble in the Gulf, dozens of foreigners were herded into hotels and Saddam's attitude to them became more menacing. In an open letter to the families of his 'foreign guests', he made it clear that he intended 'to play host to the citizens of these aggressive nations as long as Iraq is threatened by war.'[7] To deter attack, selected hostages would be placed at key military and civilian installations as 'human shields'.

Once the phone lines were restored to Kuwait, Michele was able to track down most of the New Zealanders there. She also got the names of the three New Zealand passport holders aboard BA 149. Someone had told her that some New Zealanders were among the passengers who had been brought to Baghdad and on the morning of 8 August, she knocked on nearly every door in Baghdad's multi-storey Mansur Melia Hotel in search of them. Eventually she discovered the Halkyards, who were overjoyed to see her. For a few days, they were able to exchange messages with their children. But it was a short-lived respite and on 16 August they were among the group of British hostages who were taken to act as 'human shields' at a nuclear facility attached to Iraq's nuclear weapons programme. Meanwhile, the Lovegroves and Ngaire Campbell were still languishing in Kuwait.

Throughout this chaotic period, the Embassy was getting mixed signals from the Iraqis about New Zealanders. At a press conference on 6 August, Prime Minister Geoffrey Palmer had condemned the invasion of Kuwait as an act of 'jack-booted thuggery'.[8] But although New Zealand had supported the UN call for economic sanctions, it had stopped short of joining the military coalition. According to the Iraqi Foreign Ministry, however, 'attitudes' mattered just as much as 'military contributions' and on 18 August John Clarke was categorically informed that New Zealand passport holders were on exactly the same 'no-go' footing as other Westerners.[9]

Early on in the piece, Michele and Geoff decided that they had to try and visit Kuwait. According to their key contact, Alistair Lane, who had become a leading figure among the New Zealanders there, the situation was becoming 'critical'.[10] Westerners were being seized from cars and hotels and looting was on the increase. But no one was sure that they would be any better off in Baghdad, where the choice would be between sleeping on a mattress at the Embassy and becoming a sitting duck at a hotel. From the stream of messages between the Embassy and Wellington, it is also clear that the New Zealanders in Kuwait were very wary of moving to Baghdad, especially as there was no guarantee that they would get through the checkpoints en route.

After several false starts, Michele and Geoff finally managed to obtain the necessary permits for the seven-hour drive to Kuwait. Following several weeks of confusion, the travel restrictions on diplomats had been lifted and 'to give him some status in Iraqi eyes',[11] Geoff had been appointed to the rank of Third Secretary and Vice Consul. Belatedly both he and Hong were also added to the Embassy's pay roll. On 29 August the Woods were due to leave at dawn, but the night before their departure, their plans were put on hold by an extraordinary U-turn by Saddam, which transformed their consular visit into a rescue mission.

Six days earlier, Saddam had made a grotesquely smiling appearance on Iraqi state television with a group of anxious-looking British hostages. During the encounter a courageous woman doctor had argued that the younger hostages should be liberated to continue their education. But no one had expected Saddam to respond and his announcement late on 28 August that the women and children were free to leave was initially greeted with disbelief. It took Geoff and Michele another forty-eight hours to establish that it was true – but in order to get their exit visas, all the dozen or so New Zealand women and children trapped in Kuwait would have to be brought to Baghdad.

Early on 31 August the Woods set out for Kuwait. They took the official Mercedes, which had the additional protection of diplomatic number plates, and Geoff did the driving: 'It all looked quite normal – perhaps slightly fewer people on the road ... You just go through Basra, glance past it and hang a right for Kuwait ... The Iraqi Army was on the border, but we had no problems. Our papers were all in order and we were probably stopped for about ten minutes.' 'Weren't you nervous?' I asked. Geoff shrugged: 'Obviously we felt a little less confident, not really knowing what to expect ... and there were a few tanks around ... But for me it was a sort of Boy Scout adventure.' Nevertheless the tension of the drive took its toll and when they finally reached Alistair Lane's apartment, Geoff crashed out early and did not wake up until late the following morning.

Kuwait City seemed surreally calm. Thousands of inhabitants had fled and, apart from the odd truckload of soldiers, there were few signs of the invasion or of damage to buildings. Kuwait City was the jewel of the Gulf and Saddam wanted to keep his prize intact. Throughout their visit, Michele was fully occupied with her consular duties. Before leaving Baghdad, she had sent a message to Wellington listing her objectives, of which 'sort out the movement of women and children'[12] was by far the most pressing – before Saddam had a change of heart. Geoff recalls her performance admiringly: 'Michele was always so practical and her immediate focus was to do what needed to be done as diligently as possible'.

Geoff and Michele originally intended to transport all the women and children themselves. The Embassy's Land Cruiser had been undergoing repairs in Kuwait when the invasion took place and during their visit the Woods picked it up from the garage. In the meantime, however, a safer option had emerged in the form of a designated 'Irish/Italian' convoy, in which four of the New Zealand women and three children could travel overnight to Baghdad. They arrived without mishap. But the Lovegroves, who drove separately, were less fortunate. Anne later described their journey as terrifying and Ngaire Campbell's story has yet to be told. Of the few remaining New Zealand women in Iraq, Daphne Halkyard was the only one who chose to stay. Henry had cancer and she had no intention of leaving him.

At 4.00 a.m. on 3 September, Geoff and Michele set off for Baghdad in the two Embassy cars with the remaining New Zealand women. As they headed out of the city to join the road that later became known as the 'Highway to Hell', they were stopped and searched by an Iraqi patrol. This was no time for standing on diplomatic dignity and Michele flipped open the boot of the Mercedes without protest, while Geoff followed suit in the Land Cruiser. The soldiers rifled through the women's bags and helped themselves to a camera before waving them on. Apart from what Geoff calls 'a bit of negotiation' at the border, this was their only incident.

The next morning Geoff caught a plane to Jordan. His mission to Amman is outlined in a series of classified messages from the Communications Division in Wellington. The Ministry was in the process of switching over to a new PC-based operating system and the clunky telex machines in Baghdad were already long past their sell-by date. With the phone lines liable to be cut at any time, the Embassy also needed a satellite phone system and a secure telephone. Geoff's task was to meet up with a safe hand courier at the Marriott Hotel in Amman. The courier would be flying out the same day and John Clarke was instructed to make contingency plans for storing the equipment at the Australian or British Embassy in case Geoff was delayed.

He flew on Iraqi Airways, which was still making regular flights to Amman, and later that day the Embassy in Baghdad received a cryptic message from London stating that all had gone well.

The new communications system came in a small suitcase about the size of a sewing machine, which Geoff carried back to Baghdad, together with a portable generator and the two telephones. As usual, he plays down his role: 'I had no trouble bringing them in. Things like that simply weren't a problem. Anyway, the Iraqis knew exactly what they were.' From Mexico, he was already familiar with the new system and installing it held no fears for him – especially as 'Coms' had assured him that if he ran into difficulties, they would talk him through over the secure phone. But Geoff had no trouble and, throughout the crisis, the Embassy's communications never missed a beat.

By 10 September, seventeen New Zealanders (plus the two Halkyards) were still in Iraq and Kuwait. Four were in semi-hiding in Baghdad, eleven were in Kuwait and two were staying with the Clarkes. On 26 September, the Iraqi Foreign Ministry circulated a note to all the embassies stating that sheltering a foreigner was now against the law and that 'anyone committing such a crime shall be executed.'[13] Nobody took it seriously, but John Clarke had long suspected that in Saddam's crazy world the Vienna Convention, which guarantees the inviolability of diplomatic premises, counted for nothing. In a cable to Wellington over a month earlier, he had foreseen the situation: 'If we do have NZers to stay, we would propose not to cooperate with the Iraqis on any call for foreigners to assemble … and refuse entry by Iraqi authorities to Embassy premises.' Of course, he would 'protest vigorously', but 'in the last resort' he and his staff would be unable to resist.[14]

While Michele was trying vainly to obtain a second travel permit to Kuwait, in New Zealand another woman was doing everything in her power to bring her husband home. Attractive, forceful and intelligent, Karen Lane, like her husband Alistair, emerges as a key figure in the story. Inspired, no doubt, by the example of the wives of the American hostages in Iran, she had set up a Gulf Crisis Support Group for the families of the detained men. Her first appearance in the Ministry's files comes in a typically upbeat letter thanking the head of the Consular Division for the 'Family Gathering' day that had been organised for the Support Group in Wellington. 'A flawless programme enabled every member to depart with a lighter heart,' she writes, 'you guys are doing one heck of a job … See you at the Homecoming Party – if not before.'[15] Despite being in the build-up to an election campaign, Prime

*Freed hostages celebrating aboard a Virgin flight to Gatwick from Baghdad.
New Zealanders Henry Halkyard (standing far left) and his wife, Daphne
(in a red shirt), with former British Prime Minister, Edward Heath, who
negotiated their release.* (Press Association)

Minister Geoffrey Palmer and Foreign Minister Mike Moore had made a
point of meeting the families. Three days later, at Karen's suggestion, Palmer
made a stirring broadcast to the men in Iraq and Kuwait on Radio New
Zealand International.

The Support Group's next gathering with the Ministry took place in an
atmosphere of high excitement. On 22 October, after nearly three months
in captivity, the Halkyards had been set free. A joyful photograph shows
them celebrating with other hostages aboard the Virgin Airways flight that
Richard Branson had sent to collect them. Almost the only woman, Daphne
is waving what looks like a large gin and tonic beside a rubicund Edward
Heath, who had negotiated their release.

Edward Heath was one of the stream of foreign dignitaries who paid
court to Saddam in return for the release of hostages. Others included Kurt
Waldheim, the Rev. Jesse Jackson and the pop star Cat Stevens. Very early
on, Saddam had realised that taking hostages was only consolidating the
ranks of the opposition and he was delighted to have a face-saving means of

getting rid of them. It took Karen no time at all to work out that this might also be a way to free the New Zealanders.

While the Support Group was plotting its next move, Geoff and Michele were enjoying a brief break. Despite the massive build-up of British and American troops in Saudi Arabia, Saddam was digging in. Negotiations over Kuwait were going nowhere and at the Embassy the frenetic pace of the previous three months had subsided to an uneasy lull. With the arrival of an extra diplomat, a selfless bachelor named Graeme Eskrigge who had been a Red Cross volunteer in Vietnam, Geoff and Michele seized their chance: 'We drove to Amman in our own car, and then we popped through to Syria and from there to Turkey and all the way across to Istanbul ... We reckoned if we didn't do it then, we would never get another chance.' When they crossed back into Iraq in early November, they were the only people driving in their direction. It never seems to have crossed Geoff's mind that he might return to New Zealand.

Karen's approach to former Prime Minister David Lange was on the advice of the Ministry. The 'Baghdad hostage bazaar' was a tricky business, in which no Western government wished to be perceived as making one-off deals with Saddam. But since his resignation in 1989, Lange had ceased to be a member of the government. Moreover, his anti-American stance would give him a certain lustre in the eyes of Saddam. 'I had the gut feeling he was the right man for the job', Karen told the *Dominion*, 'We are only going to get one shot at this ... and we don't know if Saddam Hussein has even heard of New Zealand, but we can only try.'[16] The newly elected National government had just offered the military coalition a forty-person medical team and a couple of aircraft, but this would barely have featured on Saddam's radar.

Lange agreed without hesitation. It was just the sort of high-profile escapade at which he excelled – and the chances of success were high. Saddam was revelling in the attentions of so many eminent emissaries and, according to Geoff, 'all Lange had to do was turn up and say the right things'. But it did not look so simple from New Zealand, and when Naomi Lange discovered that her husband would have to travel on a regular passport, she wrote an outraged letter to the new Prime Minister, Jim Bolger, accusing him of denying Lange 'the protection of a diplomatic passport'.[17] Although Lange was well aware that the government had to distance itself, he was furious about the passport. But history does not relate whether he asked Naomi to write the letter. In the meantime he and his new companion, Margaret Pope, set off for Baghdad.

As they waited for their visas in Amman, Lange and Margaret enjoyed an idyllic three-day interlude, during which they were handsomely entertained by New Zealand's Honorary Consul, a prominent Jordanian businessman named Maurice Khalaf. Lange's romance with Margaret was blossoming and in his account of their overnight trip to the Dead Sea, he muses on 'how it was possible to be so happy'. He also gave a press conference in Amman, at which he denounced 'the debilitating influence of American diplomacy in the region'. When he and Margaret eventually reached Baghdad, they were lodged in the luxurious Al Rashid Hotel as the guests of the Iraqi 'Friendship Organisation'. In his memoir, Lange describes it as 'a bizarre experience made tolerable only by our meeting with some of the hostages whose release I hoped our presence might achieve'. [18]

His meeting with the hostages took place over dinner at the New Zealand Residence, where the Clarkes had gathered the six remaining New Zealanders in Baghdad and the Woods to meet him. 'He certainly had zero complaints during our lovely meal together,' Geoff told me. After a series of meetings with Iraqi officials, Lange and Margaret dined again with the Clarkes the following evening. Although he never met Saddam, Lange's mission was a triumph. The New Zealanders were allowed to leave and he returned home in a blaze of glory.

The front-page photograph of the *Evening Post* for 13 November shows Karen enfolded in Lange's arms at Wellington Airport. According to the report, she was in floods of tears and Lange's voice was 'choked with emotion'. The headline reads: 'They're coming home'. [19] The press was out in force and at an impromptu press conference Lange, still fuming about his passport, could not resist taking a swipe at the Ministry. 'A patriotic Jordanian,' he said, 'is quite easily the most effective representative of New Zealand abroad that I have experienced in any connection with the Ministry of External Relations and Trade'. Maurice Khalaf had been forwarded Lange's visa by the Embassy in Baghdad, but Lange chose to give him the credit: 'He does a better job for New Zealand than any professional diplomat I have met and if our people were in any sense as good as he is, our country could hold its head high in international forums'. Accusations of inaction and obstruction followed, with the finger clearly pointed at the staff in Baghdad. The new Government took a similar drubbing. 'I don't think it has the wit, the ability or discrimination to do anything about it all,' [20] said Lange. Within a few hours his tirade was all over the media.

*Basking in the limelight: David Lange embracing Karen
Lane after his successful mission to free the remaining
New Zealand hostages in Iraq, 1990.* (Evening Post *13 Nov 1990,
Dominion Post Collection, Alexander Turnbull Library, Wellington, EP/1990/3926/14*)

For the two couples who had been holding the fort in Baghdad, it was a devastating kick in the teeth. 'I'm not quite sure what Lange's circumstances were at the time,' Geoff told me, 'but he obviously felt the need to lash out at somebody … maybe to build himself up.' He and Michele were bitterly hurt and the Clarkes, who bore the brunt of Lange's venom, never got over it. When I asked to speak to Hong about Baghdad, John told me that 'the bad old days' were something that she preferred not to think about. She had been sheltering New Zealanders at the Residence for months and, after Lange's attack, the warm letter from one of them thanking her and John for all their 'kindness and assistance' must have seemed like balm to the soul.[21] A huge amount of paperwork remained to be done before the men could actually leave, but on 17 November John Clarke was able to report that all but one (who had chosen to stay) had left. Most of the Kuwaiti contingent were flown out by the Americans.

New Zealand's small part in the drama was over. But Saddam was still refusing to back down on Kuwait. On 29 November, the UN Security Council issued an ultimatum threatening the use of force if Iraq did not withdraw by 15 January. The countdown to war had begun and, amid fears that Saddam might once again resort to chemical weapons, the Embassy staff and spouses were instructed by a New Zealand Army officer on the use of gas masks and Atropine injections. It took another month to close down the Embassy and Geoff and Michele did not leave until a couple of weeks before the bombing started. For both of them, the past five months had been a rollercoaster ride during which they, too, had been little more than hostages. 'But when the war started,' said Geoff, 'our main emotion was one of pity for the Iraqi people.'

John Clarke and the gallant Michele* were both awarded the New Zealand 1990 Commemoration Medal.

---

* Michele died in 2010 after a courageous struggle against breast cancer.

CHAPTER 19.
. . . .

Conduct Unbecoming

Even diplomats – and their partners – sometimes behave badly and New Zealand's envoys are no exception. Among the career officers, a leading contender for the bad behaviour prize has to be the Ambassador who was caught 'in flagrante' with the Swedish wife of a British diplomat during a visit to the Ming Tombs. Deeply shocked, the Chinese promptly put heavy security on the Tombs which, in addition to the fury of the cuckolded husband, earned 'our man' the hearty dislike of the whole Diplomatic Corps in Beijing. When he confessed his misdemeanours to the Secretary in Wellington, they prompted a stern instruction for his recall, which through some clerical oversight was circulated to staff on the Ministry's weekly cable clip.

Despite the damage done to New Zealand's reputation in Beijing, the scandal was largely confined to diplomatic and official circles. But the same could not be said of the antics of a later envoy, whose indiscretions were broadcast in every major broadsheet in Britain, as well as in all the leading papers in New Zealand. The story has never been forgotten and fifteen years later it still elicits smirks and sniggers at the expense of the country's oldest and most historic diplomatic mission, the New Zealand High Commission in London.

From the earliest days, the position of High Commissioner to the United Kingdom has been regarded as a safe haven, to which long-serving politicians or party supporters could be sent as a reward for their services. Of New Zealand's twenty-five High Commissioners in London to date, twenty-two have been political appointees, with the senior career diplomat at the post being relegated to the rank of Deputy High Commissioner and doing most of the donkey work.

As representational figures, some political appointees and their wives have served New Zealand admirably, but according to an article in the Wellington *Dominion*, the former National Party President, to whom the lady in question was attached, was not among them. 'Mr Collinge', the article states baldly, 'is not regarded as having been a successful high commissioner.'[1] An earlier piece in the *Sunday Star Times*, entitled 'Why Collinge got the job' is equally unflattering: 'In ancient Greece, when any senator or prominent citizen was proving an embarrassment to the government, he was banished to an outer province. The appointment of John Collinge to a post in London is a modern day analogy.'[2] Collinge clearly had few friends in the press, but whatever the true reasons for his appointment to London in April 1994, the government could hardly have foreseen what a major embarrassment he and his female companion, Barbara Stones, would prove to be.

Although she was never graced with the title of 'partner', as Collinge's escort Barbara undertook many of the duties of a diplomatic wife. Described variously as 'mistress' and 'lover', she accompanied him to official functions, including such high-profile occasions as Royal Ascot. She also acted as his hostess at parties and dinners at the elegant, three-storey house in Chelsea Square that served as the High Commissioner's Residence. With no background in diplomacy, Barbara was disappointed to discover that the supposedly glamorous lifestyle of a diplomatic hostess was often far from exciting. Once the novelty of playing 'Mrs High Commissioner' had worn off, she found many of the official functions deadly dull, especially the dinners at the Residence. 'The times I sat at that dining-room table and was bored to tears',[3] she complained, apparently unaware that diplomatic entertaining is primarily intended to further New Zealand's interests overseas, rather than to amuse the hostess. Such fine points of protocol as the seating at dinner also eluded her. Consumed with jealousy, she was deeply suspicious when Collinge, quite correctly, placed her on the far side of the table rather than beside him. 'The problem was he wanted me – and all the other women too', she declared, and 'would always put himself beside a single, attractive woman'.[4]

Both divorced, the couple had met several years earlier in New Zealand, when Barbara became part of the team that was campaigning for Collinge to become the National Party President. Although Collinge was still married at the time, the attraction between them was instantaneous: 'Every function that he was at, he made sure he came and talked to me. He was very strong [and] … he swept me off my feet.'[5] According to Barbara, a five-year relationship followed, during which she stood unsuccessfully as the National Party candidate for Palmerston North.

Shortly before Collinge left to take up his appointment in London, their relationship ended. But when Barbara reappeared in England a few months later, Collinge seems to have been more than happy to resume it. 'John gave me the impression he was head over heels in love',[6] she claimed, and their reunion had been his initiative. Collinge's version is rather different: Barbara had followed him 'and it became very scary. She bombarded me with love letters and letters that said why she was right for me … It wasn't a proper relationship. To be blunt, she threw herself at me.'[7] Despite his reservations, however, Collinge continued to pursue their love life with a vigour and inventiveness whose details were later shared with most of the population of Britain and New Zealand.

In the meantime, by early 1995 Collinge had found a replacement for Barbara, a decorative British socialite with the unusual name of 'Posselthwaite', who was later revealed to have been a professional model widely known as Maggie O'Grady. For a couple of months, Collinge managed to field both women. Barbara was not in full-time residence, but with her bat-like antennae for infidelity she soon sensed that her man was straying. A quick glance at the Residence visitors' book confirmed her suspicions: 'She [Margaret Posselthwaite] had been there three or four times for dinner. That's when I started thinking … What's going on here?'[8]

Up to this point, there had been nothing to suggest that Barbara was in any way unusual. In photographs she appears as an attractive brunette, with deep-set eyes, whose demeanour gives no hint of instability. But as Collinge was to learn to his cost, 'hell has no fury like a woman scorned' and for the next two and a half years she pursued a stalking campaign against him and his new lover that was little short of obsessive. Lurking in the gardens opposite the Residence, she would spy on the comings and goings of her successor. Whatever traces of diplomatic propriety that she may have possessed were cast to the winds, and on one notable occasion she even managed to give Margaret Posselthwaite a hefty kick in the auction room at Christies. 'I just winced', Margaret said, 'I've been kicked by horses before and that's worse.'[9] Later Barbara 'pounced' on her at night, outside her country home in Wiltshire.

Barbara's attempted assaults were ludicrous rather than dangerous, but her abusive phone calls and hate mail were more serious. Seizing on the ambiguity of the term 'model', she accused Margaret point blank of

Left: The spurned lover: John Collinge's former girlfriend, Barbara Stones.
(Dominion *28 Jun 1997, Alexander Turnbull Library, Wellington, N-P-1712-1)*

Right: Moving on. Margaret Posselthwaite shows off her engagement ring with fiancé, John Collinge, at her side. (Fairfax New Zealand, Sunday Star Times, *31 Aug 1997, Alexander Turnbull Library, Wellington, N-P-1713-A4)*

John Collinge relaxing in his Auckland apartment with a copy of the Daily Mail. (New Zealand Herald *27 Jun 1997. Photo Yanse Martin, Alexander Turnbull Library, Wellington, N-P-1711-13)*

being a prostitute and scattered the pavement outside the Residence with notes reading 'The Whorehouse of Chelsea Square, Madame Margaret Posselthwaite'.[10] She also sent prostitutes' visiting cards to the exclusive Hurlingham Club, of which Margaret was a member. To Collinge, however, Margaret always seemed a perfect lady and when the Queen and the Duke of Edinburgh came to dine at Chelsea Square, she probably helped him to entertain them.

By the time Barbara had poured oil on the steps of the High Commission, and sprayed 'Whore Posselthwaite' on the road outside the Residence, her harassment was common knowledge among High Commission staffers and neighbours. Yet Collinge insists that this undignified side show in no way disrupted his work or detracted from his effectiveness as High Commissioner. But after over two years of what she describes as 'a real terror campaign'[11] Margaret had had enough, and on 25 June 1997 her appeals to the police finally resulted in a prosecution at the Westminster Magistrates Court in Horseferry Road, to which the press came in droves.

When Barbara entered the court, accompanied by her lawyer, Margaret must have eyed her with interest. Apart from the scuffle at Christies and their night-time encounter in Wiltshire, the two women had never met. After the hearing, Barbara confessed to reporters that she had found it 'absolutely terrifying to have to face Miss Posselthwaite across a courtroom'.[12] Only Collinge was conspicuously absent. His posting had ended in April and he had returned to Auckland, leaving Barbara and Margaret to slug it out on their own.

The charges against Barbara ranged from 'criminally damaging the High Commission building' to 'common assault'.[13] She was also accused of distributing offensive notes and pamphlets, which were displayed by the prosecution. But by far the most sensational evidence was the abusive eight-page letter that she had sent to Margaret shortly before Collinge's departure. As its contents were read aloud to the court, the press started to scribble furiously. Much of it was mindless ranting, laced with terms like 'pariah' and 'parasite' and suggestions that Margaret spent her time 'stalking the corridors of the Hurlingham Club, looking for the next opportunity to be a whore.'[14] But when it came to describing her own sex life with Collinge, Barbara adopted a softer tone: 'The best times were when J.C. wined and dined me then made love to me – once on the dining room table. You can remember that next time you sit down to eat from it. In fact we made love in most of the rooms in Chelsea Square … I particularly enjoyed the bathroom as it had a spa bath and wonderful views over the harbour'.[15]

Diplomatic misbehaviour always makes for good copy and the following morning almost every major daily in Britain, including the *Times*, *Telegraph*, *Guardian*, *Daily Mail* and *Daily Express*, was carrying the story: 'Public revenge of diplomat's spurned lover', 'Ex-mistress stalked high commissioner', 'Envoy's hate mail ordeal', 'Diplomat's spurned lover sent hate mail'.[16] The general public saw no distinction between political appointees and career diplomats and as further headlines poured from the press, New Zealand and its Diplomatic Service became the laughing stock of London.

Some of the most spiteful coverage appeared in the *Evening Standard*: 'Is he the Casanova of the dullest little country on earth?' asked the columnist A.N. Wilson as he puzzled over Collinge's 'erotic allure'. 'A rubicund, bespectacled old codger of 58 who looks dull enough to be the family solicitor – or the High Commissioner of New Zealand'. Further on, he notes that many Britons would struggle to name '10 good things to come out of New Zealand ... We'd start humming and hawing after we'd said "lamb chops, Katherine Mansfield, and sauvignon blanc"'.[17]

The New Zealand media had also picked up the story but, as Collinge had felt no need to alert the Ministry to the forthcoming court case, the first that the Secretary of Foreign Affairs knew of it was when the Wellington *Dominion* asked him to comment. Meanwhile, back in London, Collinge's hapless successor (who for once happened to be a career diplomat), was left to cop the flak – along with the sly asides about what he did on his dining table. Even after the infamous table had been sold at auction, the sniggers and the smirks continued. 'It was a nightmare,' he told me, and he preferred not to talk about it.

For Barbara, the story ends here. Although she pleaded guilty to sending an offensive letter, she was discharged with a reprimand. Collinge had 'used' her, so her solicitor argued, and she had already suffered enough. 'You have misbehaved yourself', the woman magistrate told her, 'and caused a certain amount of harassment and distress to the new lover.' But she accepted her solicitor's arguments and advised Barbara to forget Collinge 'and look elsewhere'.[18]

For Collinge and Margaret, however, the affair was far from over. Within twenty-four hours of the hearing, Margaret was on a plane to New Zealand, where Collinge had become known as the man 'who served up more than dinner on the table at the High Commissioner's London residence'.[19] Their photographs were splashed across the Auckland papers, with Margaret in a dainty Chanel-style suit and pearls, cradling a bouquet of flowers. She had brought her walking boots and her paints with her. After all, what else would there be to do in 'the dullest little country on earth'? 'So young and attractive, she is too', said a mischievous letter to the *Evening Post*, 'could be his daughter … Maggie O'Grady has won this round and is hanging in there … Sure and begorrah, you have to hand it to the Irish; they never give up.'[20]

According to the press, the couple were very much in love. 'She completes me', said Collinge, 'it was love at first sight and my feelings haven't changed'.[21] Before long, Margaret was sporting 'a rock-sized emerald and diamond ring' with which she and Collinge posed for the newspapers. 'It's a bit like a traffic light',[22] Margaret told reporters, presumably hoping that it would give the green light to their as yet undisclosed marriage plans. Smiling serenely from the pages of the *Sunday Star Times* she, at least, was behaving beautifully. Barbara, in contrast, had brought ridicule on New Zealand's Diplomatic Service, including on all those wives and partners who accept discretion and restraint as part of their diplomatic role. She had, as she later admitted, 'gone a bit far', but the man she loved had 'used her for his own convenience'[23] and then treated her rottenly.

In 2001, the house in Chelsea Square was put on the market. But any hopes that the Collinge story might die a natural death with the sale of the house were soon dashed. As soon as the news became public, the *Dominion* rehashed the affair under the headline 'NZ to sell notorious London house'.[24] Two weeks later, the *Christchurch Press* followed suit. In March 2002, when the property was under offer, the *Dominion* referred to the story yet again, provoking a sharp response from Collinge, who denied any impropriety whatsoever during his term as High Commissioner. But, to the best of my knowledge, he has never denied that he and Barbara once made love on the dining-room table …

CHAPTER 20.

Coming Out

'The level of homophobia in MFAT is so high it may not be safe to sign names.'[1] So runs an agitated memo, dated April 1994, in response to the suggestion that a note of thanks should be sent to the Ministry's Senior Management Group on behalf of gay and lesbian staff. The occasion was the Ministry's groundbreaking decision to give same sex partners the same overseas allowances as their heterosexual counterparts.

The so-called 'wife allowance' dates back to the earliest days of the Ministry, when many wives mistakenly believed that it would be withdrawn if they took a job. In fact, it was (and remains) part of a cost-of-living allowance which is paid to married officers to offset the higher costs of a couple living overseas. In those early days payment was strictly limited to wedded women, but by the 1980s the Ministry had been obliged to include the partners of the growing number of staff who were living in de facto relationships. Same-sex partners, however, would have to wait for another decade before they too received 'married' benefits.

Despite the formation of the Gay Liberation Front in 1972, New Zealand was slower than many like-minded nations to tackle the issue of gay and lesbian rights. In England, male relationships were decriminalised in 1967. Two years later, Canada followed suit. In Illinois, gay relationships were legalised in 1962 and during the 1970s over twenty other US states passed similar legislation. In South Australia, gay relationships were decriminalised in 1975, although law changes in other states (most notably Tasmania) took rather longer. But in New Zealand, the Homosexual Law Reform Act was not passed until 1986 and only after a bitter fourteen-month battle, during which thousands of petitions opposing the bill were sent to the Statutes Revision Committee.

Earlier efforts to bring New Zealand into line with the new English legislation had met with implacable hostility. In 1970, for example, a request for a revision of the law by The Young Nationals was denounced as an attempt 'to whitewash the disgusting act of sodomy'.[2] Much of the rhetoric that emerged during the 1986 debate was equally virulent; until the passing of the New Zealand Human Rights Act in 1993, many members of the gay and lesbian community continued to face abuse.

Against this background, the reluctance of the author of the memo to reveal his (or her) identity becomes more understandable, particularly if the writer was male. Lesbianism has never been criminalised, but gay men lived under the threat of imprisonment for decades – as witnessed by the infamous trial and imprisonment of Oscar Wilde. Explanations for this discrepancy range from the claim that Queen Victoria refused to sign the legislation against lesbianism because she did not believe it existed, to the more plausible suggestion that the male-dominated judiciary never considered lesbians worthy of their attention. On the other hand, the writer's repeated assertions that MFAT was a hotbed of homophobia verge on the melodramatic, especially as there are good historical reasons for believing that the Ministry has always been sympathetic to homosexuals.

In his moving tribute at the funeral of Sir Alister McIntosh, Frank Corner not only describes the New Zealand Foreign Service as McIntosh's creation, but also as 'his chief monument … because it was there that the official and the private man came closest together and exercised their most profound joint influence'. Corner cites McIntosh's many qualities: 'Sagacious, discreet, modest' and hails him 'as one of the great public servants of New Zealand.' Above all, however, he emphasises his humanity and the lasting imprint that he left upon the Ministry:

> 'Mac' was the father of the family. He took upon his own shoulders and conscience the problems of all his officers … McIntosh aimed at the highest standards. But [he] also understood human frailties. He made people feel he understood them, that he estimated their worth accurately.[3]

McIntosh was all too familiar with human frailty, which would cost him the crowning glory of his career.

When McIntosh died in 1978, his homosexuality was still a closely guarded secret. Official disclosure did not come until 2000, when the historian, Ian McGibbon, openly confronted the issue in the *New Zealand Dictionary of Biography*:

The founding father of New Zealand diplomacy, Alister McIntosh, with his wife, Doris, at his investiture with the CMG, Wellington 1957.

(Dominion *7 Jun 1957, Dominion Post Collection, Alexander Turnbull Library, Wellington, F-58682-1/4*)

McIntosh's private life was complicated by his homosexuality – 'that glorious indiscretion', as he once described it. McIntosh grew to maturity in an era when even the suspicion of homosexuality could destroy a career. So, like many similarly situated individuals, he chose concealment and discretion.[4]

An important part of McIntosh's 'concealment' was his marriage to Doris and the production of a son, which enabled him to merge seamlessly into heterosexual society. But the bulk of his time was spent at the office in the company of the growing band of clever young men whom he was recruiting for the Ministry. According to Frank Corner, 'Mac' 'delighted in encouraging his officers, particularly his young officers, to spread their mental wings and explore and argue about unreceived ideas and possibilities.'[5] But like the aristocratic Dorians, his mentoring role to younger men also exposed him to emotional entanglements.

The tragedy of the 'boy typist' who became the object of McIntosh's affections is not referred to by McGibbon. Nor is there any documentary evidence of their relationship in the public arena. But at least one member of the Ministry (who caught them in bed together) was aware of it. The boy had started work at the Ministry at the age of fifteen and went on to become McIntosh's Personal Assistant, followed by a two-year stint as Private Secretary to the Minister of Foreign Affairs. In this latter capacity, he and McIntosh travelled together to the Commonwealth Foreign Ministers' Conference in Colombo in 1950 where, like many others far from home, McIntosh seems to have let down his guard. On the return journey he was caught 'in a compromising situation'[6] by British police at a gay bar in Singapore, which was duly recorded on the files of MI5. In a letter to Carl Berendsen shortly afterwards, McIntosh refers to it as an 'appalling incident' for which he blamed himself: 'shame prevents me from describing what happened.'[7]

Doris probably heard nothing about it either. Nor would anything in McIntosh's three-page statement under oath of 22 May 1959 have led her to suspect that her husband had any special relationship with the 35-year-old officer who had been found dead in the front seat of his car. In his right hand was a green plastic hose which had been taped on to the exhaust. Like McIntosh, he had married and fathered a child and the stated reason for his suicide was concern about his job. But the suppression and concealment of his homosexuality may well have been contributing factors. McIntosh remained at the helm until 1966, 'patiently shaping' what Corner describes as 'a particular <u>kind</u> of foreign service' that was distinguished by 'decency, humanity, modesty'[8] – and where there were few traces of homophobia.

Shortly before McIntosh's retirement, his name was put forward to become the first Secretary-General of the Commonwealth – a highly prestigious position for which he was the front runner. But on the day before the election, he mysteriously withdrew from the race, pleading his increasing deafness. The real reason, however, was that his fall from grace in Singapore had come home to roost. At the time, homosexuality was still a criminal offence, leaving McIntosh open to blackmail, and after an approach from MI5, Holyoake had been obliged to withdraw his nomination on security grounds.

Judging from the photographs of the lavish farewell party given by the Diplomatic Corps in Wellington, the McIntoshes concealed their disappointment well. At his own request, McIntosh had been appointed

Putting a brave face on it. Alister and Doris McIntosh as guests of honour at a farewell dinner given by the Diplomatic Corps in Wellington, 1966.

(Evening Post *23 Aug 1966,* Dominion Post *Collection, Alexander Turnbull Library, Wellington, EP/1966/3492)*

New Zealand's first Ambassador to Italy, where he could lick his wounds against a soothing backdrop of fountains and classical ruins. Whether or not he told Doris the truth is impossible to know, although it is tempting to link the slightly plaintive tone of her interview with the *Evening Post* to a sense of betrayal. Entitled 'Rome Exciting Prospect For Stay-Home Wife', the interview quotes her extensively: 'So many people who hear of my husband's travels on Government business think that I go too … never … never … never.' Even their modest-three week leave was rarely spent together. 'We have not been able to do this for thirty years', Doris told the reporter, 'occasionally we have begun a quiet holiday … then after a few days, my husband has had to pack for London, Lagos or some other place.'[9] Like her husband, Doris was intensely private and perhaps the most telling fact that emerges from the interview is that in over twenty years of constant travel, McIntosh had only once taken his wife on a proper holiday.

Apart from Lyn Corner's affectionate recollections, the main source of information on Doris is the large collection of letters that she received from the crime writer, Ngaio Marsh, who came to stay with her in Rome. The visit was a resounding success and resulted in another superb crime story, *When in Rome*, which Ngaio dedicated to the McIntoshes. In her recent biography of Ngaio, Joanne Drayton describes her as Doris's 'confidante and her emotional support, and possibly more'.[10] The two women were certainly intimate friends and to a modern reader, Ngaio's effusive 'Dearest Dossy' and 'Darling D' could well be misleading. With her close-cropped hair and no-frills style, Doris could also have appeared rather masculine. But while Drayton's question mark over Ngaio's relationship with her long-term companion, Sylvia Fox, seems justified, it is clear from Ngaio's letters to Doris that their friendship was a sympathetic meeting of minds – and nothing more.[11]

Despite McIntosh's liberal legacy, the Ministry did not extend full recognition to same-sex partners of its own volition. The decision was imposed by the passing of the Human Rights Act, which made discrimination on the grounds of sexual orientation unlawful. The Ministry's caution over same-sex relationships was not due to any bias, but rather to the sensitivities of posting same-sex couples overseas – especially to countries such as Saudi Arabia and Iran where homosexuality still incurs the death penalty. Even under less extreme regimes, same-sex relationships could run counter to the Ministry's Code of Conduct, which stipulates that officers serving overseas should avoid behaviour 'whether connected with their official duties, personal relationships or otherwise … which may offend, or appear to offend, against local laws or customs'.[12]

In his memo to the Senior Management Group of 22 October 1993, the Director of Personnel wrestled manfully with these problems. By far his greatest concern was the impact that the new legislation would have on the Ministry's core business of diplomacy, not to mention the practical difficulties of gaining visas and work permits for same-sex partners. 'Much larger issues include the attitude of the host country, consequences for immigration and diplomatic status and possible damage to New Zealand's international reputation … We cannot expect that our national legislation and standards can apply without restriction in other countries', he notes, adding gloomily that 'there would be little point in trying to establish a policy to cover any jail circumstances that could arise'. In comparison, the question of partners' location allowances was a minor matter; in his view only a small number of officers would be involved and the costs would be negligible. All that would be required was 'a simple change'[13] to the *Overseas Service Handbook*, which would delete the word 'spouse' and replace it with the term 'partner', thereby removing all traces of the institution of marriage from the Ministry's statute books for ever.

In conferring equal status on heterosexual and homosexual partners, the Ministry was in the forefront of diplomatic services worldwide, second only to the Netherlands. For gay and lesbian staff, it was a turning point. Of course the money was welcome, but what mattered far more to them was that it signalled a recognition of their rights. Since the passing of the Human Rights Act, the Ministry's gay and lesbian community has become far more visible. In 1994 there was no support group of any sort, but today the Ministry has an active gay and lesbian network, which operates through the MFAT intranet. According to the network co-ordinator, Rosie Walsh, all overseas post reports now include information on the local gay and lesbian scene. Equally, when the Ministry is recruiting new staff, a gay or lesbian representative is included in the recruitment team.

In response to my questions about ongoing issues for partners, Rosie confirms that most of their concerns are related to overseas postings. Even in places where a reciprocal or Dependant Employment Agreement (DEA) exists, same-sex partners are often debarred from working. A glance at the Ministry's register of agreements and DEAs underscores the problem. In Paris, for example, the agreement specifically excludes same-sex partners while in other posts, such as Rome, Santiago and Warsaw, the agreements do not cover them. If a partner wishes to find employment – and most do – this can present an insuperable obstacle that can complicate an officer's career path.

So what is it actually like for the women who accompany their same-sex partners overseas, I wonder, and are they really as interchangeable with spouses as the *Overseas Service Handbook* would suggest? Rosie and I are sitting in a café in Wellington, just opposite the imposing entrance to MFAT. She has only been at MFAT for five years and has never been on a diplomatic posting, but she is quite willing to put me in touch with a female partner overseas.

With her face wiped clean of make-up, Ayesha Verrall looks younger than her photo on Twitter. Dark haired and with a strong, attractive face, she is nursing a mug of coffee as we talk against a background of crashes, which are later revealed to be a violent electrical storm. Ayesha is speaking from Singapore and we are meeting for the first time on Skype.

Thanks to the internet, I have been able to do some homework. Until her partner Alice's posting to New Zealand's Permanent Mission to the UN in

New York in January 2010, Ayesha was a doctor at Wellington Hospital. In a scholarly contribution to an online 'think-site', she argues cogently for the earmarking of revenue collected from alcohol to pay for the costs of alcohol-related harm (which she would have seen plenty of at Wellington Hospital). Online she describes herself as 'an infectious diseases doctor and bioethicist currently at large in New York.' 'I wrote that back in 2010,' Ayesha comments, when time was hanging heavily on her hands and the term 'at large' covered not only loneliness and boredom, but also intense frustration.[14]

New York is not Ayesha's first experience of an overseas posting. She and Alice have been together for thirteen years and when Alice was seconded to the Australian Foreign Ministry in 2006, Ayesha accompanied her to Canberra. In terms of size and cultural outlook, Canberra is not dissimilar to Wellington and for Ayesha it was an ideal introduction to living overseas. But New York, with its population of eight million, is on a very different scale and even without the complications over her status, she might have found it a culture shock.

As the first same-sex partner at MFAT to be granted a US diplomatic visa, Ayesha arrived in New York with high hopes. Before her departure, she had been assured by the Ministry that an amendment to the existing DEA was in the pipeline and she should be able to work. But within the US attitudes to homosexuality are still widely polarised and in the vast US bureaucracy, the paperwork was going at a snail's pace. As a result, Ayesha faced rejection after rejection from New York's hospitals, despite their crying need for good doctors. 'HIV/AIDS is my field', Ayesha tells me, 'and outside the hospitals I could see lines of AIDS sufferers queuing up for treatment.' But with the amendment still pending (plus the problem of entering the workforce at the level she had reached in New Zealand), any employer would have to undertake the lengthy process of obtaining a work permit for her, which no hospital was prepared to do.

While friends emailed enviously from home ('it must be fantastic living in New York'), Ayesha plodded dutifully round the sights: 'I visited the MOMA and the Met and became an expert on cut-price shopping.' But, after the constant interaction of her job at Wellington Hospital, it seemed a pretty empty existence. As she speaks, the memories of my own first year in Rome come flooding back. Like her, I was unable to work and, despite being in one of the world's most beautiful cities, I was utterly miserable.

'But what about your involvement with the Mission?' I ask, recalling my early attempts at diplomatic entertaining, 'as a diplomatic partner don't you

An evening at the ballet. Ayesha Verrall (right) with MFAT partner, Alice Revell, outside the Lincoln Centre, New York 2012.

(By kind permission of Ayesha Verrall)

feel some obligation to represent New Zealand?' Ayesha looks at me blankly and I realise that I am talking to another generation. 'Not at all,' she says, 'I am very proud of Alice's achievements and I am keen to support her in her job,' but this does not take the form of networking and entertaining. 'In any case,' she adds, 'at the UN most of the official entertaining takes place over lunch and none of the partners are involved.' What she refrains from mentioning is that most of the wives are working. 'Are you ever invited to official functions?' I ask. Ayesha shakes her head 'Never.'

'There must be a UN Women's group,' I suggest. 'There is,' replies Ayesha, 'but I've never got in touch with it.' A glance at the activities of the UN Women's Guild online reveals that their fundraising activities are impressive. But I can see why Ayesha might have felt that events like the 'Brides of All Nations' gala, at which traditional bridal wear was 'modelled by spouses and daughters of ambassadors', was not quite her scene.

Towards the end of her first year, Ayesha managed to find some voluntary work with Amnesty International. By this time, however, she was running up against the deadline to complete her medical training and when a suitable position came up in Singapore, she had little choice but to take it. Back in the buzz of hospital life, with a pager that beeps every minute, Ayesha is loving the job. But the eighteen-month separation from Alice has been tough and she is looking forward to rejoining her in New York. For the remainder of their posting, she is developing strategies for survival, such as a research project on infectious diseases and a road trip to Mongolia.

As a same-sex partner overseas, Ayesha's problems are very similar to those of the diplomatic wives of the 1970s and '80s, who were also fighting for the right to work. But unlike them, she does not have recourse to the traditional wives' world of networking and charity work. Even in New York, where homosexuality is widely accepted, this is not an environment where a same-sex partner would fit in easily. Today many younger wives have also shunned the voluntary activities of their predecessors. But, in contrast to the same sex partners, their right to work is now universally acknowledged and in all but a few ultra-conservative countries they are free to take gainful employment.

Within the Ministry in Wellington, the position of gay and lesbian staff has improved immeasurably since the days when 'coming out' could spell professional downfall. McIntosh (and his companion) were casualties of that era. But, as Ayesha's difficulties show, it is a different story overseas and while Pierre Trudeau's claim that 'the state has no business in the bedrooms of the nation'[15] may be true of New Zealand, this is not the case in many of the countries where it conducts its diplomacy.

CHAPTER 21.

9/11

At 9.52 am on 11 September 2001, Maria MacKay sent the following email to her closest friends and family:

> I'm sitting in the staff room at UNIS. A few seconds ago in my class we noticed a lot of smoke and fire. I have just been told that the World Trade Center, and now the Pentagon have been hit by terrorist planes. I am just letting you know that I am alright, and I think that Don was at his office which is also not near the site. There is a lot of chaos and fear around me at the moment, as many of the people who work with me have friends and family in the financial district, not to mention the children whom we teach.
>
> It is very scary as you can imagine BUT WE ARE ALRIGHT. The radio announcers are saying the planes were probably hijacked and that America is under siege ...[1]

Seven minutes later the South Tower of the World Trade Center collapsed in ten seconds flat, killing everyone inside it. Thirty-six minutes later the North Tower crumbled in a massive cloud of smoke and debris, killing everyone on the upper floors and claiming scores of victims at lower levels.

September 11 was Maria's fourth day teaching at the United Nations International School (UNIS) on Manhattan, with a class of twenty super-bright twelve-year-olds hand-picked from the cream of the UN and New York intelligentsia. Among them were Dash Spiegelman, son of the cartoonist Art Spiegelman, whose book *Maus* won the Pulitzer Prize, and Roberto Rossellini Junior, son of the actress Isabella Rossellini, whose mother was Ingrid Bergman. At UNIS, famous parents were two a penny, but it was the children who interested Maria ('because you are so involved in your teaching that you don't actually care whose parents are what').[2] They were far more sophisticated than her pupils in Wellington and she was determined to get the measure of them:

> I was teaching English and we were reading The Light in the Forest by Conrad Richter … Suddenly the children were charging across the room – some of them left their seats and went to the window … and they kept saying 'there's smoke coming'.

From her place in front of the class, Maria was unable to see out of the window, but over the weekend there had been fires in Queens and she reckoned it was something similar: 'I took no notice at all … You have to realise what teaching is like. It's a completely focussed activity and I'm always intensely focussed on the job … There has to be a lot going on to distract me.' The children soon returned to their seats and even when a second immense column of smoke billowed into the cloudless sky, Maria advised them to ignore it and carried on with her lesson. Looking back, she realises that 'it was the best thing I could have done'.

But as soon as she entered the staff room, she knew that something was wrong. Instead of chatting around the coffee machines as usual, the teachers were in huddled groups gazing out of the windows. 'Haven't you heard about the plane?' someone asked her. All the other staff had been alerted by the Principal, but for some reason he had overlooked Maria. Earlier, in his eagerness to 'take the teaching moment', he had even led over a hundred of the older children up to the roof to witness what he believed was a minor incident. But at the sight of the blazing towers, the children had all turned tail and fled screaming down the stairwells.

By this time live coverage of the inferno was being shown on television and to spare the children from any further trauma, the school had switched to radio. 'The news came in dribs and drabs', Maria recalled afterwards, 'confusing at first and then the whole picture and the true horror started to emerge'.[3] As the tension levels in the staff room mounted, she emailed her nearest and dearest. But, looking around at the dazed faces of her local colleagues, she realised that most of them were not even registering what was happening: 'When the twin towers collapsed it was so horrific that there was disbelief', she told me.

Apart from her husband, Don, Maria had no family to worry about and when the decision was taken to evacuate the school, she volunteered to stay on:

The high school kids were told that they could go ... but the primary and middle school kids had to wait for their parents to come and that's where I came in because I was able to stay, whereas the other teachers were breaking their necks to get out of there ... Most of the parents didn't work in the financial district. But they all came to get their kids. We didn't have to call them – in a crisis the first thing you do is go and get your kids.

Maria was thinking about her kids too and in the middle of the afternoon, she finally got the message that she had been longing for:

London: 19.00

Hello Mummy

I can't tell you how relieved I am that you are both okay, but I'm not comfortable about you staying in New York ... I've been trying to ring you both but it's impossible to get through ... There must be thousands of people over there right now who are experiencing utter hell waiting to hear how their families are. Please be very, very careful.

Lots of love
Andrea XXX[4]

Andrea had just moved to London and Maria knew that she would be worried sick about her parents.

New York: 15.03

Hello darling,

It is time you went home and went to bed. Remember ... lightning doesn't strike twice at the same place so we're probably going to be safe. Our school was evacuated (along with the UN) because they thought that UN places would be likely targets. But I'm still here and nothing has happened. I am just about to walk to Don's office and then we will get home. Don't worry about ringing us. I'll send you an email from home tonight.[5]

Earlier in the day, the neighbouring streets had been jammed with cars fleeing from the financial district. But by the time Maria set off for home shortly after 3.00 p.m., the area was closed to traffic and she had to walk the sixty blocks back to her apartment on 84th Street. In a message to family and friends the following day, she describes the scene: 'There was an eerie silence. Most people just looked stunned. Lots of ambulances were rushing up and down with sirens screaming. The streets were blocked off with yellow marker tape.'[6] On her way home, she passed three major hospitals: 'I'll never forget seeing all these young people standing on the pavement in green scrubs. They had set up the triage to deal with the injuries and they were waiting for people to come. But they were all standing there doing nothing … because either you were killed or you were fine.'

When she reached the apartment, Maria found that her husband, Don, and the entire staff of the New Zealand Mission to the UN had decamped there from the office. As Ambassador, Don was co-ordinating the mammoth task of tracking down the New Zealanders and the lines were running hot from the Ministry's crisis centre in Wellington: 'There were so many rumours about people who were supposed to be missing,' Maria told me, 'and half of them weren't even in New York.' The media was also clamouring for information: 'I remember a television crew coming and interviewing Don in the front room … They kept wanting high profile stories – not facts … How many New Zealanders are lost – it must be thousands. But Don insisted that we should not announce any New Zealanders lost until we had a body count.' With hundreds of people still unaccounted for, nobody had any idea of the casualty figures.

As soon as she could, Maria emailed Andrea:

GO TO BED!!!

I am home now and so is all of the NZ mission to the UN. They will be here all night as the building Don works in is closed and people will be contacting us … There is a lot of fear about NZers who worked in the Wall Street district. It was eerie walking home; the streets were all blocked off so ambulances could rush through. Siren and sighs were the only sounds in normally raucous NY. I have to go as I don't want to tie up the phone lines as they need them to field calls from NZ.

Sleep tight love,
Mummy[7]

Throughout the night the staff worked in shifts, trying to locate New Zealanders, some of whom got a call in the early hours telling them to 'phone home' immediately. But although Don managed to avoid a 3.30 a.m. stand-up with TVNZ's Paul Holmes, neither he nor Maria got much sleep: 'I did go to bed,' Maria recalls, 'and so did Don because he realised that he had to be on the ball. But there was the odd phone call.' Outside, the streets were dead and on the East River, usually swarming with pleasure boats, the only craft were police patrols.

Next morning the staff returned to the office, leaving Maria to field a stream of enquiries on her home phone number, which 'some nut' had given out as an information line. Many of the callers were time-wasters and Maria found her patience tested to the limits: 'I'm trying to be courteous, but it is hard'. Meanwhile the realisation that 'something truly horrendous happened yesterday, just four miles down the road from our apartment'[8] was starting to sink in and to clear her thoughts she decided to take a walk. It was another glorious September day and, unlike the previous night, quite a few people were about. But the mood was sombre. New York was in mourning and people were going about their business unsmilingly, knowing that at the bottom of the island, the bodies of countless New Yorkers were entombed beneath tons of rubble and twisted metal.

When Maria arrived home, she poured out her feelings in a message to her family:

12 September 2001

I think today has really changed the way Americans think about the world and themselves. There is a sense of the essential vulnerability of a free society … How were four planes able to be simultaneously hijacked? How come a country that spends billions on intelligence and security had no inkling that this would happen? And most of all, what happens next? With such madmen around, who are intelligent, but irrational and fanatical in a way we didn't imagine possible, what will be next? Nuclear or germ war terrorism?

… Good luck to everyone. NZ … way down at the bottom of the globe isn't looking too bad at the moment.

Love,
Maria[9]

The following day the schools re-opened and Maria returned to work. No one knew what state the children would be in and the Principal had asked all the teachers to sit and talk to them. As one teacher was absent, Maria took over her class: 'I didn't know the children at all. They were about thirteen and I sat them in a semi-circle … We were told just to get them talking.'

Although none of the children had lost a parent, some of them were badly shaken. But once Maria had gained their confidence, they talked non-stop about the attacks all morning. By the afternoon, they were less voluble and by the next day, they were pleading to do something else.

Many of the teachers were equally shaken and within the space of a few days, Maria found herself being promoted from a newly arrived part-timer to the Principal's right-hand woman. Typically she makes light of her contribution: 'Everyone else was allowed to have a nervous breakdown, and couldn't do counselling and couldn't come to school, but I was always there. I could come at six o'clock in the morning and I never said no … I didn't need to. I wasn't involved in searching for people. Don had it all under control.' After several days of working around the clock, Don and his staff had located 900 New Zealanders, most of whom had never bothered to register at the Consulate.

As the scale of the tragedy emerged, the Americans were shell-shocked. It was the first hostile attack on the US mainland since the British had burnt the White House in 1814 and the largest loss of life on its soil in history. Thousands had died, but until their bodies were identified, the anguished search for survivors continued:

15 September 2001

On my bus yesterday people looked stunned and grim … There was a deathly still on the bus when we passed the New York Medical Centre with all the refrigerated trucks parked outside …

When I came out of school on Thursday, bus shelters, walls, in fact on all available spaces, flyers had been posted, pleading for information about missing people. Some were typed, others handwritten, all showing photos of the missing at weddings, with babies, wearing graduation gowns with messages such as 'If you see her please tell to phone her Mom' …

Downtown there are still tragic scenes. Desperate people trying to get past the National Guards, convinced that if they are only allowed in they will find their loved one under the tons of collapsed steel and concrete. Others still wander from hospital to hospital, or places where their loved ones used to go with flyers and posters hoping to find someone 'who worked above the eightieth floor' or 'on the ninety-second floor' knowing that if they did, they could keep their hope alive a little longer.

The saddest … no, not the saddest … these things are unquantifiable … are the stories of the firemen with their hoses and fire fighting equipment rushing into the building as everyone else was pouring out. Everyone cheered them on. Eyewitnesses say that there was no fear in their eyes. 300 of these men, traditional NY heroes, were lost, trapped when the buildings cascaded like waterfalls.[10]

The New York Fire Department lost 343 men, which is more than any fire brigade on record. But there was also another group of heroes, namely the passengers of United Airlines Flight 93, who stormed the cockpit to prevent the hijackers from hitting their target. Among them was a 48-year-old New Zealander named Alan Beaven, whose role was later immortalised in the film *United 93*. He and US-born John Lozowsky were the only New Zealand fatalities.

Ever since the terrorist attacks, the New York authorities had been tackling the psychological aftermath. Churches and synagogues were wide open and the museums had waived their charges. At UNIS, supporting the children became a top priority: 'Focus on the good' was the advice from the psychologists and when the Principal suggested teaching a unit on heroism, Maria needed no second bidding: 'I put one together … That's what I'm skilled in doing. It's my job – like an artist being asked to paint a picture'. Quite apart from the gallant firemen and the heroes of United 93, she had abundant material to draw on, such as quotes from the Mayor, Giuliani, and songs like Mariah Carey's *Hero*. The children loved it – especially the pop music – and so did the Principal: 'I hear there are some great things going on in your classroom',[11] he told Maria. But she was one of the few who bothered to respond. Most of the other teachers preferred to stick with their usual lesson plans.

Alongside her teaching and counselling, Maria was juggling her diplomatic role. By 2001, the days when diplomatic ladies gave tea-parties and baked cakes for the local charities were largely over, especially in New York where diplomatic life revolves entirely around the UN. Even at Head of Mission level, working wives are not uncommon, with ambassadresses jetting in from board meetings to attend their husbands' dinner parties.

But, for women like Maria, who had been raised in the old school, traces of guilt remain: 'I was a very bad diplomatic wife,' she told me, without the glimmer of a smile, 'but I actually found that if you've got well-trained staff they can do it. You've just got to turn up and look happy and relaxed … On my first postings … I used to do all the cooking and the table – making sure that everything was beautiful. But at the end of each posting, I felt well ... was that worth it?'

Nevertheless, reading between the lines, it is clear that Maria still kept a close eye on her household: 'I don't fuss about little things and my attitude is that the home staff know all about the flowers and the menu, so I'd give them the cook books. But if I didn't like something, I'd say "let's try this". She also kept open house for a non-stop stream of official visitors. 'It was never a problem,' she said, 'because the place was so big and they weren't sleeping in the bedroom next to you. The last thing you want is to meet the Minister of Foreign Affairs in your pyjamas.' Foreign Minister Phil Goff turned up to stay just twelve days after September 11, but Maria does not reveal whether they met in their pyjamas.

For over thirty years the official Residence in New York had been at 10 Gracie Square, which is one of Manhattan's most prestigious addresses. 'It was very old New York,' Maria told me, 'with a huge entertainment area and a huge kitchen. Madame Chiang Kai-Shek lived upstairs. In fact it was always said that there were only three poor people in the building and they were the Ambassadors.' But it incurred a crippling capital charge from the New Zealand Treasury and a year after the MacKays arrived, it had to be put on the market: 'I think the Madoffs bought it off us and we had to move temporarily to another place ... and then to the Deputy's house, which is now the Residence.'

Housing was not the only area in which the Ministry was tightening its belt. Entertainment budgets were also leaner and most of the representational duties now fell to the Head of Mission. 'We did a lot of entertaining,' Maria said. But although she chatted her way through countless dinner parties and receptions, being an ambassadress was not the all-consuming role for her that it had been for earlier wives. What mattered far more to her was her teaching.

Over the next two and a half years, Maria became the school's expert on teaching traumatised children. In 2003, she represented UNIS at an international conference in Poland and in March 2004, after a spate of bombings world wide, she and her class were filmed by Japanese television. A clip of the programme captures the scene:

Maria is completely absorbed in her task. She is smiling and as she outlines the topic, her eyes never leave the children's faces: 'So what's happened in the world recently?' she asks, 'if you opened up the paper this morning, you would have seen that something horrendous has

Completely focused on her class: Maria MacKay as she appeared on prime time CNN. New York 2005.

happened.' Seated at square tables in groups of five or six, the children are listening intently. When Maria finishes, half a dozen hands shoot up. Bombers have attacked the Madrid metro and she is talking to the children about terrorism. 'Write down one word', she continues, 'that says how you feel when you hear that somewhere in the world there has been a terrorist attack.' As the children start to write, she strolls between the tables glancing from child to child. One has scribbled 'Sad' and another has written 'Confusion'.

Maria nods to a clever-looking boy at the back. 'I wrote "mad",' he says, 'because the terrorist groups want to achieve something for the people, but actually they're going to make everybody die.' Maria turns to a slim, dark girl with a ponytail. 'I wrote "anxious",' she says, 'because you never know, they could be coming to New York and America again, so it makes me nervous.' As the camera pans across the children's artwork, a Japanese voiceover drowns out the lesson.[12]

For visiting media, Maria's class was an obvious choice and when another film crew arrived – from CNN – the Principal once again sent them straight to his New Zealand teacher. They spent the whole morning in her classroom, filming for a prime time programme that was to be shown later that day. Beaming into millions of homes, in a soft grey jacket and a double row of pearls, Maria looks a picture of elegance. But although she admits to dressing up (just a little) for her debut on CNN, she appears oblivious to the cameras. As usual, she is engrossed in her teaching and the warmth of her smile is not for the viewers, but for the children. Nor is there any mention of her role as the wife of an ambassador. Instead she is described as 'Maria MacKay, Teacher.' And that is how she would have wanted it.

Postscript

When I embarked on this book in 2009, New Zealand's diplomatic envoys rarely rated a mention in the media. By early 2012, the situation had changed radically and the staff of MFAT – and their wives and partners – had become front-page news, thereby giving my subject a topical relevance quite unforeseen at the outset. The origin of this sudden interest was a proposed 'restructuring' of the Ministry, including the culling of hundreds of staff, which many feared would leave New Zealand without a viable foreign service.

As the extent of the cost-cutting became public, a furious debate ensued. Not only was the Ministry to lose over 20 per cent of its staff, but on their return home officers would be consigned to a 'surge pool' with no guarantee of future employment. In addition, provision would no longer be made for the extra cost of supporting partners and children at posts and 'married' allowances would cease. Since nearly three-quarters of the Ministry's offshore staff have partners, reactions were outraged and in the extensive media coverage that followed expressions like 'a giant stuff-up' and 'a shambles' feature regularly.

At the forefront of the fray were the partners on whom the cuts would have a devastating impact. Excluded from the consultation process, they were venting their feelings on Facebook and, in a stinging letter to the *Dominion Post*, the redoubtable Gillian Green echoes the views of many:

> *Who in his or her right mind would be prepared to uproot children from their schools and friends, to destroy a partner's career structure and leave the family home to the frequently thoughtless hands of tenants to serve in a diplomatic post … for no recompense, with the very real likelihood of no employment for either adult on their return?*

Much of her wrath was directed at the two men at the top:

> *The basis for this shambles lies not only with an unsympathetic minister, but with a chief executive who has no knowledge or experience of service overseas.*
> *This Government has put the castration of MFAT into the hands of the ignorant.*[1]

In an open letter from the partners to the CEO, lawyer and diplomatic spouse Bronwen Golder was equally forceful:

> *We consider that the proposed changes, if implemented, will bring the Ministry to a point where partners will no longer be able to support their spouses continuing their careers with MFAT ... [and] to that end we have no choice but to encourage our MFAT partners to pursue a career beyond MFAT.*[2]

The letter was handed over at a stormy meeting attended by a large number of partners. Tempers flared on both sides and by all accounts there was plenty of blood on the carpet. But the threat of a mass staff exodus certainly hit home and within hours the Government had backed off. In his first public statement on the affair, the Prime Minister admitted that there were some 'genuine issues' and that the cuts were 'a bit aggressive'.[3] For the partners, this was a major victory. It also signalled the Government's tacit acknowledgement that unless New Zealand's diplomatic service was to become an order of celibates, it could not afford to ignore the partners.

In light of the Prime Minister's comments, the cull was reduced and some of the more extreme measures were toned down. Undoubtedly the partners' intervention aided the process, but it would be misleading to suggest that they were the only players. Smoke was also rising from the Ministry's staff association and in the face of a full-blown mutiny, the CEO took the unprecedented step of recalling all the heads of mission from their overseas posts for a two-day consultation in Wellington.

Although fewer details have emerged on Facebook, this too was a highly charged occasion at which New Zealand's top diplomats went head-to-head with the CEO and extracted some further concessions. At the time of writing, however, the restructuring is far from over and much unhappiness and uncertainty about the future remains.

NOTES
....

Chapter 1.

1. Ruth Fry, *Maud & Amber: A New Zealand Mother and Daughter and the Women's Cause 1865 to 1981* (New Zealand: Canterbury University Press, 1992), p. 23
2. London *Times*, Friday 6 Dec 1907, p. 8.
3. *New Zealand Graphic*, 27 Aug 1892, p. 853.
4. Hall MS, quoted by Keith Sinclair, *William Pember Reeves: New Zealand Fabian* (Oxford: Clarendon Press, 1965), p. 180.
5. Ibid., p. 243.
6. *Times*, Fri 6 Dec 1907, p. 8.
7. Quoted by Raewyn Mary Blackstock, 'The Office of Agent-General for New Zealand in the United Kingdon, 1870–1905 (PhD. Thesis, VUW, 1970), p. 94.
8. Ibid., p. 214.
9. Sinclair, *William Pember Reeves*, p. 285.
10. Beatrice Webb, *Visit to New Zealand in 1898: Beatrice Webb's Diary with Entries by Sidney Webb* (Wellington: Price Milburn & Co., 1959), pp. 54–5.
11. Norman & Jeanne MacKenzie, eds, *The Diary of Beatrice Webb*, Vol. 2, 1892–1905 (London: Virago in association with the London School of Economics and Political Sciences, 1982), p. 147.
12. Ibid., Vol. 2, p. 320.
13. Sinclair, *William Pember Reeves*, p. 313.
14. G.P. Wells, ed., *H.G. Wells in Love: Postscript to an Experiment in Autobiography* (London: Faber and Faber, 1984), pp. 70–1.
15. Quoted by Fry, *Maud & Amber*, p. 37.
16. G.P. Wells, ed., *H.G. Wells in Love*, p. 74
17. Ibid., p. 73.
18. Ann Phillips, ed., *A Newnham Anthology* (Cambridge: Cambridge University Press, 1979), p. 68.
19. H.G. Wells, *Experiment in Autobiography: Discoveries and Conclusions of a Very Ordinary Brain (Since 1866)*, Vol. II (London: Victor Gollancz Ltd., 1934), pp. 435-6.
20. Ibid., p. 464.
21. G.P. Wells, ed., *H.G. Wells in Love*, p. 82.
22. Wells papers, Illinois, quoted by Ruth Brandon, *The New Women and the Old Men: Love, Sex and the Woman Question* (London: Secker & Warburg, 1990), p. 184.
23. Quoted by Fry, *Maud & Amber*, pp. 49–50.
24. Phillips, *A Newnham Anthology*, p. 68.
25. G.P. Wells, ed., *H.G. Wells in Love*, pp. 74–5.
26. N. & J. MacKenzie, eds., *The Diary of Beatrice Webb*, Vol. 3, 1905–1924, pp. 98–99 entry for 15 Sep 1908.
27. Brandon, *The New Women and the Old Men*, p. 187.
28. G.P. Wells, ed., *H.G. Wells in Love*, pp. 77, 73 & 76.
29. J.R. Hammond, ed., *H.G. Wells: Interviews and Recollections*, 'Dramatising a Wells Novel' Compton Mackenzie (London: Macmillan Press, 1980), p. 33.
30. G.P. Wells, ed., *H.G. Wells in Love*, p. 80.
31. N. & J. MacKenzie, eds., *Diary of Beatrice Webb*, Vol. 3, p. 125.
32. Ibid., p. 132.
33. Maud Pember Reeves, *Round about a pound a week* (London: Virago, 1979), p. 215.
34. G.P. Wells, ed., *H.G. Wells in Love*, p. 73.

Chapter 2.

1. 'Mrs Boswell visits grim Stalingrad Scene', Auckland *Herald*, 10 Dec 1949, p. 8.
2. Ibid.
3. Ibid.
4. 'Life goes on in Ruins of Stalingrad', Auckland *Herald*, 17 Dec 1949, p. 8.
5. ATL, MS-Papers-8661-1, Memoir of Doug and Ruth Lake by Sarah Lake, Appendix II, p. 75.
6. ATL, MS-Papers-8752-206, Tribute by Frank Corner to Sir Alister McIntosh, 5 Dec 1978.
7. Templeton, M., *Top Hats are Not being Taken: A Short History of the New Zealand Legation in Moscow 1944–1950* (Wellington, NZIIA) 1988, p. 13.
8. Ibid., pp. 25 & 26.
9. ATL, MS-Papers-8896-5, undated letter from Jean Boswell to Mrs Dodd, c. 1946 and letter to Mrs Dodd of 10 Mar 1947.
10. ATL, MS-Papers-8661-1, Memoir of Doug and Ruth Lake by Sarah Lake, Appendix II, p.69 (Letter from Ruth Macky to her parents of 29 Jan 1945).
11. ATL, MS-Papers-8752-206, Letter to Dan Davin from Michael King, 24 Sep 1982.
12. Ovenden, K., *Fighting Withdrawal: The life of Dan Davin, Writer, Soldier, Publisher* (Oxford, OUP, 1996), p. 174 & footnote: diary entry 4 Nov 1963.
13. McNeish, J., *The Sixth Man: The Extraordinary life of Paddy Costello* (New Zealand, Random House, 2007), p. 119.
14. ATL, MS-Papers-8896-5, Letter to Mrs Dodd from Jean Boswell of 14 Apr 1946.
15. ATL, MS-Papers-6759-235. Top Secret telegram from Charles Boswell to Alister McIntosh of 9 Apr 1946.
16. ATL MS-Papers-6759-260, letter to Paddy Costello from Alister McIntosh of 22 Mar 1945.
17. Ibid., letter to Alister McIntosh from Paddy Costello of 29 Apr 1945.
18. McNeish, J., *The Sixth Man*, p. 215.
19 ATL, MS-Papers-8752-204, declassified SIS papers, report of Detective Sergeant Jones re Patrick Costello of 9 Oct 1950.
20. ATL, MS-Papers-8896-5, letter from Jean Boswell to Mrs Dodd of 14 Apr 1946.
21. ATL, MS-Papers-6759-260, letter from Paddy Costello to McIntosh of 7 Mar 1946.
22. Ibid., letter from Paddy Costello to McIntosh of 2 Nov 1945.
23. ATL, MS-Papers-8896-5, undated letter from Jean Boswell to Mrs Dodd c. 1946.
24. Ibid., p. 2.
25. Ibid., letter from Jean Boswell to Mrs Dodd of 14 Apr 1946.
26. ATL, MS-Papers-6759-260, letter from Paddy Costello to Alister McIntosh of 31 Oct 1946.
27. *Southern Cross*, 'Boswell Articles "one-eyed"', 6 May 1950 (no page).
28. ATL, MS-Papers-6759-292, letter from Alister McIntosh to Ruth Lake of 18 Mar 1950.
29. ATL, MS-Papers-8661-2, Lake, D. 'Goodbye Diplomacy', p. 25.
30. *Dominion*, 20 Sep 1999.
31. ATL, MS-Papers-8752-204, letter from the Director of Security to Michael King of 20 Dec 2002.

Chapter 3.

1. Christopher Hassall, *Rupert Brooke* (London: Faber & Faber, 1964), pp. 426–7.
2. Rupert Brooke 'Some Niggers', *New Statesman*, 19 September 1914.
3. Letters from Eileen Powles to Dick Powles of 14, 26 Jan 1946 & 19 Feb 1946, ATL MS-Papers-9351-094.
4. Ibid.
5. Letter from George Laking to Dick Powles of 28 Sep 1948, p. 2. ATL MS-Papers-9351-042.
6. Letter from Dick Powles to John S. Reid of 31 Aug 1949, p. 1. ATL MS-Papers-9351-032.
7. Letter from Col. Voelcker to Dick Powles of 19 & 20 Oct 1948. ATL MS-Papers-9351-032.
8. Letter from Dick Powles to John S. Reid of 31 Aug 1949. ATL MS-Papers-9351-032.
9. Letter from Col. Voelcker to Dick Powles of 20 Oct 1948. ATL MS-Papers-9351-032.

10. Speech by Dick Powles c. Mar 1960, p.1. ATL MS-Papers-9351-049.
11. Eileen Powles Interview. ATL Sound Archives.
12. Letter from Dick Powles to John S. Reid of 31Aug 1949. ATL MS-Papers-9351-032.
13. Letter from Dick Powles to Carl Berendsen of 10 Aug 1950, p.1, ATL MS-Papers-9351-033.
14. Letter from Dick Powles to Walter Nash of 12 May 1958, p. 2. ATL MS-Papers-9351-?026.
15. Tim Beaglehole, *A Life of J.C. Beaglehole: New Zealand Scholar* (Wellington, Victoria University Press, 2006), p. 389.
16. Letters from Lord Cobham to Dick Powles of 12 Oct 1959 & 8 Feb 1960. ATL MS-Papers-9351-049.
17. Eileen Powles Interview. ATL Sound Archives.
18. Report on 'Farewell Malaga to Savai'i by his Excellency the High Commissioner and Mrs Powles – 13 March to 16 March 1960', p. 4. ATL MS-Papers-9351-049.
19. Letter to Eileen Powles from an unidentified Samoan friend of 1 April 1960. ATL MS-Papers-9351-049.

Chapter 4.

1. *New Chronicle* (London), 2 June 1953, p. 1.
2. Interview with Lyn Corner 30 Oct 2009.
3. Ed., Brian Lynch, *Celebrating New Zealand's Emergence* (Wellington: New Zealand Institute of International Affairs, 2005), p. 75.
4. Ian McGibbon ed., *Undiplomatic Dialogue: Letters between Carl Berendsen & Alister McIntosh 1943–1945* (Auckland: Auckland University Press in association with MFAT, 1993), p. 35 (letter from McIntosh to Berendsen of 29 Oct 1943).
5. Malcolm Templeton, ed., *An Eye, An Ear and a Voice: 50 Years in New Zealand External Relations 1943–1993* (Wellington: Ministry of Foreign Affairs, 1993), p. 73.
6. François de Callières, trans. A.F. Whyte, *On the Manner of Negotiating with Princes* (Boston & New York: Houghton Mifflin Co., 1919, pp. 23 & 61.
7. Harold Nicolson, *Diplomacy* (London: Geoffrey Cumberlege, Oxford University Press, 1950), p. 126.
8. Templeton, *An Ear, An Eye and a Voice*, p. 189.
9. Ibid., p. 190.
10. Ibid., p. 116.
11. Ibid., pp. 121–2.
12. Interview with Lyn Corner, 30 Oct 2009.
13. Templeton, *An, An Ear and a Voice*, pp. 190–1
14. Interview with Merv Norrish 25 Nov 2010.
15. Interview with Lyn Corner 11 Sep 2009.
16. Ibid.

Chapter 5.

1. Based on interview with Alison and Jim on 27 Nov 2009.
2. Unpublished typescript of Alison's letters. Letter to her parents of 2 Dec 1967, p. 2.
3. Ibid., 'Jim's Notes' of 26 Dec 1967, p. 16.
4. Interview with Alison and Jim on 27 Nov 2009.
5. Unpublished typescript of Alison's letters. Letter to her parents of 26 Dec 1967, p. 10.
6. Based on interview with Alison and Jim on 29 Nov 2009.
7. Unpublished typescript of Alison's letters. 'Jim Jottings' sent with letter of 6 Feb 1968, p. 36a.
8. Interview with Alison and Jim on 27 Nov 2009.
9. Unpublished typescript of Alison's letters. Letter to her parents 6 Feb 1968, p. 33.
10. Ibid. Letter to her parents of 13 Feb 1968, p. 35.
11. Ibid., Jim's Jottings, sent with letter of 6 Feb 1968, p. 35d.
12. *Dominion*, 2 Feb 1968, p. 1.
13. Interview with Alison and Jim on 27 Nov 2009.
14. Ibid.
15. Unpublished typescript of Alison's letters. Letter to her parents 20 Feb 1968, pp. 50–51.

16. Ibid.
17. Unpublished typescript of Alison's letters. 'Jim's Effort' of 4 Jun 1968, p. 41.
18. Comment to JMW by a former diplomatic colleague of Paul Edmonds.
19. Interview with Alison and Jim on 27 Nov 2009.
20. Unpublished typescript of Alison's letters. Letter to her parents of 30 Oct 1968 p. 4.
21. Ibid., Letter to her parents of 13 Nov 1968, p. 2.
22. Ibid., letter to her parents of 20 Nov 1968, p. 2.
23. Ibid., letter to her parents of 26 Dec 1968, p. 3.
24. Ibid., letter to her parents of 4 Feb 1969.
25. 'History of a Hospital', *Te Manu Rere: The International Magazine of the VSA*, December 2001, p. 8.
26. Unpublished typescript of Alison's letters. Letter to her parents of 21 Apr 1969, p. 3.
27. Ibid., letter to her parents of 7 May 1969, p. 2.
28. Ibid., letter to her parents of 24 Sep 1969, p. 3.
29. Ibid., p. 2.
30. Interview with Alison and Jim on 27 Nov 2009.

Chapter 7.

1. Marguerite Scott, draft of *Handbook for Foreign Service Families* of 13 Aug 1974 (MFAT Archives, FSA 3/17).
2. Marguerite Scott, *Reminiscences of Service in the Wrens, 1942–1945* (Unpublished typescript).
3. Ibid., p. 12.
4. Ibid., p. 6.
5. Marguerite Scott, interview with Ian McGibbon of April 2001 (ATL Oral History).
6. Ibid.
7. *Overseas Service Handbook*, B.6, Dept of External Affairs, c. 1968.
8. Marguerite Scott, draft *Handbook*, ch. 5, p. 8.
9. Interview with Roger Peren of 19 May 2010.
10. Letter and recommendations from Marguerite Scott to Peter Adams, Secretary of the FSA, of 13 Apr 1981 (MFAT Archives FSA 3/17.)
11. Interview with Veronica Scott of 18 Dec 2009.

Chapter 8.

1. Unless otherwise indicated, all quotes are from the author's meeting with Jane Eyre on 16 June 2010.
2. *New Zealand Herald*, Thursday 24 Nov 1966, p. 3.
3. Jim Weir, *Eat, Drink and be Wary: A New Zealand diplomat looks back* (Wellington: Dunmore Publishing Ltd., 2011), p. 80.
4. Unidentified newspaper clipping, London c. 1973.
5. *Globe and Mail*, 19 April 1979 (page no. missing).

Chapter 9.

1. Unless otherwise stated, all quotes are from the author's meeting with Piera McArthur on 24 February 2010.
2. James McNeish, *The Sixth Man: The Extraordinary Life of Paddy Costello* (Auckland: Random House, 2007), p. 233.
3. Jeffery Grice, Personal Entry, My NZ Music Connections,jefferygrice.net/events/diary/view.asp?id=6
4. T.J. McNamara, review of 'The Holy Ghost among the Fantails' (Studio of Contemporary Art, Auckland), 16 Nov 2005.

Chapter 10.

1. All quotes are from the author's meetings with Janine Hunn on 13 April and 4 May 2010.

Chapter 11.

1. All quotes are from the author's meeting with Greta Keur on 28 February 2010.
2. Jim Weir, *A New Zealand Ambassador's Letters from Moscow* (Auckland: Hodder and Stoughton, 1988), p. 18.
3. Quoted by Brian Easton's paper 'Trying to understand Sutch', Stout Research Centre Seminar Series, 2 Sep 1998.
4. Weir, *Letters from Moscow*, p. 141.
5. Ibid., p. 117.
6. Ibid.,
7. *Christchurch Press*, Tuesday 18 Oct 1977, p. 1.
8. Weir, *Letters from Moscow*, p. 117.
9. Ibid., pp. 117–8.
10. Ibid., p. 121.
11. Funeral tribute by Keith Sinclair, 27 March 1984.

Chapter 12.

1. All quotes are taken from Penny Klap's letters to her parents from 1978–81.
2. Phillip Klap, *What a Life!* (Auckland: Kalamazoo, 2010), p. 127.

Chapter 13.

1. *Code of Conduct* (Wellington: Ministry of Foreign Affairs).
2. *Overseas Service Handbook* (Wellington: Ministry of Foreign Affairs), Chapter L, 'Compassionate Assistance' & Chapter B, 'General Instructions'.
3. Ibid., 'General Instructions'.
4. Vienna Convention on Diplomatic Relations 1961, Article 42.
5. Letter from T.P. Davin to NZ High Commissioner in Kuala Lumpur of 27 Jun 1961, MFAT, FSA 3/17.
6. Handwritten note from Lloyd White to Norm Farrell c. Oct 1966, MFAT FSA 3/17.
7. Letter from Norm Farrell to Paul Edmonds of 9 Nov 1964, MFAT FSA 3/17.
8. Telegram from Malcolm Templeton to P.G. Millen of 14 Jul 1970, MFAT FSA 3/17.
9. Airgram from Department of State to All Posts, Washington, 22 Jan 1972, National Archives, RG 59, Central Files 1970-73, PER 1.
10. Malcolm Templeton, ed., *An Eye An Ear and a Voice*, Wellington: MFAT, 1993, pp. 198–200.
11. Letter from Denis Dunlop to David McDowell of 3 May 1973, MFAT FSA 3/17.
12. Letter from Pat Caughley to Denis Dunlop of 7 May 1973, MFAT FSA 3/17.
13. Letter from Lloyd White to David McDowell of 9 Jul 1973, MFAT FSA 3/17.
14. Letter from David McDowell to Frank Corner of 4 Dec 1973, MFAT FSA 3/17.
15. MFA response to FSA submission of 19 Apr 1974, MFAT FSA 3/17.
16. Ibid.
17. Cited in MFA's response to Women's International Forum Questionnaire c. 1977, MFAT FSA 3/17.
18. *General-Anzeiger*, Bonn , 24–26 Dec 1976 (trans).
19. 'Dippy Wives and their views are not to be ignored' *Times* of 12 Sep 1977
20. 'And One Wife's Story', *New York Times* of ?9 April 1984 (newspaper clipping MFAT FSA 3/17).
21. 'The New Breed of Foreign Service Wives', *Washington Star* of 26 Apr 1981.
22. Letter from Moina Simcock to her mother of 13 Nov 1981. Family papers.
23. *Washington Post*, Wednesday 7 Mar 1984, 'Mrs Foreign Service Deserves to Be Paid Too', Marlene Eagleburger.
24. 'Foreign Service Wives: What Price Service?' Judy Mann, *Washington Post* of 27 Jul 1979.
25. Letter from Geoff Randall to Richard Grant, FSA President, of 30 July 1986, MFAT FSA 3/17.
26. *Overseas Service Handbook*, Ministry of Foreign Affairs 1982–
27. Letter from Margaret Farrell to Nancy Mullins, FSA President, of 5 Oct 1981, MFAT FSA 3/17.

28. Letter from David Lackey to Richard Grant of 27 Oct 1986, MFAT FSA 3/17.
29. P.M Caughley, Notes on FSA Submission of 11 May 1973 (MFAT Archives FSA 3/17).
30. Tania Domett 'Soft Power in Global Politics: Diplomatic Partners as transversal Actors', *Australian Journal of Political Science*, vol. 40, Issue 2, 2005, pp. 289–306.

Chapter 14.

1. Taken from the author's meeting with Judith Paulin on 30 Dec 2009.
2. Letter from Irvine Paulin to his parents of 23 Jan 1987.

Chapter 15.

1. All quotes from June Hillary are taken from the author's meeting with her on 18 Feb 2010.
2. Edmund Hillary, *View from the Summit* (London: Doubleday, 1999), p. 201.
3. Ibid., p. 208.
4. Ibid., p. 209.
5. Ibid., pp. 240 & 241.
6. Ibid., p. 272.
7. *Evening Post*, 'A spouse writes', letter from Gillian Green, 18 June 1990.

Chapter 16.

1. All quotes are from the author's meetings with Jill Caughley on 21 and 24 December 2009.
2. William Shawcross, *The Quality of Mercy: Cambodia, Holocaust and Modern Conscience* (London: Andre Deutsch, 1984), p. 239.

Chapter 17.

1. All direct quotes from Barbara are taken from her typescript 'Fiji Memories' (1 May 2010) and her follow-up to questions (16 Aug 2010).
2. *Dominion* 15 April 1987, p. 5.
3. John Sharpham, *Rabuka of Fiji: The Authorised Biography of Major-General Sitiveni Rabuka* (Queensland: Central Queensland University Press, 2000), p. 97.
4. Eddie Dean & Stan Ritova, *Rabuka: No Other Way* (Australia: Doubleday, 1988), p. 67.
5. Ibid., p. 70.
6. Ibid., p. 72.
7. This and other comments by Rod Gates are taken from an interview on 24 Jan 2010.
8. Kenneth Bain, *Treason at Ten* (London: Hodder & Stoughton, 1989), p. 5.
9. Ibid., p. 7.
10. *New Zealand Herald*, 20 May 1987, p. 2.
11. Gerald Hensley, *Final Approaches: A Memoir* (Auckland University Press, 2006), p. 300–1.
12. Sharpham, *Rabuka of Fiji*, p. 122, citing Paul Lynch in the *Australian*, 22 May 1987, p. 1.
13. Bain, *Treason at Ten*, p. 8.
14. *Fiji Times*, 23 Sep 1987, p. 1.

Chapter 18.

1. MFAT Travel Advisory, Iraq. www.safetravel.govt.nz
2. All quotes from Geoff Wood are taken from the author's meeting with him on 8 Nov 2011.
3. Daphne Halkyard, *Unscheduled Stopover in Iraq* (Sussex: The Book Guild Ltd, 1993), p. 10.
4. *Washington Post*, 15 August 1990.
5. Malcolm Templeton, ed., *An Eye, An Ear and A Voice: 50 Years in New Zealand's External Relations 1943–1993* (Wellington: Ministry of Foreign Affairs and Trade, 1993), p. 185.
6. MFAT Archives, MERT Consular Division 45/9/3/1, Part 1, cable from Baghdad of 13 Aug 1990.

7. Lawrence Freedman & Efraim Karsh, *The Gulf conflict, 1990–1991: Diplomacy and War in the New World Order* (London: Faber and Faber, 1993), p. 137. (Saddam paraphrased by Iraqi Speaker, Sa'di Mehdi Saleh.)
8. MFAT Archives, MERT Consular Division 45/9/3/1, Part 1, Geoffrey Palmer, Post Cabinet Press Conference, 6 Aug 1990.
9. Ibid., Part 2, cable from Baghdad of 18 Aug 1990.
10. Ibid., Part 3, Letter from Alistair Lane via London of 19 Aug 1990.
11. Ibid., cable from Wellington of 21 Aug 1990.
12. Ibid., Part 4, cable from Baghdad of 29 Aug 1990.
13. Ibid., Part 6, cable from Baghdad of 26 Sep 1990.
14. Ibid., Part 3, cable from Baghdad of 21 Aug 1990.
15. Ibid., Part 2, letter from Karen Lane to Graeme Ammundsen of 16 Aug 1990.
16. *Dominion Post*, 5 Nov 1990, p. 1.
17. MFAT Archives, MERT Consular Division, 45/9/3/1, Part 8, letter from Naomi Lange to Jim Bolger of 5 Nov 1990.
18. David Lange, *My Life* (Auckland: Viking, 2005), p. 280.
19. *Evening Post*, 13 Nov 1990, p. 1.
20. MFAT Archives, MERT Consular Division, 45/9/3/1, Part 8, text of David Lange's press conference in Wellington, 13 Nov 1990.
21. Ibid., letter from Geoff Frost to John Clarke of 20 Nov 1990.

Chapter 19.

1. *Dominion*, 4 Mar 1997.
2. *Sunday Star Times*, 18 Aug 1996, p. A.2.
3. *Dominion*, 27 Jun 1997, p. 12.
4. *Otago Daily Times*, 28 Jun 1997, p. 3.
5. *Christchurch Press*, 28 Jun 1997, p. 20.
6. *Otago Daily Times*, 28 Jun 1997, p. 3.
7. *Otago Daily Times* 27 Jun 1997, p. 3 & *Dominion* 27 Jun 1997, p. 12.
8. *Christchurch Press*, 28 Jun 1997, p. 20.
9. *Sunday Star Times*, 29 Jun 1997.
10. *The Times*, 26 Jun 1997, p. 11.
11. *Christchurch Press,* 28 Jun 1997, p. 20.
12. *Dominion,* 27 Jun 1997, p. 12.
13. *The Times*, 26 Jun 1997, p. 11.
14. *Dominion*, 27 Jun 1997, p. 1.
15. *Evening Post*, 26 Jun 1997, p. 2.
16. Headlines of: *Daily Mail*, 26 Jun 1997, *Daily Telegraph*, 26 Jun 1997, p. 9, *Daily Express*, 26 Jun 1997, p. 29, *The Times*, 26 Jun 1997, p. 11.
17. *Evening Standard* quoted in *Christchurch Press* 30 Jun 1997, p. 5.
18. *Dominion*, 27 June 1997, p. 12.
19. *Evening Post*, 30 Jun 1997, p. 2.
20. *Evening Post*, 3 Jul 1997, p. 6.
21. *Sunday Star Times*, 29 Jun 1997.
22. *Sunday Star Times*, 31 Aug 1997, A. 4.
23. *New Zealand Herald*, 27 Jun 1997, News Review, p. 13.
24. *Dominion*, 23 Feb 2001, p. 1.

Chapter 20.

1. Unsigned memo re Support Services Circular of 14 April 1994. Family Liaison Office files, MFAT.
2. *Dominion* 8 June 1970, p. 1.
3. Tribute by Frank Corner, Secretary of Foreign Affairs, given at the funeral of Sir Alister McIntosh on 5 Dec 1978.
4. Ian McGibbon, 'McIntosh, Alister Donald Miles 1906 - 1978', *Dictionary of New Zealand Biography,* vol. 5. Auckland University Press & Dept of Internal Affairs, 2000, p. 314.
5. Frank Corner, tribute to Sir Alister McIntosh.

6. James McNeish, *The Sixth Man: the extraordinary life of Paddy Costello* (Auckland: Random House, 2007), p. 373.
7. Ian McGibbon, ed., *Undiplomatic Dialogue: Letters between Carl Berendsen & Alister McIntosh 1943–1952* (Auckland University Press, 1993), p. 204.
8. Frank Corner, tribute to Sir Alister McIntosh.
9. *Evening Post,* 18 Jun 1966, p. 27.
10. Joanne Drayton, *Ngaio Marsh: her life in crime* (Auckland: Harper Collins (New Zealand) Ltd., 2008), p. 221.
11. ATL, MS-Papers-1946.
12. Code of Conduct, MFAT, 2009, p. 31.
13. MFAT, O/S Staffing Policy 19/6/2, part 2, memo from Adrian Macey to SMG of 22 Oct 1993.
14. All quotes from Ayesha are from a SKYPE interview with the author on 28 April 2012.
15. Pierre Trudeau as reported in the *Globe and Mail* on 22 Dec 1967.

Chapter 21.

1. Email from Maria Mackay to friends and family, 11 Sep 2001.
2. All direct quotes are taken from the author's meeting with Maria MacKay on 19 Apr 2011.
3. Email attachment from Maria MacKay to friends and family, 12 Sep 2001.
4. Email from Andrea MacKay to her mother, 11 Sept 2001.
5. Email from Maria MacKay to her daughter, Andrea, 11 Sept 2001
6. Email attachment from Maria MacKay to friends and family, 12 Sep 2001.
7. Email from Maria MacKay to her daughter, Andrea, 11 Sep 2001.
8. Email attachment from Maria MacKay to friends and family, 12 Sep 2001.
9. Ibid.
10. Email attachment from Maria MacKay to friends and family, 15 Sep 2001.
11. Email from Maria MacKay to Cathy Keating, 23 Sep 2001.
12. Transcribed from TV coverage of Maria's class on Japanese television, 12 Mar 2004.

Postscript

1   *Dominion Post*, 16 Mar 2012, B.6.
2   Open letter to John Allen from partners' representative, Bronwen Golder, 12 Mar 2012.
3   *Dominion Post*, 13 Mar 2012, A.2.

SELECTED BIBLIOGRAPHY

....

1. *Alexander Turnbull Library*

Manuscripts and Archives Collection
Letters from Jean Boswell. MS-Papers-8896-5
Paddy Costello – Death certificate etc. MS-Papers-7950
<u>Michael Bassett Papers</u>
  Biography of Peter Fraser. Ref. No. 2000-094-1
<u>Dan Davin Papers</u>
  Correspondence – C. MS-Papers-5079-008
  Correspondence: Wendy Campbell-Purdie. MS-Papers-5079-416
  Papers relating to Paddy Costello. MS-Papers-5079-426
  Paddy Costello draft of memoir. MS-Papers-5079-434 & 435.
  Papers & Correspondence relating to Paddy Costello. MS-Papers-5079-436, 437, 438 & 443.
<u>Michael King Papers</u>
  Proposed book on SIS. MS-Papers-8752-203, 204 & 206.
<u>Lake Family Papers</u>
  Douglas Lake: Correspondence from Moscow. MS-Papers-8661-7
  Douglas Lake memoir: Goodbye Diplomacy. MS-Papers-8661-2
  Memoir of Parents: Sarah Lake. MS-Papers-8661-1
<u>Alister McIntosh Papers</u>
  Personal Correspondence: Charles Boswell. MS-Papers-6759-235
  Personal Correspondence: Doug and Ruth Lake. MS-Papers-6759-292
  Personal Correspondence: Paddy Costello. MS-Papers-6759-260
  Personal Correspondence: Jean McKenzie. MS-Papers-6759-313 & 314
<u>Powles Family Papers</u>
  MS-Group 0480

Oral History Collection
Interviews with Sir Guy and Lady Powles

Video Collection
A view from the top: Hillary written and researched by Tom Scott, (Vid 0874)

2. *Ministry of Foreign Affairs and Trade*

General
Lists of New Zealand Representatives Overseas 1944–1987
Foreign Service Wives Manual (Ottawa: Dept. of Foreign Affairs, 1970).
Guidance to Diplomatic Service and other Officers and Wives, posted to Diplomatic Service
  Missions Overseas. (London: FCO, Diplomatic Administration Office, 1965).
Notes for Wives of Officers (Canberra: Dept. of Foreign Affairs, 1971).

Archives
Employment of Spouses (1954–1981), file 0049113 8/1/2
Employment for spouses and dependents, file 0141314 19/6/2
Role of spouses and women officers (1975–), file 0160205 FSA3/17
Spouses: role in overseas service (1981–), file 0160203 FSA3/17
Spouses (1987–1993), file 0160276 FSA3/17
Spouses Role/Recompense, file 0160273 FSA3/17/1
MERT Consular Division, file 45/9/3/1 – 5
Iraq/Kuwait Relations File 267/2/16/4

MFAT Family Liaison Coordinator
MFAT Partners' Newsletters

3. Theses

Blackstock, R. 'The Office of Agent-General for New Zealand in the United   Kingdom, 1870–1905' (PhD. Thesis, Victoria University of Wellington, 1970).
Caughley, J. 'Humanitarian, International Nursing and the New Zealand Recipients of   the Florence Nightingale Medal 1920–1999' (MA Thesis, Victoria University of Wellington, 2001).
Domett, T. 'Soft Power in Global Politics: Diplomatic Partners as transversal Actors' (from MA Thesis, University of Auckland) cited in *Australian Journal of   Political Science,* vol. 40, no.2, Jun 2005).

4. General Reading

Agents Abroad: the story of the New Zealand Trade Commissioner Service (New Zealand: Penguin, 2009).
Ammundsen, A. *From Pillar to Post* (London: Minerva Press, 1996)
Andrew, C. & Mitrokhin, V. *The Mitrokhin Archive: The KGB in Europe and the West* (London: Penguin, 1999).
Asbridge, G. *Funny Foreign Affairs: A View from the Middle* (Wellington: G. Asbridge, 1991).

Bain, K. *Treason at Ten* (London: Hodder & Stoughton, 1989).
Beaglehole, T. *A Life of J.C. Beaglehole: New Zealand Scholar* (Wellington: Victoria University Press, 2006).
Bickerton, I. & Pearson, M. *43 Days: The Gulf War* (E. Melbourne: text publishing in association with Australian Broadcasting Corporation, 1991).
Boswell J. *Dim Horizons* (Christchurch: Whitcombe & Tombs, 1955).
Boswell J. *Ernie and the Rest of Us* (Christchurch: Whitcombe & Tombs, 1960).
Brandon, R. *The New Women and the Old Men: Love, Sex and the Woman Question* (London: Secker & Warburg, 1990).
Brickell, C. *Mates & Lovers: A History of Gay New Zealand* (Auckland: Godwit, 2008)
Brown, B. ed. *New Zealand in World Affairs III 1972–1990* (Wellington: Victoria University Press in association with the New Zealand Institute of International Affairs, 1999).
Buckingham, L. *My First 40 Years* (Wellington: L. Buckingham, 2009).
Burgess, M. *Nursing in New Zealand Society* (Auckland: Longman Paul, 1984).

Callières, F. trans. Whyte A. F. *On the Manner of Negotiating with Princes* (Boston & New York: Houghton Mifflin Co., 1919).
Clark, M. ed. *For the Record: Lange and the Fourth Labour Government* (Wellington: Dunmore Publishing, 2005).
Cole, M. *The Story of Fabian Socialism* (London: Heinemann, 1961).
Craw, C. *Work of a New Zealand Diplomat.* Text of address. (Wellington, MFAT, 1970).

Dalziel, R. *The Origins of New Zealand Diplomacy; The Agent-General in London, 1870–1905* (Wellington: Price Milburn for Victoria University Press, *c.* 1975).
Dean, E. & Ritova, S. *Rabuka: No Other Way* (Australia: Doubleday, 1988).
Denman, C. *Diplomatic Incidents: Memoirs of an (Un)Diplomatic Wife* (London: John Murray, 2010).

Freedman, L. & Karsh E. *The Gulf Conflict, 1990–1991: Diplomacy and War in the New World Order* (London: Faber and Faber, 1993).
Fry, R. *Maud & Amber: a New Zealand Mother and Daughter and the Women's Cause 1865 to 1981* (New Zealand: Canterbury University Press, 1992).

Gore-Booth, Lord ed. *Satow's Guide to Diplomatic Practice* (London: Longmans, 1957).
Gwyn, R. *Northern Magus: Pierre Trudeau and Canadians* (Toronto: McClelland and Stewart, *c.* 1980).

Halkyard, D. *Unscheduled Stopover in Iraq* (England: Book Guild, 1993).

Hammond, J. ed. *H.G. Wells: Interviews and Recollections* (London: Macmillan Press, 1980).

Hammond, J. *A Robert Louis Stevenson Companion: A Guide to the Novels, Essays and Short Stories* (London: Macmillan Press, 1984).

Hassall, C. *Rupert Brooke* (London: Faber and Faber, 1964).

Hensley, G. *Final Approaches: A Memoir* (Auckland: Auckland University Press, 2006).

Hensley, G. *Beyond the Battlefield: New Zealand and its Allies 1935–1945* (New Zealand: Penguin, 2009).

Hickman, K. *Daughters of Britannia: The Lives and Times of Diplomatic Wives* (London: HarperCollins, 1999).

Hillary, E. *View from the Summit* (London: Doubleday, 1999).

Holroyd, M. *Bernard Shaw*, vol. 2 (New York: Random House, 1989).

Keesing, F. *Modern Samoa: Its Government and Changing Life* (London: George Allen & Unwin Ltd., 1934).

Klap, P. *What a Life!* (Auckland: Kalamazoo, 2010).

Lake, R. *My Years in Mrs Boswell's Moscow* (Wellington: NZ Society for closer relations with U.S.S.R., 1950).

Lange, D. *My Life* (New Zealand: Penguin, 2005).

Locke, E. & Matthews, J. eds. *Stick Out, Keep Left/Margaret Thorn* (Auckland: Auckland University Press; Bridget Williams Books, 1997).

Lynch, B. ed. *Celebrating New Zealand's Emergence* (Wellington: New Zealand Institute of International Affairs, 2005).

Lynch, B. ed. *Celebrating 75 Years: Proceedings of the NZIIA 75th Anniversary Series of Addresses and Lectures,* vol. I (Wellington: New Zealand Institute of International Affairs, 2010).

McGibbon, I. ed. *Undiplomatic Dialogue: Letters between Carl Berendsen & Alister McIntosh 1943–1952* (Auckland: Auckland University Press in association with MFAT and the Historical Branch, Dept. of Internal Affairs, 1993).

McGibbon, I. ed. *Unofficial Channels: Letters between Alister McIntosh and Foss Shanahan, George Laking and Frank Corner 1946–1966* (Wellington: Victoria University Press in association with MFAT and the Historical Branch, Dept. of Internal Affairs, 1999).

MacKenzie, N. & J. eds. *The Diary of Beatrice Webb,* vols. 1–3 (London: Virago in association with the London School of Economics and Political Science, 1982, 1983 & 1984).

McKinnon, M. *Independence and Foreign Policy: New Zealand in the World since 1935* (Auckland: Auckland University Press, 1993)

McNeish, J. *The Sixth Man: The Extraordinary Life of Paddy Costello* (New Zealand: Random House, 2007).

Marsh, E. *Rupert Brooke: a memoir* (London Sidgwick & Jackson Ltd, 1918).

Nicolson, H. *Diplomacy* (London: Geoffrey Cumberlege, Oxford University Press, 1950).

Ovenden, K. *Fighting Withdrawal: The Life of Dan Davin, Writer, Soldier, Publisher* (Oxford, Oxford University Press, 1996).

Overseas Service Handbook (Wellington, MFAT).

Phillips, A. ed. *A Newnham Anthology* (Cambridge: Cambridge University Press, 1979).

Pollock, D. *Third Culture Kids* (London: Intercultural Press, 2001).

Pope-Hennessy, J. *Robert Louis Stevenson* (London: Jonathan Cape, 1974).

Post, E. *Emily Post's Etiquette: The Blue Book of Social Usage*, revised by Elizabeth L. Post, 11th revised ed. (New York: Funk & Wagnalls, 1965).

Rabel, R. *New Zealand and the Vietnam War: Politics and Diplomacy* (Auckland: Auckland University Press, 2005).

Radwanski, G. *Trudeau* (Toronto: Macmillan of Canada, *c.* 1978)

Reeves, M. *Round about a Pound a Week* (London: Virago, 1979).

St Cartmail, K. *Exodus Indochina* (Auckland: Heinemann, 1983).

Shawcross, W. *Quality of Mercy: Cambodia, Holocaust and Modern Conscience* (London: Deutsch, 1984)

Simpson, J. *The Wars against Saddam: Taking the Hard Road to Baghdad* (London: Macmillan, 2003).

Sinclair, K. *William Pember Reeves: New Zealand Fabian* (Oxford: Clarendon Press, 1965).

60 years ago: Celebrating the Anniversary of Diplomatic Relations between New Zealand and France (Wellington: French Embassy, 2005)

Smedley, B. *Partners in Diplomacy* (England: Harley Press, 1990).

Stevenson, F. & R.L. *Our Samoan Adventure* (New York: Harper & Brothers, 1955).

Templeton, M. *Top Hats Are Not Being Taken: A Short History of the New Zealand Legation in Moscow 1944–1950* (Wellington: NZIIA, 1988)

Templeton, M. ed. *An Eye, An Ear and a Voice: 50 years in New Zealand's External Relations 1943–1993* (Wellington, MFAT, 1993).

Templeton, H. ed. *Mr Ambassador: Memoirs of Sir Carl Berendsen* (Wellington: Victoria University Press, 2009).

Trotter, A. ed. *Fifty Years of New Zealand Foreign Policy Making* (Dunedin: Otago University Press in association with University Extension, Dunedin, 1993).

Webb, B. *Visit to New Zealand in 1898: Beatrice Webb's Diary with Entries by Sidney Webb* (Wellington: Price, Milburn by permission of the Passfield Trust, 1959).

Weir, J. *A New Zealand Ambassador's Letters from Moscow* (Auckland: Hodder & Stoughton, 1988).

Weir, J. *Eat, Drink and be Wary: A New Zealand Diplomat Looks Back* (Wellington: Dunmore Publishing Ltd., 2011).

Wells, G. ed. *H.G. Wells in Love: Postscript to an Experiment in Autobiography* (London: Faber & Faber, 1984).

Wells, H.G. *Ann Veronica* (London: J. M. Dent & Sons Ltd., 1943)

Wells, H.G. *In the Days of the Comet* (New York: Airmont Publishing, 1966).

Wilson, A. *New Zealand and the Soviet Union 1950–1991: A Brittle Relationship* (Wellington: Victoria University Press in association with the New Zealand Institute of International Affairs, 2004).

Wood, F. *New Zealand in the World* (Wellington: Dept. of Internal Affairs, 1940).

Wood, F. *The New Zealand People at War: Political and External Affairs* (Wellington: Historical Publications Branch, dept. of Internal Affairs in association with A.H. & A.W. Reed, 1971).

Wood, J. & Serres, J. *Diplomatic Ceremonial and Protocol: Principles, Procedures & Practices* (London: Macmillan 1970).

Zolf, L. *Just Watch Me: Remembering Pierre Trudeau* (Toronto: J. Lorimer, 1984).

INDEX

....

Page numbers in **bold** refer to illustrations.